For Linda

CHEFFIN'

from potatoes to caviar

Brendan Cronin

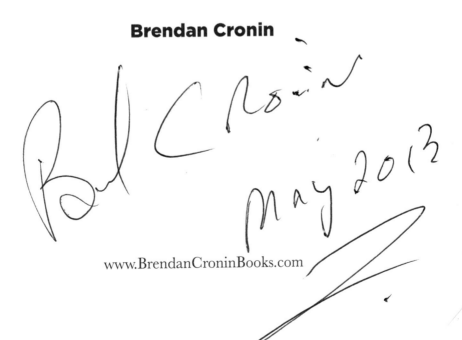

Bud Cronin

May 2013

www.BrendanCroninBooks.com

Set in Baskerville and Helvetica

First published in 2012 by
Falmore Enterprise
All rights reserved.

ISBN 9780985144500
Library of Congress Control Number 2012933285

Cover Design: by Aaron Mahnke / Wet Frog Studios

Cover pictures and authors picture: Shannon Cronin
www.shannoncroninphotography.com

Editing: Tom Richards

To my mother, Agnes Cronin

And in memory of my father, Harry Cronin

With my deepest appreciation for the foundation you both provided for my life.

Harry and Agnes – my parents – photographed during their honeymoon on O'Connell Street in Dublin. This picture was taken by a street photographer in October, 1948 as they rushed to catch a bus. It was their only wedding picture.

Contents

Acknowledgements

If this book was a pot of water on a gas burner, then it surely took a long time to boil. But boil it did!

I had the idea for this book in my mind for many years and could not have completed it without the help, support, and encouragement of so many people, friends, and family. I am grateful to Enid Larson who first taught me to write in her Assessment of Prior Learning class. To my mother, who told me to "just write the book," and to my brother Louis, who then challenged me to complete the book in one year, I am indebted to your insistence. To my brothers John and Fred for helping me to keep the perspective we shared so many years ago.

My thanks to the many reviewers around the world who painstakingly read every chapter as they were completed and gave me precious comments for improvement. To Joy Greedy, thank you for your global perspective, encouragement, and valuable advice on the book structure. To Linda Bassett, my thanks for your culinary wisdom, recipe formatting guidance and constant support. I also thank the reviewers − whom I never met − who were handed a completed manuscript out of the blue through a third party and asked for their opinion. Your feedback motivated me to cross the finish line.

Words can't express my feelings for my wife Christine, who saw me leave the house every weekend for twelve months to write − while encouraging me on. Your love and support has been a major force reflected in every word, in every chapter propelling me on to completion. To our children, Shannon and Ryan, your feed back was all the more appreciated as you watched your old man re-discover his younger days. My apologies that the book was a constant subject dominating many of our conversations. Thank you Shannon for your advice and for taking the cover photographs; you are an emerging talented photographer.

To Tanya Strahlendorf, Ryan Cronin, and Henric Persson, thank you for your assistance with the main cover photograph. To Aaron Mahnke of Wet Frog Studios for your expertise in designing the cover, and for your patience with me during the process as I changed my mind so many times. My thanks to TNC Holding Company LLC, owners of Tsar Nicoulai Caviar, San Francisco, CA for the use of their logo on the cover.

Finally to my editor: Tom Richards. My deepest appreciation for the many hours of hard work you put into reading and re-reading the manuscript with such enthusiasm as if it was your own. You have enabled me to tell my story and for that alone, I thank you!

Prologue

Nothing could have prevented the waiter from catching fire. It happened in an instant, what you would call a kitchen accident – and it was my fault! I refilled the fondue burner the waiter just brought back from the guest's table and did not see it was still burning as I poured more fuel into it. Flame shot out from the burner, fuel got on his jacket sleeve which caught on fire and now he was jumping around, screaming at the other waiters in a mixture of Italian and French: "Le chef veut me tuer!" – "The chef tried to kill me!" The kitchen was busy, the grill brimming with steaks, flame licking their edges, chefs calling out to me for main course pick-up times, more orders coming – two raviolis, one frog legs, one veal escalope. I had no time to mess around with this hysterical waiter in the middle of a very busy service time, so I poured a jug of cold water on his sleeve to put out the flame, gave him a new jacket, told him in very decorative language that he was a rotten idiot for thinking like that, and sent him back to his table with a new burner.

There was always friction between waiters and chefs in all the kitchens I worked in around the world. There is almost an ingrained expectation that one would hate the other, yet we depended on each other to take care of the third person in the equation – the guest. Guests are the very reason chefs and waiters get out of bed in the morning, the person we care about, kowtow to, strive to please and make happy, whatever it takes!

My mother taught me how to make guests happy with food. I saw how she took great care of the lodgers and tourists who stayed in our farm house in the west of Ireland. Guests always left our house happy; some even wrote thank you cards to her from as far away as America. When I was still a boy, she taught me how to cook the guests' breakfasts, their dinners, and pack lunches. We made brown soda bread together, delicious black pudding, Christmas cakes, plum puddings, homemade butter, and of course, her delicious coffee cake. As time went by, she encouraged me to train to be a chef, an unseemly job for a man at that time in rural Ireland. Cooking was a woman's job!

But cooking would become my avenue out of rural Ireland of the 1960's. A place with no future other than the pub, the dole, and developing a love affair with boiled food – an Irish staple. Cooking would provide a long and successful career allowing me to travel the world and cook for wonderful people, some famous, some dubious, and it all began with me standing on a little wooden stool by our turf-fired range, helping my mother fry Irish breakfasts for our guests. Even as a young lad, with my mother by my side and using a little wooden stool to reach the cooker, I fried the rashers in the pan on the range so they rendered the fat needed to fry sausages and the slices of black pudding, then lastly the eggs, still warm when I collected them the same morning from the hen house. By God they had flavor!

My mother saw something in me that I didn't and got me accepted to a hotel school in Galway, where I began my chef's training. The boarding school was a daily grind where I learned the fundamentals of cooking. I learned to make succulent brown stews, hollandaise and béarnaise sauce; soups like consommé royale, mulligatawny and brown onion soup. I saw spaghetti for the first time, made Sheppard's pie, steak and kidney pie, roast duck, and desserts like bread and butter pudding, chocolate éclairs and the revered 'Bavarian cream' – which literary dissolved on the tongue.

A summer placement in County Donegal gave me my first insight to a professional kitchen. Seamus, a great head chef, taught me to slice smoked salmon so thin that the plate was visible through it. The long hours and the hot kitchen were an endurance test. After college, I joined the Intercontinental Hotel in Limerick City. Eddie, the Sous chef, encouraged me to work in Germany. He told stories of the great dishes they prepared, such as "Schwarzwalder Kirschtorte" – the famous Black Forest cherry cake, and the 'schnitzel', not to mention the women. "There are lovely women in Germany," he said.

Later in the Intercontinental Hotel in Dublin, at the bottom of the brigade hierarchy, I roasted chickens, geese, turkeys by the dozen for the Cabaret which featured famous Irish entertainers like Hal Roach and Maureen Potter, performing every night to a packed house. But I thought there must be more to cooking than grilled T-bone steaks, deep fried plaice, boiled vegetables, boiled spuds, sherry trifle, and apple custard, so thoughts of working on the Continent kept coming back to me. Eventually through contacts, I found a job in a hotel in Switzerland and bid farewell to Dublin and boiled food.

What follows is a story about cooking from a professional chef's perspective: how I began my career at my mother's side; the great times, and the not-so-great times along the way, and the constant struggle against the misconception of "The Irish can't cook." This is also a story about the degradation of always being a foreigner, a second class citizen living so far away from my Irish home, and my dream of becoming a master chef. It is a story of the beautiful countries I visited, the wonderful people I cooked for, and the recipes, cooking tips, and tricks I learned along the way. And this is a story of the highlights of meeting famous people, the staff who helped me, who took me into their homes and into their hearts, and showed me that the world is really full of "just nice people" – if you know how to listen to them, guide them, and let them do their work.

And yes, the Italian waiter really did catch on fire!

Cheffin' by Brendan Cronin

CHAPTER ONE

My Coffee Cake

"Harry! Harry! Come in quick! The cooker is on fire!"

My mother was in a state. She ran outside to the byre where my father was milking cows. She had just put a cake in the oven of the new gas cooker. A special cake for the priest, as he was coming home from the priesthood and would be looking forward to a home baked cake and now that cake was burning.

It was the early 1960's and we had just got the cooker delivered from McIntyre's store in Belmullet, County Mayo, Ireland, a town about one mile from our house. Now it was standing proudly beside the turf range in our kitchen with a cylinder of Calor gas beside it when the flame and smoke started coming out around the oven door. My father opened the door and jumped back as a big red flame with a huge puff of black smoke roared out and rose up to the ceiling. Using the oven gloves, he carried the burning cake outside to put out the flame. All that was left of the cake and the brown paper lining of the baking tin was a blackened lump resembling carbon paper. My mother was mortified; burning a cake was not in her repertoire. Mam never burnt a cake when she used the traditional, old fashioned turf-fired oven in the range.

Well, the delivery man had to come back again the next day to readjust the oven setting. He admitted that the oven temperature dial was set incorrectly, allowing the oven to get so hot that the paper lining in the cake tin caught on fire. So my mother and I baked a new cake and the priest – my mother's brother – had a nice slice of his sister's cake when he got home. He said it was a welcome change for him from the shop cake they got in the priesthood. This was one of my first baking encounters in my long cooking career.

Growing up on a dairy farm in Ireland on the outer edge of the western seaboard involved a lot of hard work. Farms were small and money was scarce. My father, a very savvy man, guided the family through tough times while remaining at home on the farm. Many of my school friends would see their fathers leave for England or Scotland only to come home once a year for a few weeks, and leave again. But the money they sent home was a Godsend. As soon as the eldest child was old enough, even if they were not finished school, they followed the immigrant lives of their fathers. There was no future for the young generation in the west of Ireland at the time other than to inherit the farm and go on the dole. We were fortunate to have 'the Boss', as many farmers referred to my father, at home all the time.

My mother told me that when they got married, my father did not know how they would get by. Yet without leaving the country or even the farm, they both worked together to provide for us. We grew most of our own food, killed the odd hen, had a calf butchered or a pig killed, and there would be fresh eggs every day. We had fresh fish and shellfish and of course the auld spud was always around and mostly boiled. Later in life I often wondered if the Irish would have starved to death if it wasn't for boiling water, because at times it seemed everything was boiled.

The Boss, the youngest of six, took over the family farm in the village of Carne, in County Mayo, when he married my mother. Then his two sisters moved out of the family home to a house near the town called Seafield, a sensible name as the house was in a field by the sea. It was big enough for my aunt Birdie to open a bed and breakfast while my aunt Kate taught at Aughleam National School eleven miles away – a journey she completed every day by bicycle. My mother, one of nine children, moved directly from her home – also in Carne – to our house which was only 400 yards and two fields away. There were only seven houses and six farms in Carne. The seventh house was the Parish Priest's and even though he had one white cow, it couldn't be called a farm.

My father began supplying vegetables and potatoes to the local hospital which provided a weekly income, a rarity in the 1950s rural Ireland of my childhood. He also began supplying milk to the hospital and over time, to many of the town's people. Demand increased and we eventually became a dairy farm and so the majority of my childhood revolved around the biological clock of twenty dairy cows. They were our bread and butter. We took care of them night and day. We even gave them names, like the Red Heifer, the Blue Cow, or the Big Friesian, and talked to them as if they were part of the family. We brought them water, hay, and grass. We kept them indoors during the winter cold and let them stay out under the stars in summer. If one got sick, we all worried: my father would be up all night attending to the cow. His veterinary training became incredibly valuable when animals got sick. We celebrated when the cow got better and if it died, it was almost like a funeral – sadness would fill the house. And with a cow's death came the shame of not been able to take care of your animals.

The kitchen was the hub of family life. The dominating turf-fired range took up an entire corner of the kitchen. The fire, visible through a cast iron grill in the front, affected the atmosphere. It was like watching a film, the flame dancing around in the grate, never the same shape or size. We looked at the fire as a focal point; it influenced our mood especially at night when the paraffin-fired tilly lamp gave the only light we had to make the tea. Visitors were given a seat by the fire, clothes were hung to dry by it, and all our food was cooked on it. The range had a built-in hot water boiler, our only means of hot water. The first thing my father did every morning at half-six after waking us up was to light a fire in the range so my mother could fry the breakfast and heat water for the boarders and lodgers that we took in to make some extra money.

I would help her to bake bread and roast chickens and cook the Christmas turkey in that turf-fired oven. Later, when she got the gas cooker and despite burning the priest's cake the first day, we could boil water for the tea in the morning before lighting the fire.

It changed the way we prepared meals. It provided instant heat, and just as important, eliminated residual heat, something I valued later during my chef's career – the power of gas over electricity for cooking is favored by many chefs.

When I was about six we installed the "electric", as some neighbors called it. The Irish Electricity Supply Company was building an electric power line down the center of the local peninsula and it was going to cross through the field above our house. My father got them to connect the wiring to our home. It was a tremendous change to have a light in every room and even an electric plug although we had no appliances to plug into it.

Even though it took some time to get used to it, electricity changed the way we used the house. Prior to this I would help my mother cook the lodgers' dinner by the light of that simple, single-wicked tilly lamp. Now in the evenings, despite our ability to switch on the light, we would wait until it was almost dark before switching on the electric because of our habit with the tilly lamp. The electric light gave a warm feeling to the kitchen and was a blessing for doing our homework. While we always had running water and an inside toilet and a bath which was above the kitchen beside our room, the advent of electricity was cause of celebration. My father even bought an electric radio which was placed on the kitchen window sill. We could listen to the weather, music, and storytelling on it at night after our homework was done.

As I was too young to be working outside with the cows, I mostly helped my mother in the kitchen. She always needed help with the lodgers' dinners, and then after that, the cooking of three meals a day for the rest of us. In the colder months she often made a stew for the lodgers. To make it she would set some stewing beef in cold water on the range early in the afternoon, add an onion, a few parsnips, a carrot or two, a head of cabbage cut into slices, a bay leaf, a grain of salt and a few peeled potatoes. While it simmered on the range she would from time to time remove any froth or fat that would rise to the surface with a large metal spoon. By the time the lodgers came home from work the wonderful smell of the stew would have drifted throughout the house. The lodgers always ate in the dining room, downstairs facing the bay with Belmullet town in the distance. We ate in the kitchen. The dining room had a large table with eight chairs which was constantly set with homemade butter, sugar, milk, salt and pepper shakers, and a bottle each of HP sauce, YR sauce and Coleman's mustard. Next to that were a few armchairs for the lodgers to sit around the fire in the evenings. When they sat down at the table I would carry the large plates of stew – which my mother divided equally – to the lodgers in the dining room. They always complimented her on the flavors: "Mrs. Cronin, that was a lovely meal," they would say every time.

Our kitchen was alive with life and good cheer! It was where I began my career with food as my mother taught me how to make brown soda bread, succulent stews, fried steaks, and breakfast for the lodgers. Our family had breakfast, dinner, and tea in the kitchen every day. Breakfast was a porridge affair with tea and my mother's homemade brown bread together with homemade butter and marmalade or sometimes homemade jam. She would make the porridge the night before in a double boiler: oatmeal, water and a grain of salt. The double boiler prevented any burning on the bottom of the pan. Then she would reheat it in the morning. We ate it sprinkled with sugar and a drop of milk. Dinner, usually served after we came home from school, could be a stew, or a steak, or a few lamb chops, or perhaps pan-fried mackerel with boiled potatoes and vegetables. Tea was around six o'clock and consisted of brown bread, homemade butter, homemade jam, and maybe a slice of cold roast lamb with homemade apple raisin chutney.

My parents made a great team. The Boss took care of the animals and the outside and my mother, the inside, the lodgers, cooking, and cleaning. Although my two brothers and I worked very hard from an early age, we were content with our lot. We slept in one big bed in a tiny room above the kitchen. John, the eldest, slept on the outside; me, the youngest, against the wall and AJ in the middle. There was a narrow unlit stairs hidden behind the dresser leading from the kitchen to our bedroom and my parent's room so we could get to our room without using the front stairs, which was reserved for the lodgers.

Local visitors and farmers always came to the kitchen door, never the front door, asking Mam for my father. "How ya Missus Cronin, is himself in?" they would enquire. Depending on who they were, they might call her Agnes. The Priest, however, was a different matter. A man of the cloth, he always got the best of everything. "How are ya Father?" my mother would state. "Come on in, sit down and take the weight off your feet." He would be greeted with great respect, served tea in a china cup, with biscuits and homemade currant cake, and was usually brought into the "dining room", a kind of upgrade from the kitchen due to his station in life.

Uncle Peter, my mother's brother who lived in the homestead located a few hundred yards across the Priest's field, would come to our house nearly every day and sit in the kitchen to listen for any news. A quiet man who often whistled under his breath, he farmed sheep and cattle and thought forever over every decision before he made it. He would sit on a chair just inside the door and promptly fall asleep.

If we had the fortune to get a letter from my two aunts who lived in the United States and therefore referred to as "The girls in America", my mother would give it to him. Uncle Peter would then borrow her reading glasses and settle down to read all the news from the great city of New York. This particular day Auntie Grace, who worked in one of the big hotels in New York City, wrote that she and Auntie Kathleen were fine and she herself had been nominated for an employee award at the Waldorf Astoria Hotel where she worked.

"Wasn't it a great achievement for my aunt, a girl from the small village of Carne, to be given the recognition of such a fine hotel in the city of New York?" I remember thinking. Of course, for me, any hotel in New York was a fine hotel, and what did I know? My aunts always finished their letters hoping the good Lord and his Holy Mother would bless us all, and if Joseph, the Holy Mother's practical husband could lend a hand in the affair, that would be a blessing altogether. Then as quietly as he came in Uncle Peter would get up, and still whistling under his breath, leave the letter on the kitchen dresser and walk out without saying a word.

Like the cows, the lodgers were a constant so there was always another job for my mother to do. One evening as my mother was adding turf to the fire in the dining room didn't one of the lodgers make a sly remark about him being disturbed by the racket she was making. She was upset and told my father who was just finishing his tea. He jumped up from the kitchen table, went straight in to the dining room and told the lodger to pack up and get out right this minute! "Ah now Harry," says the others. "Sure he was only jokin'…" The Boss cut them off, asking if they also wanted to join the unruly lodger in packing their bags? "How dare you insult the woman of the house, you are a blaggard!" he shouted at the lodger. And so the lodger spent the night in the local hotel and the rest of them shut their mouths. The Boss would never allow anyone to insult our mother. It was seldom we would see him upset, and even when he was, he never used bad language. He might call us *eejits* or *Umadans* – fools – but never *fecking eejits.*

When I was about seven, my mother told us we were going to have a new baby in the house. While she was in hospital getting the baby, I helped my father with the lodger's meals. I could do some of the cooking, set the table, and wash the dishes and he helped with the fire and boiling water for tea and some of the frying. We all went to the hospital to see my mother and the new baby. While we waited in the ward for the nurse to bring in the new addition, AJ and I began winding the big wheel under the bed, raising the back part so my mother could sit up. We wound it so far that it came off the thread and the top of the bed fell back with a big bang, our mother with it! The long threaded bar hit the floor with another loud bang; my mother nearly fell out of the bed and she shouted at us, "God almighty! Will ye leave that bed alone!" Then the Boss shouted at us: "Yeer pure umadans." The nurse came in with the baby and gave us a quare look when she saw the broken bed and wheel lying on the floor. The baby was asleep and looked all wrinkled and pudgy. My mother called him Louis. He had red hair like the Boss. The three of us were named after uncles on both sides of the family. Uncle John, the headmaster and the Boss's brother, Uncle AJ, and Father Brendan O'Malley – two of Mam's brothers.

The baby was brought home and put in the cot at the foot of my parent's bed, the same one I vacated a few short years earlier. Dr. Conway – our family doctor – told my father to get a few bottles of Guinness and give my mother half a bottle mixed with milk every morning and evening to strengthen her up. So we got used to the baby in the house; he slept most of the time, and we only saw him when he was awake and downstairs as we seldom went into my parent's bedroom. When it was time to feed and change the baby Mam would bring him down from their room to the kitchen and sit before the range to keep him warm while she changed the nappy. When she changed the baby it was like she was trussing a chicken. She would lay the baby on his back across her knees very close to the fire for warmth, and remove the nappy. Then to put on the clean one, she would hold one ankle between the thumb and forefinger and the other ankle between the three other fingers and lift the baby, then lay him down again on the clean nappy all while she held two big open safety pins between her teeth. The baby never once fell on the floor or into the fire.

As I helped my mother with the cooking, we would cook a full Irish breakfast for each lodger every morning: two fried eggs, one streaky rasher and one back rasher, two sausages and two slices of black pudding. Streaky bacon was cut from the pig's belly and back bacon from the loin with more lean meat in it. Standing on a little wooden stool, I fried the rashers in the pan on the turf fired range, so they rendered the fat needed to fry the eggs, still warm in my hand because I collected them the same morning from the hen house. Mam showed me how to tilt the pan slightly, take the hot bacon fat with a metal spoon and pour it over the egg yolk cooking it further. She never flipped the eggs – the result was a beautifully cooked egg with a slightly opaque yolk which contrasted well on the plate with the bacon, sausage and slices of black pudding. The lodgers would also have grapefruit juice, homemade brown soda bread, white shop bread, homemade butter, and fresh milk for the tea. While they were eating breakfast we would prepare a packed lunch for each one with flasks of tea, ham and cheese sandwiches made with homemade butter and Coleman's mustard – a powder that we mixed with a little water to form a paste. When they came home at half-five in the evening, I would help again with the dinner, a meal with homemade vegetable soup, maybe a fried steak or pork chop or a stew with potatoes and vegetables. Some days there would be a piece of fresh fish, maybe a mackerel fried in the pan, or a slice of salmon that my father would have bought at the street market in Belmullet.

In the evening after most of her work was done she still wasn't finished: my mother would sit by the kitchen fire darning socks. But despite her long hours, she took delight in teaching me the joys of cooking, a passion she ignited in me and that I have enjoyed all my life. For instance, she instilled in me a sense of Irish hospitality. I learned from an early age that the gift she gave to our lodgers was true hospitality, offered from the heart and with a real concern for the guests' comfort. My mother's simple warmth was, I discovered later in my career, a precious gift that cannot be taught. Either you have it or you don't.

On the farm we were self sufficient in many areas, notably food. We grew most of what we ate. Planting spuds was a tedious job, but necessary, as most of our meals contained this most noble of starches and it was essential to be self sufficient. Years later, in hotels around the world and while working with some great chefs and Master Chefs, I learned to prepare many different types of foods that relied on the lowly potato: potatoes au gratin, pommes savoyardes, and the famous Swiss rösti potato cake. But it was during my childhood that I learned just how much work was involved in bringing the spud from seed to table.

Our horse Charlie was strong, and the plough an easy pull – even against the hill. It was gratifying to see the green sod turned black by the curve of the blade – a sign of spring. We ran behind the plough to look at the worms wriggling in the furrow, some of them cut in half. They said that the two halves eventually grew into two new worms. The minute a little earth was turned the gulls would appear up from the shore as if by secret signal, screeching and swooping, fighting to get whatever worms were unfortunate enough to grace the surface of the upturned earth. So if worms wanted to grow back they had to be fast. The Boss would talk to the horse. Horse and man were in perfect unison; there was a calm sense of achievement as the horse effortlessly pulled the implement through the ground. The field would be left for a few days before being harrowed.

The harrow was made from six wooden beams about 4 feet long with six-inch steel spikes sticking out of each side. When it was harnessed up to Charlie it travelled over the sod sideways like a crab looking for a rock to hide under. The spikes broke up the sod and raised a cloud of dust when the soil was dry, which wasn't often. Then we prepared the sprouting spuds for planting.

Picking out the good sprouting potatoes was very important. They had been carefully selected by the Boss over the last few weeks, each potato with a few fragile sprouts sticking up like an antenna in search of light. When planting day arrived – or 'setting potatoes' as we called it – once again Charlie was harnessed up, this time to the driller. This implement was pulled through the loose soil to form a drill about a foot deep in which we would place the sprouts. Drilling was the most precise job of all. If the horse and his master were not in unison the lines would be crooked and trampled, not a great view for passing farmers. So up and down the field they went, Charlie guided by the Boss with only a few clicks of the tongue and a few gentle words, walking perfectly straight until all the drills stood out in beautiful lines, like a work of art. We placed the sprouts one foot apart in the drills with farmyard manure. Half way through the day the Boss harnessed Charlie to the driller and started to close the drills. It was early evening when the last drill was closed. We would have to wait several months before we could begin to eat the potatoes and that crop would have to last us the entire winter. Then we had our tea. My mother had made apple cake with cooking apples from our orchard which she stored during the winter months. It had big juicy chunks of apples in it and the dough had extra sugar which allowed the top to brown. Needless to say, it got a sudden death. Apple cake and apple tarts were very special treats for us, and so was a sandwich made with white shop bread and homemade butter and sprinkled with sugar because we ate mostly homemade brown soda bread for breakfast and tea. White shop bread was reserved for the lodgers.

Potatoes were a staple, eaten at every meal except breakfast. We never ate any other starch. The three main potato varieties we had were Home Guards, Arran Banners, and Kerr's Pinks. The latter were a floury variety when boiled and they also mashed very well. Once they were boiled – in the skin – my mother would strain off the water, put a clean tea towel over them, put the lid back on the pot and set them on a warm area of the range. The towel absorbed the moisture from the boiling process so that when the potatoes were served, the skin would have split revealing a white floury interior that was a great match for the homemade butter. I was the only one at the table who would eat the potato skin. Everyone else peeled them and gave the skins to the dog. To this day I still eat the skin of boiled potatoes, mostly to the distain of my fellow diners.

We often visited my grandmother's house. These visits were always eventful as my uncles and grandfather would be either shearing sheep, branding cattle or stacking turf or Gran would be baking large cakes of her homemade currant cake. There was a spring well at the bottom of the Priest's field next to her house and Gran would only use water from that well for the tea because it had great flavor. She always sent one of us down to the well for some water during our visits. The well – about two feet deep – was covered with a piece of rusty galvanized metal and the stones around it were whitewashed. The water was crystal clear, the bottom covered in white sand. We had to be careful not to stir the water to avoid getting sand in the bucket – something Gran would be annoyed with and would send us back for a cleaner bucket with no sand if we did so. We would get a big slice of her currant cake with hot sweet tea for our help. Unlike my mother who sliced bread on a wooden board, Gran would hold the big homemade currant cake against her chest with one hand and using a large bread knife slice it towards her, and then just before the slice would fall she'd catch it between her thumb and the blade and place it gently on the table. I always waited for it to fall but it never did. She used to spread it with her own homemade butter which had a lovely yellow color and a rich texture. Its saltiness and smooth mouth feel contrasted with the sweetness of the currant cake and the crunchiness of the currants which had browned on the surface.

On these visits I would help Uncle Peter to gather sheep with his sheep dog named Cap. He was a beautiful black and white dog who spent most of the time sleeping outside the kitchen door. When he did not obey while rounding up sheep, Uncle Peter would call the dog by a choice name extracted from the Irish dictionary. Cap would be far down the field moving the sheep, and my uncle would call out to him to "go outside" the sheep; when it did not happen he would mutter another few choice names for Cap under his breath as if Cap could hear him and respond accordingly. This was a time in the spring when he would move the sheep to the hill field, overlooking Blacksod Bay and the Bangor Mountains in the distance. Every year he would have a few lambs butchered for their own use and my mother would make black pudding using the sheep's stomach and pig's blood. This was a big task, taking up half a day, and I was in charge of washing out the sheep's belly. The stomach would be left to soak for a few days in a bucket full of salt water and lime to clean it and kill the germs. I would peel the onions, my mother would chop them and I would fry them on the range. We would add the fried onions, cubed pork back fat, oatmeal, and spices to the blood and mix it until it became a thick liquid. Then we filled the mixture into the cleaned stomach using a tea cup.

I would hold the stomach flesh open with both hands while my mother filled it up. Drops of the mixture would spill over my hands onto the table leaving red blood streaks on my skin. When we were finished, the stomach resembled a large balloon filled with liquid. While I was still holding the stomach, she sewed up the opening with a darning needle and together we lifted the stretched stomach into a large pot of simmering water, being careful not to puncture the tightly stretched flesh. While the pudding cooked we made tiny pin pricks with a thinner sewing needle to let any air out and so prevent the pudding from bursting. When the pudding was cooked, we removed it from the water to let it cool. We served slices of it pan-fried for the lodger's breakfast. They loved the taste; it was delicious, much better than the black pudding from the shops. I liked the pudding but did not eat the skin. I would leave it on the side on my plate. My father, seeing the rim of my plate covered with pieces of black pudding skin would mention how wasteful that was, reach over with his fork and move it to his plate, and promptly ate it all the while reciting the rhyme:

> *"Jack the sprat would eat no fat, his brother*
> *would eat no lean. They killed a pig and*
> *between them both they licked the platter*
> *clean."*

My mother taught me how to make her coffee cake. It was a sponge cake with a coffee butter cream filling and icing sugar sprinkled on top. After helping her to make it many times, she asked me one day to make one by myself for some visitors she was expecting. So I made the cake on my own, weighing the ingredients on a small green scale with a maximum capacity of 8 ounces. Then I whipped up the eggs and sugar to foam like she showed me, folded in the sieved flour and poured the mixture in two shallow round baking tins. I baked them for three quarters of an hour at gas mark 7 (about 180C, 350F), and then removed them from the tins to cool on a wire rack. While they were baking I creamed together the butter and sugar and added a thick liquid coffee flavor. When the cakes cooled down I spread one side with the butter mixture, placed the second cake on top and spread a little mixture around the side, sprinkled the top with icing sugar and that was that. When her visitors arrived, she served them tea and a slice of the coffee cake. They would not believe her when she told them that her son Brendan had made the cake. After all, cooking was a woman's job and all a lad of my age was supposed to do was work on the farm. I was out working in the field at the time so she called me in to explain to the visitors that it was me who made the cake. I was very surprised when the wife of a local doctor, Mrs. Kelly, asked my mother if I could make her a coffee cake. She couldn't believe a boy would be cooking instead of farming.

One day, my mother told us she was going to get another baby at the hospital in Belmullet. This time when we went to visit her, the Boss made sure we did not touch the bed. The hospital was on a hill overlooking Belmullet with a great view of Blacksod Bay, Claggan Head and our house across the bay. She told us she could even see the cows in our field from her bed. We saw the baby for a few minutes: he had blonde hair and she called him Fred after Uncle Fred, my father's brother who lived in County Leitrim. When he was brought home he was put in the cot at the foot of their bed and my mother got another six bottles of Guinness.

In the meantime, I continued with my schooling. Even though my uncle was the school's Headmaster, national school was a fearful place for me. I was not good at my lessons and had trouble with my sum tables. Everybody called Uncle John – the Boss's brother – "The Master." Our national school had five classrooms. Some rooms held two classes all the time. When the teacher taught one class, pupils would sit at the desks while the other class stood around the wall silently learning off by heart. There was no running water in the school. There were dry lavatories at the end of the playground which no one used unless it was an emergency. The Master would pick up my brothers and myself at our gate at ten to nine every morning and bring us back at three o'clock in the afternoon. A tall man, with a fine lock of white hair and a spring in his step, the Master was always dressed in a suit and tie. An Army man in his younger days, he walked as if he were walking only on the tips of his toes. With AJ I ate my lunch every day in his classroom before going out to play with the lads. We had a flask of hot sweetened tea and sandwiches made with homemade soda bread and homemade butter. We would sit around his desk and he gave us his lunch which was always the same – slices of Galtee cheese between two Jacobs Cream Crackers spread with shop butter. We never saw him eating; he just sat there chatting with us and chain smoked. Nearly every day during play time some lad would come in to complain that he got hit by another lad in the playground. It was a big deal to go to the Master's classroom to complain and took a certain amount of courage. "Sir, Sean hit me," was a common complaint. My uncle would then enquire, "Where did he hit you?" "In the 'stomuk' sir." "Do you know where the gear lever is?" "Yes sir," was the response. "Well go out now and give him a kick in the gear lever and tell him I said to stop hitting you." And the lad would leave saying, "All right sir." At the time, I did not know what he meant by the gear lever: none of us knew. Every morning, two pupils from second class would go to the local well in a neighboring farmer's field for a bucket of water to make the teachers tea. To make the tea – using the fireplace at the top of the classroom – the teacher would balance a kettle on four small hot coals of turf until it boiled, then rinse out the teapot with some of the boiling water, add a few spoons of tea leaves from the tea caddy and fill it with boiling water. Then she put the teapot back on the four coals to draw for a few minutes before pouring cups for each of the teachers and the Master.

Despite her tea making abilities, our teacher was quick with the bamboo cane if we answered questions incorrectly. We had to recite all the sums tables off by heart. When we had a sums table test, we were told that if we couldn't recite the answers correctly we would get two slaps of the bamboo cane, one on each hand. Two times two is four, three times two is six and so on until we got to twelve times two is twenty-four. God help us if we got one wrong. The girl sitting beside me started on the nines: they were harder. When she got them wrong and the teacher shouted in Gaeilge – our national Irish language, "Níl sé sín chéart! – that's not right, come up here," we were all afraid. Then she took the bamboo cane from a press behind the blackboard. The hinges of the press door made a squeaking noise that we associated with the pain that was to follow. We were all nervous that we would get the same treatment.

There was a lot of fear in the classroom. For that reason alone, I never liked National School.

We also had music lessons at school. We were asked to choose a musical instrument and so I began to play the mouth organ. The fourth class teacher was very easily upset: one day one of the lads made squeaky noises with his wet Wellington boots. The teacher, thinking it was me, came straight over to my desk and asked, "Brendan Cronin, are you making strange noises?" I said: "No Mrs." "Don't lie to me," the teacher yelled. Then she hit me with the palm of her hand right across the face. The force of the blow nearly knocked me over. I was determined not to cry, and I never ratted on the lad that did the dastardly deed.

In sixth class, the Master would often tell us stories to clarify a point in class. One day he was explaining the importance of telling the truth. He told us a story of an old man on his death bed who had not made a will. Realizing the consequences, his family decided to write the will and get him to sign it before he died. Well, while they were writing the will, didn't the man die! Not willing to let their legacy get away from them, the family devised a plan. They caught a fly on the window, put it in the dead man's mouth and closed it shut. Then they put a pen in his hand and signed the will. Later, when the will was read, the barrister asked the family if the man was alive when he signed the will. They answered, "Sure there was life in him!" The Master explained to us that the family was not telling a lie, but they were not telling the truth either.

We never learned about cooking in the National School and I never volunteered any information, or even told my friends that I cooked at home with my mother. Cooking was a woman's job and I would be made fun of. Farming was a man's job. When school finished at 3 o'clock we headed home to begin the evening farm work. Before starting the car the Master would light up his pipe, filling the car with a cloud of smoke. Droplets of tar hung from the sun visor and the floor beneath his feet was covered in cigarette butts, pipe ash, and burnt matches. Some afternoons he would come in to our kitchen, exchange greetings with my father in Irish, and ask my mother for a 'drop of soda' for his stomach was acting up again. She would take a spoon of regular baking soda, and mix it with warm water. He would drink that, feel better, and be on his way. I later learned that it was the alkalinity of the baking soda that neutralized the stomach acids, eliminating the discomfort.

On the farm, summer brought other jobs. In June, July, and August hay making was the priority except on Sunday. Making butter was also a summer job because we had more milk than in the winter and the best way to store it was to make butter. I would take all the milk we did not need for sale and separate the cream from it. This was done in a separating machine using centrifugal force. The separating machine was bolted to a table in the dairy, a small room next to the kitchen. It had a large cast iron arm with a wooden handle on the end. I would spin this and as the skim milk was heavier than the cream, it was projected further through a system of pipes and flowed into a bucket on the floor. It was fed to new born calves. The cream was collected in a large earthenware bowl on the table. It was left to sour slightly in the pantry and when the tartness was just right – the cream would be thick and yellow, almost like custard – my mother would pour it into the churn and then I could spin it. As the butter began to 'gather', the churn became harder to spin and rocked back and forth with the lumps of butter hitting the inside. I would then drain off the butter milk through a valve in the bottom of the churn. Butter milk was great for the thirst because it had a sharp taste. Workmen helping with the hay would enquire if we had any and they would drink a glass in no time.

Standing on a chair, I would reach into the churn and remove the butter. My mother would mix in a grain of salt and knead the butter in a wooden bowl using two grooved wooden butter spades. Then with the spades she would take a piece of butter the size of a pearl onion and make perfect round butter balls for the lodgers' breakfast table. Every ball was the same size and she never measured a bit. I often tried to imitate her use of the butter spades but never managed to make a butter ball as perfect as hers. Summer was also a time we would go to the strand on a Sunday with my parents. My mother would sit on the sand reading the newspaper and my father would wade out into the big waves. We were afraid to go with him, so despite living by the ocean during my childhood I never learned to swim until later in life.

October, when the darkness came early, was usually the time for picking the spuds we planted in the spring. It would be nearly dark when the Master would bring us home from school. My mother would have a plate of stewed beef or lamb ready for us. It had great flavor: there were chunks of vegetables and potatoes in it. The meat was so tender from hours of stewing that we could eat it using only a spoon. "Sit in there," my mother would say, referring to the kitchen table with the plates of steaming stew. "Get that into your bellies. It'll keep the wolf from the door while ye'er out picking."

Now the drills we planted in the spring were turned into neat rows of potatoes of all sizes by the workmen and not one of them was cut or spliced by the spade. We had to pick all the spuds that were dug that day for the frost would ruin them by the morning. The spuds were put into pits located around the field, piled in heaps about two feet high and ten feet long on a bed of rushes. They were covered with a layer of rushes and then, at the end of the evening, the workmen started to cover it with clay. The spuds remained in the field like this late into the winter, well protected from the frost.

My two brothers and I would still be in the field after dark, the frost creeping in and our fingers getting numb with the cold. We would tell each other jokes and ghost stories to keep us from thinking about the length of the row of potatoes. We each had a metal bucket with a wire handle. When it was full we would walk to the pit with it – the weight straining at our arms – and pile up the potatoes, then start again on the row where we left off with the empty bucket. The cold metal numbed our hands. When the last bucket of potatoes was put in the pit we left the workmen to close it up and headed down to the house to start the milking. My mother would bring out a bucket of cold water from the kitchen sink to the back yard and we dipped our hands to wash off the clay. She told us that cold water was better for getting the feeling back to numbed hands and many's the person that had their fingers fall completely off from using hot water instead.

In our kitchen, my mother baked Christmas cakes and made plum puddings well in advance of the season. She would make 3 or 4 plum puddings in late October. Once they cooled down they would be left on the very top of the kitchen dresser until it was time to eat the first one on Christmas day, then one on New Year's Day, and one on Easter Sunday. By late November every year she would also have made three Christmas cakes 12 inches in diameter and coated them with a half inch thick layer of marzipan and then another half inch of royal icing. Then with a piping bag, she would pipe a row of icing decorations around the top edge of the cake and a similar row around the bottom. In each row she would stick on little silver edible decorative beads. When the icing was dry – which took a few days – she would wrap a wide band of red ribbon around the side of each cake. This really brought the cakes to life. They tempted us for weeks just looking at them on the dresser – powerful flavor sealed in with icing. One cake was for our house, one would go to our Gran, and one would go to Auntie Birdie in Seafield house.

I helped with getting the ingredients ready for the plum puddings. They were time consuming to make because assembling the ingredients alone was a day's work. And then it usually took us another day to make them. I could peel the almonds. I put them in a saucepan of boiling water for a few minutes, strained them out and put them in a tea towel. Then when I rubbed them dry in the towel, the brown skin came off revealing the milky white nut underneath. The next ingredient was the fresh white breadcrumbs. My mother would have bought a white shop loaf and let it go stale for a few days. Then I would cut off all the crusts, slice it into large chunks and begin to grate it into breadcrumbs – in later years, when sliced bread became more common, this type of unsliced loaf was harder to find, which made the process of making breadcrumbs more difficult. All the candied peel, currants and glazed cherries were soaked in dark rum overnight in a covered bowl which prevented the rum from evaporating. On the day the puddings were to be made I would begin by creaming the butter and sugar. I used the same bowl every time, a large delft bowl, yellow on the outside with a green dot halfway up the inside that looked like a green moon on the white background.

It would take me a long time to mix the butter and sugar to a creamy consistency, and my mother would help now and again. To help speed up the process I would sit by the fire and warm the bowl to soften the butter because the sugar had to be almost dissolved in it. Once the mixture was creamy enough I would add in one egg, stir it until it was absorbed in the creamed mixture, and then add some flour. I repeated these steps until all the flour and eggs were mixed in. Then it was time to add some porter and treacle. After that, we would add the marinated fruit, and all the rum, the breadcrumbs, and now the mixture was ready to fill into bowls. Each bowl would be filled almost to the brim, a piece of greaseproof paper went on top, then covered with muslin cloth and tied with a string and a handle made from string was added so we could lift each one out of the hot water when cooked. They were each steamed in a pot of simmering water for three hours, then removed and allowed to cool.

Christmas was a lovely time in our house. The smell of baking in the kitchen, the aroma of spices like cinnamon, nutmeg and allspice, the baked ham giving off its sugary clove aroma, and the whiff of the odd hot whiskey with lemon, made the kitchen an extra special place during that season. We would have a big Christmas tree in the hall porch that touched the ceiling. It gave off a damp pine scent that was noticeable in all rooms and rose up the stairs to the landing. There was a string of round colored lights on the tree connected to the porch light in the ceiling. This is where Santa Claus would leave our presents on Christmas night. We all helped with decorations and each room had a little holly. There was even some stuck in behind the picture of Jesus which hung over the range in the kitchen. After all it was his birthday. The first people to get a slice of Christmas cake would be visitors like the Priest or a neighbor who came by to wish my mother and father a Happy Christmas. To get the first slice was considered a privilege.

They would be offered a cup of tea or a drop of the strong stuff or depending on who they were, might get a drop of Poitín (Potcheen), the local liquor distilled clandestinely from potatoes or barley, and often referred to as 'The crayture.' The crayture was mighty powerful stuff, reserved for special visitors. The bottle was always kept in a separate room – never in the kitchen. When a deserving person visited, my mother would leave the kitchen with an empty glass and return within minutes with the 'drop' – a clear potent liquid that could take the breath away – saying: "Drink that now, it'll do ye good, and a Happy Christmas to you." The bottle was never seen. Good stuff was hard to come by, poorly distilled stuff a health hazard. Never the less, a bottle of the crayture was a very special Christmas gift indeed.

By now I was about twelve years old and in sixth class, my last year in National School. It was the nicest classroom in the school – the Master did not have a bamboo cane. The entire class would recite poetry and learn our lessons out loud so there was a hum in the classroom as we all learned poetry off by heart. "I wandered lonely as a cloud…" Wordsworth would have been proud of us, learning about his daffodils. The Master would be reading the *Irish Independent* at his desk and puffing away on his pipe, a big cloud of smoke curling over him. Sitting beside the glowing fire piled high with black turf, he looked a stately figure with his suit and tie and polished shoes, his white hair always neatly combed back. The fire provided the only heat in the room. At the back of the classroom on winter days we were freezing and had to keep our feet moving to stay warm. All the time the hum of our education never stopped – it sounded like a swarm of bees.

There were five tall windows in the room and the bottom sill was above our heads. Even if we stood up, we could only see the sky through them. When they built the school, they must have thought that only the teachers needed to see out. There were wooden flower boxes filled with geraniums on the inside sill of each window. The outsides of the boxes were completely covered with seashells stuck on with putty. Now and again, the Master would go around to each plant, pruning as he went, accompanied by the humming of our learning, holding the pipe between his teeth, then throwing the dried leaves in the fire. Finishing National School was a major event for me. Now I would be joining the 'big lads' in Belmullet Technical School.

So the following September my mother bought me a pair of long trousers, a symbol of the beginning of my secondary education. My brother A.J. was already there in his second year. He was wearing long trousers too. John, my oldest brother, had already finished school and left home for a job in Galway. The two youngest brothers were in Belmullet National School. While I attended the 'Tech' I began to cook more at home. My mother, seeing my continued interest in cooking, suggested I interview at the Tech for a spot in a hotel school in Galway. I took the interview and was told to wait for an answer during the summer. I began to look forward to this, not realizing what it meant for me. As my time at the Tech neared its end, class mates each began discussing where they would go on from here. Many intended to immigrate, which was a common occurrence at the time. Countries such as England, Australia, and America offered prospects of a better life; each had established Irish communities and a common language. Sean, my class friend, told me he was leaving for Australia to join his brother. Other class mates were planning to go to England or Scotland and were sure to get 'the start' – a job from a family member. We faced few prospects of employment in the area. Thousands of people immigrated during my childhood, a heartbreak that continues to this day. When school finished for the year, I still had not heard back from the hotel school. I began to wonder what became of the interview and what prospects were in store for me. Would I also be taking the boat to a foreign land to join my class mates?

However, despite the economic gloom that persisted at that time, my big break came in July of that same year. A letter came in the post; I had been accepted to a Hotel College in Galway! My mother was crying as she read aloud; I didn't know if she cried from happiness that I would be getting a chance at a future other than farming, or from sadness because I would be leaving home. I thought of all the crying she did the day John left home for the first time. That day we thought she'd never stop as she leaned over the sink peeling potatoes for the dinner. Now it was my turn to leave the house that was my home, my only home. I had never been away from the farm. It was the only life I knew. Galway sounded awfully far away and I had no idea how I would get there. My mother read the letter again and thanked the Holy Mother and her extended family for answering her prayers. I was separating milk in the dairy when she read the news. At the time I really didn't understand what it meant for me. I kept on spinning the wheel on the separator. She was hugging me tightly and feeling very proud. After a while my father came in and read the letter. He too was happy for me but in the back of his mind he was thinking how he would manage the cows, the milking and everything else on the farm, with one less soldier around.

The work men on the farm heard I was going to be a chef and started making fun of me. "Wasn't that women's work? Cheffin'? Is that what yer going to do? What's gotten into ye at'all?" they would say. "Why aren't ye goin' over to England and be making good money workin' in the tunnels, roads, and on building sites?" "I don't want to work on the roads," I said. "I want to be a chef and learn to cook different dishes and work in hotels." "Chef me arse! Leave the cookin' to the women," they would reply. I couldn't get away from the comments because I had to help them on the farm. "And where will ye be Cheffin'?" they asked. "In Galway," said I. "You'll be sliding around on a slippery kitchen floor and break yer neck. Hotel kitchens are a devil for the grease." They would laugh. Years later I realized that they were anything but right.

My mother bought a suitcase in Belmullet and placed it on the floor inside the front hall door, and over the rest of the summer began filling it with clothes, towels, shoes, a new overcoat, and other items she believed I would need away from home. In September the Boss and Mam drove me to the school in the town of Athenry, a few miles outside Galway town. I was sad leaving my home, my parents, my younger brothers, my dog Mars, and all the other animals on the farm. Even today, I can't believe how young I was when I left my home to learn about cooking, just a few months after my 15th birthday.

My Mother's Coffee Cake

Here's how I got started cooking: with my Mother's Coffee Cake, a delicious family recipe that is still a wonderful taste memory for me.

Ingredients for the sponge cake

4 oz. (120gr.) sugar

4 oz. (120gr.) pastry flour

2 drops vanilla essence

4 eggs

2 oz. (60gr.) melted butter

Filling: (butter cream)

8 oz. (240gr.) unsalted butter   5 teaspoons instant coffee

6 oz. (180gr.) icing sugar (Confectioners' sugar)

Method:
- Whisk eggs and sugar to a foamy consistency until the whisk leaves a trace in the mixture.
- Sieve flour, and fold gently into the mixture being careful not to leave any flour residue on the bottom of the bowl.
- Gently fold in the melted butter.
- Pour mixture into a greased 9 inch (23cm) baking tin.
- Bake at 350F (180C) for approximately 40 minutes.
- Remove from tin; allow to cool on a wire tray

For the filling
- Cream the butter and sugar until very light and fluffy.
- Add instant coffee (dilute instant coffee in a few teaspoons of hot water).

Assembly
- Cut the cake in half horizontally; spread the filling on one half.
- Place the second cake on top.
- Add some filling around the side.
- Sieve the icing sugar on top and serve.

CHAPTER TWO

Cooking School and My First Job

The school – in the former Railway Hotel in the town of Athenry – was a mixture of a barracks and a prison. There were forty-eight of us, all boys between the first and second year. Some of us from the country, some from the city, some had money and some had none. I fell into the latter. Large stone steps led up from the road to a path that leveled out as it approached the entrance. There were lovely flowerbeds on both sides and beautifully manicured lawns reaching out to what looked like an extensive vegetable garden. The same man that interviewed me in the Technical College in May answered the door, shook my hand and asked, "You are Brendan Cronin from Belmullet? How are you?" It was more of a statement than a question. I wondered how he knew my name so quickly. He told me he was the principal and began showing me around the school, introducing me to some of the teachers and other students. "This is the new lad from Belmullet in the County Mayo," he said out loud.

Finally, I was shown to my room. We climbed three flights of stairs and walked down a long corridor. My room was on the right. There were seven small beds with seven wardrobes. It had two windows which provided a little light and fresh air and that was it. It was so reminiscent of the Disney story that I thought surely Snow White would jump out of one of the beds and start singing. Six beds were lined up along one wall and the seventh, on its own in an opposite corner, was mine, so I had a little privacy. The toilet and bathroom were at the end of the hall. As I unpacked my suitcase, I thought of my mother because of the way she had carefully organized it, thinking of everything. I could picture her sitting by the fire in the kitchen for hours sewing labels with my name into every garment so I would know my own clothes. I put the clothes in the wardrobe and the suitcase under the bed and went down to the kitchen to see who I would meet.

In the kitchen, directly inside the dining room door, was the dishwashing area and opposite that was the pantry where the waiters got the tea, milk, bread, butter and jam for service. Patrick, a lad from Loughrea, a town a few miles away, was showing me around and asked where I was from. "Where's that?" says he, when I told him. "It's in County Mayo. Don't you know where Belmullet is?" So I had to tell him I didn't know where Loughrea was either. The biggest kitchen I had seen up to now was my Aunt Birdie's in Seafield House where she ran a bed and breakfast, and organized weddings and special functions. She would cook lunch for the bishop every year when he came to Belmullet for the first communion mass. The school's kitchen was much bigger. A large anthracite-fired Aga cooker dominated one side. Directly opposite was a gigantic pot that could boil a pig, and was full of bubbling liquid with bones sticking up from it which Patrick said was a stock. There were six electric cookers lined up around the walls for us to use and two students could cook on the Aga.

There was a separate section at the end of the kitchen for pastry making. It had a big oven and a mixing machine for large quantities of dough. Behind this were steps leading up to the storeroom. Patrick opened the door and led me inside. He told me this was a refrigerator. I had never seen one before. We didn't have a refrigerator at home and especially not one that you could walk into and pick foods off the shelf. At the rear of the building was the prize – a vegetable garden – a veritable chef's dream. There were rows of Early York cabbages, carrots, onions, turnips, potatoes and many more kinds of vegetables. It seemed the gardener was devoted to providing us with the freshest vegetables possible for the table. This was the school where I was going to learn cookery while using the best ingredients.

The bell rang for lunch and we lined up at the bottom of the stairs before being allowed into the dining room. Then we marched single file from the kitchen through the swinging doors to our seats. The dining room had a parquet floor, a few windows, and was set up with 12 tables of four seats each. This was my first time eating in a restaurant. There were waiter's stations around the room for keeping the cutlery and some cupboards underneath for china, something that was very new to me.

The principal walked in with all the teachers and called for grace before meals. "God Bless the food we are about to receive for which we are truly thankful." We all mumbled along and finished with a loud "Amen", made the sign of the cross, sat down and dived for the bread and butter. Some of the lads were waiters learning to wait on tables; they took our orders and brought the food from the kitchen. Their teacher was dressed in a black jacket with striped trousers and he kept walking around between the tables checking their work. We were served a three course meal, but not much of it. The second year lads told us to get used to it because there was nothing else in the way of food between meals. When we finished dessert we had to remain seated until the teachers were finished eating so we could all stand up and say grace after meals, then we left back out through the kitchen.

Back in the classroom, at two o'clock, Mrs. Farley taught us nutrition. A youngish woman who spoke with a bit of an English accent, she told us about things called carbohydrates in food and explained how they gave us energy. The principal taught the next class about business methods. We would learn to write letters to hotel guests on various subjects. He would give us a scenario and we would write a response by hand. Then he would correct them and hand them back. One day while we were writing a letter to confirm reservations, he was walking up and down between the desks and looking over our shoulders inspecting our work – a frequent habit of his. Always impeccably dressed, his leather soled shoes broke the silence by grating and squeaking on the tiled floor.

He stopped at my side and I froze. He said: "Cronin, how do you spell accommodation?" "*Accamadation*, sir!" "Will you write that on the blackboard for me, like a good lad?" "Yes sir." I went to the board and wrote *Accamadation*. He went pure red in the face and shouted at me. "*Jeeesus*, Mary and Joseph! Cronin, how can you expect to work in hotels if you can't spell accommodation?" He turned to the class, jumping up and down, asking: "What will we do with him lads? Will I kill him? Will I? What lads? What? Tell me lads! What will we do with him?" No one answered him for fear of being asked another question and all the while I stood at the board, now realizing that I had misspelled the word. He gave me a clip across the ear and said I should be ashamed of myself. "Get back to your seat and check that word in the dictionary right away," he shouted. There was complete silence for the rest of the lesson. The lads were happy that someone else got the rap. After class, out in the yard, they made fun of me, saying, "Jaysus, Cronin aren't you the bastard that cannot spell the fancy word for hotel rooms. Jaysus, Mary and Joseph will ye spell it out? Will ye Cronin? Spell it out or I'll go through ye like a dose a salts! What in God's name is wrong with ye?" And we all laughed, imitating the principal.

The daily schedule never wavered. The prefect woke us at seven o'clock, and then we'd tidy the room and make the beds ready for room inspection. Breakfast was at half seven and class at nine o'clock. Dinner was at twelve o'clock. More classes at two o'clock with some free time from four to six o'clock. Tea was at six o'clock, study time at seven, bedtime at half nine, and lights out at ten. Every night one of the teachers would supervise tea time and study time from seven to nine o'clock. At nine the teacher would ask us to put away our books, kneel beside our desks and say the rosary beginning with a Hail Mary, then call out to one of us to say one decade and then move on to someone else for the next decade. Every night without fail someone would let a loud fart in the middle of the rosary and the teacher would say we were nothing but a bunch of rotten animals for farting during a holy time.

There was no radio in the school and we were not allowed to have radios in our rooms. The only time we were allowed outside the school was on Saturday afternoon from two to four o'clock and for Mass on Sunday morning. Saturdays were the most boring days because we had no classes and it was such a lot of time to pass. In the afternoons it was always a rush after dinner to clean the kitchen and wash up the dishes so we could go downtown for two hours. And then when we did, there was nothing to do. Rainy Saturdays were exceptionally long because we were forced to remain indoors. Terence, a Dublin lad who always referred to me as 'a fookin weed,' had a record player – he was allowed to use it only on Saturday afternoons – and he introduced me to the Kinks. I remembered how in our kitchen at home we listened to the Beatles on the radio my father bought, and now I learned about Dave Davis and the Kinks without any radio. I liked their kind of music. We sang my two favorites out loud every Saturday afternoon: "A Dedicated Follower of Fashion" and "Let's all Drink to the Death of a Clown."

This school was a major change for me. I had never been away from home before and I missed everyone, my family, even the animals, especially my dog Mars. He was a brown Labrador mix, what many would call the result of a "street accident" with some passing dog. He followed me everywhere, helped me gather the cows for milking and kept me company on dark evenings as I returned home along the boreen after bringing the cows to their night pasture in the hill field. I cried myself to sleep many nights and longed for the letters from home with all the news of the family, farm, and neighbors. When my mother did find time to write, I would read and reread the letter ensuring I got every bit of news out of it.

Eventually I settled in to learn more about cooking. I was very nervous on my first day in the kitchen which was about two weeks after my arrival. For some strange reason, I believed the other lads knew more about cooking than I did. We were each given a chef's uniform: blue checkered trousers, a white jacket, necktie, and a hat. We also got a set of knives. I had cooked a little with my mother over the years but not enough to tackle the first lunch menu, which was written in French:

Crème St. Germain,
***

Filets de Merlan frits
Pommes vapeur
Haricots verts au beurre
***

Salade de fruits

The instructor arrived wearing a chef's jacket, checkered trousers, and a tall white hat. An older man with graying hair and a nasal twang in his voice, he called us around to his station – a table located in the center of the kitchen – and explained the menu in English. Now it made more sense to me, even though I did not know how to prepare it: Cream of green split pea soup, deep fried fillet of whiting, buttered green beans, steamed potatoes and fruit salad for dessert. I was assigned a station with an electric cooker beside the Aga cooker. We had to collect the ingredients from a tray in the center of the kitchen and weigh out enough for four people. We started with the ingredients for the soup. The chef showed us how to make a Bouquet Garni for flavoring it. He explained that because it is a bundle of vegetables and herbs tied together, it can be removed once it has given the desired taste to the soup. Leeks, carrots, celeriac, half an onion, one bay leaf and one clove, all tied together. It was difficult to get all the vegetable lined up so it would not fall apart. The chef would shout if they fell apart. Everyone got nervous when the chef shouted. He showed us a special way to get the vegetables lined up. Then we returned to our stations to make the Bouquet Garni. First we used the clove like a thumb tack to pin the bay leaf to the flat side of the half onion, then as the chef demonstrated, we made a cross shaped incision with a sharp paring knife in the round side of the onion, and laid it flat side down on the celery carrot and leek. Then we put the string around the lot making sure it fitted in the incision on the onion to prevent it from slipping, and then tied a knot.

We reconvened at his station to learn the chopping of the other half of the onion and then the crying started. We learned that the onion has a built in defense system to protect itself, much like the thorns on a rose. Once the cells of the onion are cut they release a chemical that makes the eyes water and is intended to make us abandon the vegetable, but we persevered and finally finished chopping. The chef instructor said: "Let ye not think that was satisfactory. I'll let it pass for today because we will be straining the soup through a sieve and the onions will be mashed, but tomorrow they must be chopped much finer."

Then we started on the fish. Using a filleting knife, the chef effortlessly demonstrated filleting and then gave us four whiting each to fillet at our stations. Once we had them completely massacred, he said we were lucky they would be coated in batter or the guests would surely send them back and ask what kind of eejits were cooking today. Then he demonstrated turning potatoes. He held the unpeeled potato between thumb and forefinger of his left hand and using a small turning knife in his right hand, he placed his thumb at the bottom of the potato, slid the knife in an arc down the side of the potato until the blade touched his thumb, removing the peel and revealing the creamy white flesh. After several arcs he had a beautifully turned potato that presented much nicer than a potato boiled in the skin. It was like a miniature wine barrel, narrower at both ends with a thick center. I tried to imitate him but to no avail. My turned potatoes were more like cement blocks.

After the potato fiasco it was easier to top and tail the beans. Then they were boiled and seasoned with salt and pepper. Boiling was easy! For my fruit salad I had apples, bananas, pears, oranges and grapes. The chef showed us how to cut them nicely and how to use a little sugar syrup and lemon to keep the apples and bananas from turning black. Back at our stations, we promptly massacred them also into all shapes and sizes. The chef said he expected we would improve with time. During the lunch service, the chef called out the orders to each of us and we then presented our dish for a table of four. The fish fillets were crisp from the deep fryer, drained on absorbent paper and served on a silver platter with a white doily paper, lemon wedges, and a sprig of parsley. We added chopped gherkins, capers and parsley to mayonnaise to make Tartar sauce. This was served separately in a sauce boat. The potatoes and beans were served in silver vegetable dishes and the fruit salad in dessert bowls. Every dish was checked by the instructor before it left the kitchen and if it was not properly presented he would ask us to rearrange it.

As the weeks progressed recipes became more difficult. One day we had Bakewell Tart on the menu. We had already learned how to line a flan ring with pastry so we were left to prepare this on our own. Then it was simple to mix butter, ground almonds, castor sugar, flour and almond essence and fill it into the pastry-lined flan and cover it with strips of pastry. We began weighing ingredients according to the recipe. Johnny, a lad from County Cork, decided he wasn't going to measure the ingredients and threw everything together in a bowl. He had the tart in the oven before any of us. The chef complimented him for his speed and we thought he was sure to get away with it. The type of filling we were using is called a "frangipane" – an almond flavored tart filling, which turns semi-liquid with heat in the oven before solidifying. Half way through the baking process the liquid in Johnny's tart began to overflow the edge of the flan ring on to the oven floor and then dripped out onto the kitchen floor. Then the whispering started until everyone, except Johnny and the instructor, noticed the growing pool of raw tart filling on the floor behind him. Someone said, "Johnny, how's yer tart coming along?" Then he saw his predicament and started wiping up the filling, but it kept dripping out. He could see we were all looking in his direction and he didn't want the chef to notice. He put a cloth on the floor to catch the flow and we started making fun of him. "Johnny, did you put baking powder in the mix? You'll be in a right fix when the chef sees the shite you're making." "Will yous be quiet, leave me alone, the chef will never notice if ye shut up," he replied.

When all the tarts were baked we presented them at our stations and the chef gave each one of us a few comments on presentation and degree of baking. He never noticed the filling dripping on the floor but then he got to Johnny's tart with no filling left in it and it all dried out. "What, in God's name is this?" he said. We all started laughing and Johnny was steaming mad. "How much flour did you use?" asks the chef. Johnny couldn't remember. Eventually the chef found out he didn't measure the ingredients and went red in the face. He leaned over the table, caught him by the ear and nearly lifted him on to the table. "Are you trying to be a smart aleck?" "No sir!" "So you think you know it all?" "No sir!" "The next time I say to measure something you better measure, do you understand?" "Yes sir!" We all learned a valuable lesson that day: when making pastry, measure exactly or the recipe won't turn out right.

I learned so much about different foods and methods of cooking, as every day in the kitchen was a new experience. I was poaching fish in fish stock, braising beef in brown stock, deep frying and shallow frying and of course stewing, one of the most common cooking methods in Ireland after frying and a close relative to boiling. We made the five 'mother sauces' including béchamel sauce, veloute sauce, espagnole sauce, hollandaise sauce and tomato sauce, the different subsidiary sauces that stem from these, and the revered sauce Bercy using shallots, parsley and bone marrow. The instructor demonstrated the making of hollandaise sauce and I realized how difficult the hot butter sauces are to make because of the delicate liaison with the egg yolks.

On days of practical cooking the most anticipated and challenging dessert was without doubt, Bavarian Cream. Its creaminess, melt on the tongue consistency, and vanilla flavor had us weak with anticipation during morning classes. When it arrived at the table we picked up our spoons and nibbled at it to make it last longer savoring every mouthful and willing for it to last longer. Usually decorated with sweetened whipped cream, it was often the subject of the afternoon conversation. It was not easy to make and until it was unmolded we were never sure if it was correctly made, for if it collapsed it would look similar to a dog's dinner.

During study hours we learned culinary terms in French and had to explain their meaning in English: Au four, a la carte, mirepoix, sabayon and vol-au-vent, to name just a few. Page upon page of culinary French terms had to be learned off by heart. The instructor was increasingly incorporating them in the practical classes so we had to know what he was talking about when he asked us to cut vegetables into "Brunoise", small dice or "Julienne", fine strips, or to cut bacon into "Lardons", cubes. After many months of school – one week spent cooking, the next studying the theory of cooking – the end of the year arrived and I was assigned to The Great Southern Hotel in Bundoran, in County Donegal, for the summer. This would be my first job.

On the way there the bus traveled through County Sligo which I knew from our classes with the Master was Yeats country. W.B. Yeats – one of our most loved poets – had this genius ability to marry words that got along together and have touched so many for so long. We learned some of his poetry in sixth class and then the Master would ask us to recite it out loud. I gazed at the height of Ben Bulben in the distance, looking majestic – partially shrouded in cloud. I had never seen such a high mountain. There was so much to see traveling through this beautiful countryside that I never felt the time passing.

Bundoran is a beach resort type of town with one long Main Street and lots of amusement arcades. Carrying my two suitcases I followed the directions from the bus stop and walked to the hotel. It was situated on the cliff just outside the town and surrounded by a beautifully manicured golf course. People were playing as I walked up the road which led through the course. Golf balls were flying in every direction. I was afraid I would get my brains knocked out before I even started to work.

I asked for the manager at the reception desk. He brought me to see the chef, a big man with a thick mop of red hair and a scraggy matching beard to be known by me for the summer only as CHEF. He was very polite despite his appearance. Chef showed me around the kitchen and introduced me to the staff. They were happy to see additional help arriving for the summer. I turned up for work at nine o'clock the next morning and met James, the sous chef. My first job was to wash lettuce for one hundred people for lunch and when that was finished there were vegetables to be washed, peeled and sliced, all for the salad selection. Chef came by and, seeing the lettuce dripping wet, asked why had I not dried it? He said that if guests wanted water with their salad they would ask the waiter to pour them a glass. Even without the sarcasm, I got the message loud and clear. Every time I finished a job, I would tidy and clean the space I used. Jimmy, the Chef Garde-Manager – cold kitchen chef – said he could see I came from a training school from the way I organized my workplace. It was a nice compliment to get on the first day of work. It was also the only one I got during the summer so it was hard to judge how I was doing.

The hotel dining room opened for lunch at 12 o'clock and we prepared all the orders as they came in. Although in our home we called the midday meal dinner, in hotels it was referred to as lunch. Jimmy showed me a sample of each order and then expected me to make the next one on my own. The dishes were simple. We learned most of them with the instructor in Athenry: Smoked salmon, Russian eggs, Eggs mayonnaise and different kinds of salads. Jimmy could carve smoked salmon so thin that the plate was visible beneath each slice. He told me "The thinner the slice the more the flavor emerges." It was a pleasure to see him using the salmon knife which was also visible through the fish as it travelled underneath the slice. I practiced over the summer and eventually could use the knife like him.

After the dining room closed for lunch, the kitchen staff took their lunch break during which we were allowed to help ourselves to any dish off the menu. I had a slice of prime rib with mashed potato and a glass of water for my lunch and thought that was not bad for my first meal at my new job. As the days went by, I got used to a routine and the work became easier, only because I didn't have to ask as many questions and that gave me a little confidence. I got to know the rest of the kitchen staff, mostly during breaks and at the end of the shift. Some of us worked split shift, which started at nine in the morning and finished at two in the afternoon, and started again at five in the evening, lasting until ten. Some of the lads went to the pub for the afternoon and sometimes came back staggering from the drink. That meant we had to work a little harder because they couldn't keep up with the service. The chef worked the morning shift which covered lunch, and the sous chef was in charge for dinner. The breakfast chef worked from six in the morning until two. He took a break around ten when breakfast was over and afterwards prepared his mise-en-place – food preparation – for the next day and finished at two o'clock. The evening chef arrived at two and worked till ten. He prepared the roast for dinner and all the sauces and main courses that would be served from the sauce section. He also had the staff meal ready when we came back at five. The pastry chef worked a split shift, doing production in the morning and desserts at night.

There was a lovely beach – the Strand – beside the hotel. One day during our lunch break, Mick from the pastry asked if I would go down to the Strand with him during the afternoon. So off we went and he showed me around. We could walk through the hotel grounds and down a path along the cliff to the beach. Many hotel guests took this shortcut as well. Some days, I would go on my own and eventually there was a crowd of us that always met in the same spot. Over the summer, I met many nice people on the Strand: some were on their holidays, and some lived nearby and just came to the seaside for the day. There was always something or someone to see and it was cheap entertainment. I was getting only eight pounds a week after the taxman took his share – about sixteen US dollars. The Strand was great value for a fellow with no money.

The dinner shifts were very repetitive. The sous chef was not as strict as the chef and if the evening was quiet they would tell jokes and mess around. The lads told me he was "a horny bastard", always looking for a bit of skirt. One night we were not very busy and the sous chef got into an argument with one of the waitresses. After a while, he told the sauce chef that he would be away for a few minutes and to "keep an eye." He went into the storeroom with the waitress, closed the door, and didn't come out for a long time. When he appeared, he put on his apron and went back to work and she walked out to the restaurant smiling away to herself.

One evening as I was making mashed potatoes for the dinner menu, the lads in the main kitchen were messing around with wet towels. They would roll wet towels into a tight ball and throw them at each other. I had just finished seasoning the potatoes when I was hit in the side of the face with a wet towel. It stung the skin and made me mad. I said nothing, which translated into calm in the emotional inferno that was the main kitchen. I finished the mash, and carried it to the bain-marie. Then I took off my apron and hat, handed them to the sous chef and close to tears, told him I was walking off the job and if he could not maintain order in his kitchen, it was not my problem. There was renewed silence from all around and I walked down the corridor leading to the staff house.

The sous chef came running after me, said he was sorry and asked me why I couldn't take a joke. "If you got hit with a wet cloth across the face while doing your job, would you take it as a joke?" I asked. I went to my room and went to bed. Nevertheless I came in to work the next morning and strangely enough the staff was very nice to me. From that day until I left, I got on better with the sous chef and all the others and when I left they all wished me a safe trip home and a good second year in school.

I left Bundoran at the end of August and went home to Belmullet for a week before going back to school. A.J. had a car and we would go to the local dances. If I was lucky, I might even get a chance to dance with some girl! For some unknown reason, the women would always line up on the opposite side of the dance hall to the lads. When the music started the lads would make a run for it across the dance floor. It was like a march, a line of nervous young men ready to ask a lovely young woman if she wished to dance, and having the fear of God put in them if they received the wrong reply. Strong men were weak with anticipation – turning to jelly before the women. If the girl refused to dance – walking back to the other side of the hall without a girl by your side was the height of embarrassment – there was no other choice but to ask the girl beside her, then she'd be disappointed for coming in second. Once out on the floor, dancing and getting lost in the crowd helped to generate conversation. The next difficult bit was when the music changed to a slow dance, then many a girl would say that she had a sore foot and wanted to sit down. That could have various meanings: I don't want to dance with you anymore, or the fear of a slow dance and a close embrace. Sore feet were common.

At home, I helped out with the hay, taking care of the animals and in the kitchen with my mother. I made the Bakewell tart for her. She was so proud to have me home again. One day, she made our family a new spaghetti bolognese recipe that she'd been given. She laughed when I told her the story of my first week in Athenry, and of the spaghetti that I'd been instructed to prepare there. One of the second year lads asked me to go to the garden and pick the spaghetti off the spaghetti tree in the corner of the top garden. I almost fell for it because, growing up on meat and potatoes, I never saw spaghetti until I left home and did not know what it was. After all, in school we were often sent to the garden for various ingredients for the menu so why would spaghetti be any different? During my short stay at home, neighbors would visit our house and ask how my "cheffin'" was going. I visited the Master and he wanted to know all the details of my studies. I spent an entire evening chatting with him. He was retired now and spent most of his days at his favorite pastime, rock fishing. Any fish he caught would be brought to my mother for filleting; they were mostly mackerel – delicious when pan fried.

Before I left for school my mother gave me a paper clipping of an article she received from an American couple who stayed at the house that summer. The couple sent it to her with a lovely thank you note for making their stay so special. There was no author's name on the article and I add it here in good faith as I do not know which author to credit.

"A glowing spot of warmth among the bleakly beautiful sea-lashed moorlands of western Mayo is Harry and Agnes Cronin's Sea Call (Carne, Belmullet, Phone 47). It would be impossible to pilgrimage to the Cronin's and not feel welcomed. They are what people mean when they want to meet "the real Irish." The two story bungalow set in a 65-acre dairy farm at the edge of the sea is bright, clean and simple. Mrs. Cronin churns her own butter, cans delicious pickles and is noted for her apple tart. Harry Cronin is a grand shooter and story teller – just give him a half-bottle of whiskey (says herself) and get him telling shooting tales, and you'll be up all night. (Note: without the half-bottle and on any other subject, the result seems the same.) There are only three rooms with H&C (water) and central heating, so write or call well in advance as the Cronin's do a fantastic repeat business. Bed-and-breakfast: £2.00 ($4.64), high tea £1.50 ($3.47), weekly half-board £24.50 ($55.83). Dinners available on request. 25% discount for children."

After reading the article, my father jokingly said it was unbelievable he was available in all three rooms – making reference to his 'H&C' initials.

Eventually, the day came for me to leave for my second year in Athenry.

By now a familiar ritual any time one of us left home, my mother would get out the bottle of holy water and sprinkle some on the bonnet of the car and then on all of us and we'd bless ourselves and ask the great Saint Christopher, the patron saint of travelers, to protect us on our travels. How Christopher got that distinction I'll never know. Maybe he was a big traveling man himself? In all my years of coming and going to our house, the Boss never cried when saying goodbye to any of us. He would wrap his big arms around me, give me a huge hug and with his great smile wish me well. My mother would be so sad, all she could say was, "Sure you have to leave to come back!"

Back at school it was great to see all the lads again. We exchanged stories and compared hotels, kitchens and chefs, how we were treated and the dishes we cooked. Now we were without any radios, television or newspapers to inform us what was happening in the world. Although it was not allowed, I had brought back a little battery operated transistor radio. I would hide it under the sink during room inspection. Many lads would come to my room after lights out and listen to the Grand Duchy with the volume really low. Radio Luxembourg played the best music, not like Irish radio that went off the air after playing the national anthem at half eleven. We could listen to Rod Stewart singing that it was late September and he should be back at school with Maggie. Well we knew all about that because he was singing about us. Going back to school after a great summer doing everything we liked and now confined to the discipline of Athenry was difficult to bear, Maggie or no Maggie!

In our second year we cooked more complicated dishes such as duck á l'orange, beef consommé (a clear French soup), poached fillets of sole with white wine sauce, lobster mayonnaise, lamb cutlets reform, Rum Baba, and Profiteroles. The latter were very difficult to make because the choux pastry is semi-liquid when raw and must be piped into shape from a piping bag before baking. We learned about the fat content of meat and did calculations on the yield percentage to determine the real cost of a pound of meat. We did food costing, menu costing, and calculated labor costs for the kitchen. There were the famous chefs and philosophers to learn about such as Carême, Savarin, Soyer, and Escoffier. We learned of their contributions to the culinary profession and the impact of Cesar Ritz on the hotel industry, and his historic partnership with Escoffier in opening the Ritz hotels in London and Paris. We were taught about the historical origins of the many dish names we cooked throughout the year. Béchamel sauce named after Louis Béchamel, Maitre d'hôtel to King Louis XIV, and Parmentier, the man who introduced the potato to France.

One of the most influential people in French cuisine was actually Italian. Catherine De Medici of Florence married the Duc d'Orléans in 1533 – who later became King Henry II of France – and then moved her entire culinary brigade to the French Court thus changing the future of French cuisine forever. We studied the different types of service, learning when waiters should serve from the right or left and the proper way to pour wine. We learned about banquets and the use of round or rectangular tables and were taught how to change a table cloth without exposing the top of the table, a faux pas in fine dining restaurants. We learned about food hygiene, food poisoning, and how one can prevent the other. We examined kitchen design plans to see how they could be improved and learned how fridges worked and what temperatures they should operate at.

Near the end of our second year we began preparation for our final practical exam. We had to cook a four course menu for four people unassisted, provide the cost for each dish and a list of equipment with a detailed order of work outlining the sequential steps for the entire menu. If we failed the exam we could not graduate. My menu was a selection of four composed salads, poached fillet of sole with a white wine sauce, grilled sirloin with château potatoes and braised leeks. For dessert I had the feared and revered Chocolate Bavarian Cream. Thinking about the exam was nerve racking, so much depended on this one day. I had to calculate the ingredients for four people. Then make a work order which outlined the sequence in which I would prepare the entire menu. In addition, I had to prepare a list of the equipment required. This was part of our exam and would be corrected by the examiner afterwards.

On the day of the exam, I made the Bavarian cream first so it would have the most time to set in the fridge. I was using one large mould for four people. My biggest fear was that it would not remain in one piece once unmolded. Then I began on the four different salads. Afterwards I filleted the sole, folded the fillets skin side in on a buttered dish for poaching and using the bones, began making a fish stock for the sauce. When the skin side is on the inside of the fold, the fillets curl up when heated, creating a beautiful shape. If the skin side is on the outside, the fillets lose their shape during cooking and a nice presentation is impossible. Now it was time to turn the potatoes: each one should have seven sides and look like the next. They went in the oven in a small roasting pan with a little clarified butter. Then it was time to cut the leeks for braising and get them into a covered braising pan and in the oven. All the time the examiner was looking over my shoulder and not making any comment, which was probably worse than if he did. By now, I had the potatoes roasting in the oven, the leeks also in the oven but using a different cooking method, braising – slow cooking in a liquid. Then the fish stock was ready to strain, the salads were ready in the fridge. But constantly in the back of my mind was the thought of the Bavarian Cream spilling out of the mould instead of popping out as a beautiful tower of culinary delight.

The instructor gave us the countdown. I was second to present my dishes, four people would eat this food in the dining room and contribute to my marks for the exam. Time came to present: first up were all the salads. It was a relief to have them served. No comment from the instructor. Now he was calling for the sole, and I had a five minute window to serve it or I would be late. By now I had poached the sole using the fish stock, poured off the stock, thickened it with a roux, strained and seasoned it. It was ready to serve, and one more relief to have that out of the way, but still no comment from the examiner. Next was the sirloin. I had been instructed to prepare two of them medium and two well done. This time I had a ten minute window. I grilled them, then garnished them with the chateau potatoes and leeks and gravy – as it was called at the time – and topped it with sprigs of curly parsley and served them – still no comment.

Now, with my main course served, it was time to face the music with the Bavarian Cream. I had another five minute window. I turned the mould upside down on the silver platter and shook it to dislodge the cream. The cream would not budge, and I realized that it would not come out of the mould! I shook it again, still no movement. I gave it a more vigorous shake, but still it would not budge. I thought that if I could not get this dessert unmolded I would fail the exam. Then, after pressing down the edges of the cream with my fingertips, I put my trembling hands around the mould and the heat of my hands through the metal mould melted a very thin layer of the Bavarois and it literally "popped" out onto the platter. I was so relieved – it had not cracked or split! All the while the examiner was standing beside me he still had not made a comment, not even a facial expression. I decorated it with sweetened whipped cream and glazed cherries and sent it out to the restaurant. I waited two days to get any feedback and only then did I find out I had passed the four hour exam. I would graduate! I would become a commis chef, only one step above an apprentice but still a start on the long ladder of a culinary career.

Again the school was placing us in hotels around Ireland for practical training. Many of the lads were talking about eventually leaving for Switzerland. Some of them had friends there in Geneva, Berne and Zurich. There was great experience to be gained in Switzerland, or so it was said. Some lads told stories they'd heard of different foods, interesting hotels in beautiful resorts, and better pay than in Ireland. Out of all these discussions we had in the weeks before leaving Athenry, I made my mind up that I would go to Switzerland as soon as I could make enough money for the passage. I never thought about the difference in language, an oversight that I later realized would be one of my greatest challenges.

About two weeks before we left the College, we got our hotel assignments. I was assigned to the Intercontinental Hotel in Limerick. I was overjoyed. I was finally going to a big hotel and living in a big city. I had no idea how big it was or where I would stay, or even how I would get there, but I knew I would work it out. The name sounded very elegant. Maybe this would be fancier than the Great Southern Hotel in Bundoran. On the last day of school, we said our goodbye's at the train station and since that day many of us never met again. As the train pulled out of the tiny station, we had a final look at the school we had called home for two years. I have fond memories of the time spent there, the lads, the teachers, the jokes, the laughs, and the tears.

Before reporting to work, I went home to Belmullet to visit my family. I would often go out on the town with my brother and it was as if I was a stranger. My brother A.J. would have to tell them who I was because I had been away for two years and before that I seldom left the farm, so most people did not know me. Nothing creates more curiosity in a small town in the west of Ireland than a stranger. People want to know where you're from. Where are you staying? When are you leaving? My uncle A.J. said he once saw a black man in Belmullet and that no one had ever seen a black man walking the streets of Belmullet before. He said it was the talk of the town partly because small western Irish towns were fairly isolated at the time.

I made my way to Limerick by bus passing through all the towns on the way: Galway, Gort, Ennis. The bus driver kindly stopped the bus right outside the hotel on the Ennis road and let me off even though it was not a scheduled stop. I carried my two cases in through the front door and asked for the manager by name. A small man with thinning hair, he welcomed me and asked a porter to put my cases behind the reception desk. We immediately set off to the kitchen to meet the chef. He was a very clean cut man with a neatly trimmed moustache, slightly different from the chef in Bundoran. He shook my hand saying "Welcome!" and showed me around the kitchen, introducing me to all the staff.

Now all I needed was a place to stay. The chef had arranged something. Ah, I thought, an organized man! And he was. There was perfect order in this kitchen. He brought me to the laundry department and introduced the head housekeeper. A plump courteous woman, she had a room in her house for rent. It was two pounds ten shillings a week and I could move in right away. She was a kindly woman, never married and as the sous chef said to me later, he believed she was untouched by human hand. She drove me to her house in a black Morris Minor, took me to my room and showed me the bathroom which was down the hall. She did not want any drinking or eating in the room and visitors were not allowed. I was not to come home drunk. She wouldn't stand for it. The last lodger that rented my room got thrown out because he came home in the middle of the night, mad with the drink, singing at the top of his voice and broke down the front door when she refused to let him in. She had to have a new door put in the next day. And if that wasn't enough, he went upstairs and threw up all over the bathroom. Mary, the other lodger, and a teacher at that, came out of her room in only a night dress and gave him a wallop on the head with the brush. "Ah," the housekeeper said, "the drink is a terrible curse. Do you drink?" "No, Mrs." I replied. She said it was a real blessing that I did not drink and I should thank God and his holy mother and pray that I would never start. "The drop never passed my lips," says she, "and many's the poor soul in Limerick City had their lives ruined because of the drink. Women and children starving, while the husband would spend his days in the pub."

I got used to work quickly. Next in line to the chef was the sous chef, a Mayo man, he spent most of his working life in Limerick. When he told me he worked in Germany I mentioned my plans to go to Switzerland. "Go as soon as you can and you will learn a lot there," he said. The sauce chef was next in line to the sous chef. He cooked very well and was extremely well organized. I learned a lot just from looking at him working. He would start every day at half past two preparing the evening menu and a la carte mise-en-place. When we came back from our split shift at half past five the bain marie – hot water table for holding hot foods – would be filled with sauces and garnishes for the evening menu. Prime ribs would be roasted, horseradish sauce made, and the highest Yorkshire puddings I have ever seen would be created. It became a sort of competition to get the highest 'puds' and he would always win. He never let us see him making the recipe and to this day I do not know what he put in the mix to get them so high. It was a pleasure to see him work. His workstation was always clean and tidy and the dishes he prepared were tasty. I thought he was a better chef than the sous chef and did not understand why the kitchen hierarchy was like that. It would make sense to me that the better chefs would be in more senior positions. It took time for me to learn that the qualities of a chef encompass more than just cooking.

I spent my first few weeks in the cold kitchen preparing similar dishes to the ones in Bundoran. The kitchen was smaller and had very poor ventilation and no windows. After a few weeks the breakfast chef left and the chef asked me if I would take over her shift. I accepted, which meant walking to work in the morning at half five in the dark. My greatest fear was to be late; the guests depended on me to cook their breakfasts. Some mornings I would walk in the rain and go straight in to the warm kitchen to start up the ovens and salamanders for the bacon. My clothes would dry out as I worked. One of my favorite desserts from the menu in the Intercontinental Hotel was Steamed Apricot Pudding. It was simple to make and the guests loved it. I creamed a half pound of castor sugar with a pound of butter. Then added seven eggs and one pound of flour and poured the mixture into a paper lined cake tin with a layer of apricot jam on the bottom. I wrapped the whole thing in tinfoil and poached it in a water bath in the oven for two hours. Once it was un-moulded the jam flowed down over the pudding giving off a wonderful aroma. Apple tart and ice cream was another popular dessert as was jelly and cream and sherry trifle. I learned to make good trifle from my mother and I remember when we used to have sherry trifle for dessert when we visited Aunt Birdie in Seafield House for lunch every St. Stephen's day. She always made great trifle.

By now I was earning more than in Bundoran, about sixteen pounds a week, which left me with thirteen pounds and ten schillings when the landlady was paid. I was saving to pay for a passage to Switzerland and so I did not go out much. It was cheaper to watch television. On most evenings after the shift finished work, the chefs would go for few drinks to Martin's pub across the Shannon River. The hotel was located right next to the Sarsfield Bridge, named after Patrick Sarsfield, who was instrumental in defending the City of Limerick during the 1690 siege and eventually signed the Treaty of Limerick. One evening the chefs asked me to come along and I had my first drink. They all made a big hullabaloo about it. I did not like the taste of the first beer I had and wondered what was so special about it anyways? It reminded me of what my Uncle A.J. said to my Aunt Mary when she tasted his pint of Guinness one day in Gallagher's pub in Belmullet. Turning her face in disgust at the bitter flavor, she remarked sharply, "How can you drink that stuff?" He replied with his usual wit, "Now you know what it's like every time I come to the pub, no one knows what I have to go through!"

Some days I would be assigned to the evening shift. On one of those evenings I roasted ducks for the dinner menu; they would be carved to order. The sous chef was late for the evening shift and I was not sure how to carve the duck. I had carved a duck in Athenry once with the instructor, but neither the duck nor I remembered the details of the experience and now I did not know which end was which. Once the neck was removed the duck had a hole in each end which made matters worse. It was half six, food orders were coming in and no sous chef around to show me how to dissect the bird. The manager came in to the kitchen, as he did every evening before service, put on an apron and did a nice job showing me his method of carving. Just then the sous chef walked in and got a strange look from the manager. He was a little worse for the wear for having spent too much time in the pub. That evening – despite his excess in the pub – the sous chef told me he would ask the hotel management if they would sponsor me to go to Switzerland as part of a training course. I thought this is my chance. If they could get me a job and a visa, that would be a great start. We then began planning my transfer to the Intercontinental Hotel in Dublin where I would work in the meantime. My plan to get to Switzerland was one step closer.

On another evening the sous chef was complaining about the extractor fan over the grill and how we had been waiting for the hotel to fix it for months. It was not extracting the smoke quick enough and as a result made breathing difficult. I suppose it was the last straw for him because he was leaning over the grill with about twenty steaks on it when he turned to us and said: "That's it lads, we are walking off the job!" We were going on strike to protest poor working conditions. With that he walked out of the kitchen leaving the steaks and their new owners to fend for themselves. He was the shop steward and we were all union members, so we had to walk with him. This was my first experience with this kind of confrontation. The manager begged us to come back to work and at least finish the orders on the grill. The sous chef told him that he had begged long enough to have the fan fixed and maybe he should work on the grill for a while to see what it was like to breathe in all that smoke during the evening. The manager pleaded: "For the love a Jaysus, will ye at least finish the orders on the grill!" A polite "fuck off" from Eddie ended the conversation. It is said that in Ireland we have such an eloquent style and convincing manner for expressing this command that the recipient actually begins to look forward to the journey. Eddie's tone accomplished exactly that. It wasn't an insulting expression but more like a verbal exclamation mark. We were on strike for sixteen hours, the fan was fixed the next day and we returned to work after lunch.

Seamus was one chef who seemed to be always in good humor. He worked split shift and was always making funny jokes, mostly about the women. He had a round tanned face and a slight belly visible above his apron strings. When he was carving turkey he would ask the waitresses if they liked the breast or the leg for the guest. Then, with a big wink, he would say, "Now if that was me, I'd take a little of the breast meself, I'm partial to the breast but ye can't neglect the thigh either." The younger waitresses would laugh with him and the older ones would tell him to shut his filthy mouth, and that it wasn't right to be talking like that. One of the waiters who worked mostly evening shift was a big Dave Brubeck fan. He would call out the tables in riddles around the singer's famous song "Take Five". If he wanted table five he would ask for "one Dave Brubeck please"; for table four it was Dave Brubeck minus one and plus one for table six. It took me a while to get used to it.

Peggy, one of the older waitresses, was a great complainer and always wanted special requests for her guests. One day Gay Byrne, host of Irish TV's *The Late Late Show*, and one of the most famous personalities on Irish television, came to the hotel dining room for dinner and of course he had to sit in her section. In she came to the kitchen and went on as if she had known him all her life. "Oh isn't he only gorgeous, he's not at all like when he's on the 'Telly', he's much nicer, and he's a darlin'! Now make sure that food is done right, chef. I don't want him complaining on his first visit here." The chef told her that he wouldn't be back if she had anything to do with it, fussing over him like that. He got his food and was very happy. Peggy was telling everyone that it was because of her waitressing abilities that he was so happy with his meal.

On slow evenings, the sous chef would tell us stories about Germany and all the great things that happened there. He described some of the dishes from the Black Forest Region and how the local cherries are used to make the great "Schwarzwalder Kirschtorte", the famous Black Forest Cherry Cake. He mentioned how a simple slice of pork is introduced to some common breadcrumbs and becomes the mighty "schnitzel." This made me even more determined to work in Switzerland. He said the women on the continent were great fun and mighty drinkers.

Later in the year, the head concierge invited me to join the Shannon Rowing Club. I spent months rowing up and down the river, fourth in an eight-seater. We would row out on the Shannon River estuary as far as the cement factory, and then turn in mid-stream and row back against the current. I was nervous when we maneuvered these turns, the strength of the current, our distance from the bank, and the fact I could not swim added to the fear of capsizing. But when we were on the straight, almost gliding over the water at full speed, it was great feeling, I loved the water. It was beautiful rowing there on summer evenings with the sun a fireball in the sky and no sounds except the oars in the water and the coxswain guiding us. I found it a welcome change from the hectic life of the kitchen.

My landlady always offered me a cup of tea when I came home from work, One evening – although I was very late – she was waiting up for me. She was "very disturbed" by a poster I had put up on the back of my bedroom door. She said it was not right to have a picture of a woman wearing only wellington boots facing our Lord's picture, which of course she had hanging over my bed since the day I moved in. She could not face entering the room to change the sheets and was surprised that a lad like me would put such filth on the wall. I was to take it down that very minute. Anything for peace and quiet, I took down the poster. I would be leaving soon anyway.

A few weeks later my transfer papers arrived and I made preparations to move to Dublin to work at our sister hotel in Ballsbridge which was now renamed Jury's Hotel – while I was working in Limerick, Intercontinental Hotels sold their three properties in Ireland to Jury's. We had a great party in Martin's pub the day before I left. Even Martin put up a round of drinks and wished me luck in the big city. I told him I wouldn't stay long there because I wanted to go to Switzerland and learn a different kind of cooking. "Fair play to ye," says he and we raised our glasses and I bid farewell to Limerick and the good times I had there.

At Jury's in Dublin, a much bigger kitchen than in Limerick, I was assigned to the Chef Rôtissier – roast chef. On the roster I was called "commis rôtissier" which basically meant I was his assistant. On my first morning at work my chef showed me to a long table piled high with turkeys, chickens, loins of pork, sirloins of beef, and the odd goose thrown in for good measure. Those meats were all to be roasted by lunch time. No wonder he needed an assistant! In addition to roasting, during the lunch service I was responsible for grilling any fish that was ordered off the menu for the dining room. Grilled Dover sole-on-the-bone and salmon steaks were the main grilled fish orders.

I also worked at the cabaret in the evenings. Hal Roach and Maureen Potter, well known Irish entertainers, were playing at the time to a mainly American audience, and every night my roast chicken was served. After just three months in Dublin, my visa for Switzerland arrived. I finally had it in my hand. I could now leave for that beautiful country at anytime. I bought my plane ticket to Geneva from a travel agent in Grafton Street. On my last day at Jury's Michael, the cold kitchen chef, an older man with a moustache for whom I roasted many of the meats for sandwiches and salads, called me aside and said, "Brendan, learn all the Swiss can teach you, scrub floors if you have to, because it will open the doors of the world for you." Later in my career, I realized the power of these words.

Sitting on the Aer Lingus plane before takeoff and listening to foreign languages being spoken around me, I wondered if I would meet any English speaking people on the flight. A big fellow sat down beside me and politely introduced himself as Josef, a businessman from Berne in Switzerland. He spoke a little English with a strong accent. It was the first time I had heard someone speaking a language that was not their native tongue. He said, "I vos in Dublin for von veek and had great fun in ze pubs. In Berne ve have ze pub, but is full of Swiss!" he laughed. "Zey are too conservative to have fun and zing and dance. Ze Irish are good for ze conversation." As the plane rose out over Dublin Bay, I looked back and realized for the first time that I was actually leaving Ireland. I wondered when I would come back again. After all, I had a working visa for only one year. It was 1973, a few months before my eighteenth birthday. I had no idea what to expect in my next job.

All I knew is that it would involve food, and hopefully something other than the boiled variety!

Bavarian Cream (Bavarois)

The following is a favorite of mine. Pay close attention to the recipe so it does not turn out like a dog's dinner!

Ingredients for 6 portions

1 cup (230ml.) milk
1 cup (230ml.) cream
½ oz. leaf gelatin (or 5 leaves)

3 oz. (90gr.) sugar
3 eggs
A few drops of vanilla essence

Preparation

- Soak the gelatin leaves in cold water to soften them.
- Separate yolks and set the whites aside.
- Whisk the yolks and sugar until they are almost white.
- Bring the milk to a boil in a thick-bottomed saucepan and pour over the eggs while constantly whisking.
- Return to the saucepan on low heat and stir until it coats the back of a wooden spoon.
- Do not allow the mixture to boil or it will curdle.
- Remove from the heat and stir in the softened gelatin leaves until they dissolve.
- Strain the mixture through a fine strainer and stir it in a bowl over some ice until it is almost at setting point.
- Whip the cream to soft peaks.
- Whip the whites to a meringue with stiff peaks.

Assembly

- Fold in the cream to the egg mixture and fold in the whites being careful to eliminate any 'pockets of meringue' in the mixture.
- Pour the mixture into a mold (or coffee cups) and allow to set in the refrigerator – wet the mold with cold water before filling.

Presentation

- Once firm, release the edge of the cream from the mold by gently pressing down with the finger-tips.
- Shake the mold and turn the 'Bavarois' onto a plate – can also be served in the mold. Decorate with sweetened whipped cream and serve.

CHAPTER THREE

Irish Boy

Josef and I parted at the customs in Geneva and that was the last I saw of him. Despite my complete lack of French as I arrived in Switzerland, I found the bus from the airport to the railway station. Trains were coming and going at high speeds, stopping only for a few minutes before taking off again. Not sure which one I should take, I eventually wrote the name of my destination – the town of Biel, Switzerland – on a piece of paper and showed it to one of the men in uniform on the platform. He pointed to a train on the other side of the station. I lugged my two cases down the steps of the underpass and up the other side, found an empty seat, and settled in for the trip. As the train gathered speed and it passed through towns and countryside I was surprised at the cleanliness and neatness of everything and everyone I saw. Fields were well kept and mowed to the very edge, something that wasn't done in Ireland. Railway stations were tidy – luggage carts lined up perfectly like soldiers waiting for a call to action. Even inside the train, the absence of litter was striking. People dressed differently – almost trendier, their clothes were a better fit.

I had no idea how long the journey would take and there was no one to ask. I was afraid to fall asleep, miss the station, and end up somewhere in the Baltic. The train was much faster than the Irish trains and was noticeably quieter. Later I learned all Swiss trains are electric. Eventually the conductor came around and we had a short English lesson before I could explain my predicament. A tall man dressed in an impeccable uniform with a peaked hat wrote down the names of the towns we would pass through and lastly my destination: in neat handwriting he wrote Nyon, Lausanne, Neuchatel and then Biel. I thought the Swiss to be a friendly lot. Eventually the train pulled into Biel which I later found out was bilingual in French and German like many towns in Switzerland.

Taxis were lined up near the pavement. Not being able to speak the language I ignored them and started walking, carrying my two cases and a bag. I thought that such an elegant hotel would be on a main street. Sure enough, the Hotel Elite was located on the Banhofstrasse only a short walk from the station. As I approached the hotel steps, two porters rushed to take my suitcases and carried them to the reception. I introduced myself and stated my reason for being there to the receptionist. When the porters heard that they made themselves scarce. No kitchen helper was going to get them to carry his luggage. He can carry his own bags. The manager arrived and welcomed me in broken English. I didn't have even the most rudimentary French or German with which to answer him and he was quite content to use English. A tall man with a bald patch on the very top of his head and a graying ring of hair around the sides, he showed me to the kitchen and introduced me to Herman, the chef, a pleasant man with very short hair and an extremely strong handshake. I was surprised at the strength of the squeeze he gave my hand; he noticed me wincing but never said a word. He welcomed me, asked if I had a good trip and if I was hungry and what would I like to eat? Now, I had never been asked that question before: food for kitchen staff was always whatever was left over. "I don't know," I said. "How about a fillet steak," he asked. "That will be fine," I replied. "Mit rice or *Pommes Frites?*" "What are *Pommes frites?*" "Deep-fried potatoes." His accent was just like Josef's on the plane: he had w's and z's all over the place.

He showed me to a small dining room off the kitchen with one long table and ten chairs. "Please sit down," he said. "This is the chef's private dining room. You can have all your meals and breaks in here. What will you have to drink, a beer?" "Yes, thank you" I said. He brought the biggest beer bottle I had ever seen and opened it with the flip of his thumb. One of the chefs came in and asked in broken English how I wanted the steak cooked. The chef translated "rare" into whatever language they had in common and left.

The fillet steak arrived with a nice garnish of vegetables and chips – which now were upgraded to *Pommes Frites*. The taste was delicious. I could not believe I was actually sitting here, in a foreign country, not speaking the language and getting this treatment after just one hour in the hotel. I never received this much attention in Limerick or Dublin. Even in Bundoran where we had a little dining privacy, we were never allowed to drink beer with our meals. I was beginning to think, "So this is how the Swiss treat their workers." After my meal, one of the apprentices showed me to a staff bedroom, one floor above the kitchen, and I unpacked.

I spent my first day at work on the sauce section. Marcel, the chef saucier, spoke a little English, acquired from working for a summer in London many years ago which was probably the reason the chef put me to work with him. I was to be a Stagiaire – Intern – on that section. Marcel turned out to be a cheerful fellow and loved to talk about his stay in London. Like many Swiss chefs, he went abroad after completing his apprenticeship to learn English. Most went to London and picked up some of the language. I could see his eyebrows squeeze together at times trying to make out the Irish accent. Maybe he didn't listen too well in London after all! In all fairness, he had reason to be surprised as I had a very strong Irish accent. I pronounced many words differently to what he would have heard in London. Words beginning with a T sounded like Ch. So tuna was '*Chewna*' and Tuesday, '*Chewsday*'. Even Chocolate, I pronounced it '*chalklate*'. No wonder he was confused.

It was strange to be in the kitchen and not understand a word of what was being said. I could not ask any questions as no one spoke English except the chef and Marcel. I could smile and call them whatever I liked in English and they would probably thank me for some compliment or other, possibly thinking, "Look at the Irish boy, he is happy to be working in a warm kitchen and not out on the building sites in the cold like many of the other foreigners."

Marcel gave me a list of duties for the morning, written out in his best English, and although the shallots were written *echalottes*, I still managed to make out his writing. He put the time he wanted them completed next to each item and then showed me around the kitchen. He showed me where the ingredients were stored, the fridges, the drawers of equipment, and the fish tank. I must admit that I had never seen a fish tank in a kitchen before. It had a window in the side and I could see lovely rainbow trout swimming in circles waiting for their encounter with the frying pan. After the tour I got back to my list: finely chopped shallots, chopped parsley, freshly squeezed lemon juice, lemon segments, decorated half lemons, seasoning mix, chopped fresh tarragon, half a liter each of hollandaise and béarnaise sauce, 200g of sliced fresh mushrooms and two large bottles of cold beer for Marcel to keep him from dying of thirst during the lunch service. I started with the first item on the list: finely chopped shallots. When they were finished I put them in a container, covered them, placed them in the fridge and made a mental note for the next day to leave the chopping of the shallots until last, to avoid crying.

We had our half-hour lunch break at eleven and Marcel said I should be finished with the list by then. I started the reductions for the hollandaise and béarnaise. White wine, bay leaf, crushed peppercorns and chopped shallots for the hollandaise and the same in a separate sauteuse – saucepan – with the addition of tarragon vinegar and the stems of tarragon for the béarnaise. Reducing the wine concentrates the flavor. Then I clarified the butter by melting it and allowing it to boil slowly to evaporate the water and buttermilk. Next step was to separate the egg yolks into two bowls and once both reductions were reduced to a third of the original amount I could strain each one over the eggs making sure to whisk in order to prevent the yolks from coagulating. When the butter was clear I strained it through cheesecloth. The liquid was a beautiful amber color almost like an English pint of beer without a head. Now all that was left to do was to whisk the egg yolks and reduction to a creamy consistency over a bain marie – water bath – and add the butter at a trickle. When the sauce got too thick, I would add a few drops of white wine to keep the correct consistency. When all the butter was added, the sauce had to be seasoned with salt, white pepper powder, lemon juice and Worcestershire sauce, and then strained through cheesecloth. Now the chopped parsley and tarragon could be added to one mixture making it a béarnaise while the other remained plain for a hollandaise: their silky texture literally caressed the tongue. A spoonful of hollandaise sauce stirred into a white wine fish sauce just before serving added tremendous flavor and a silky richness. Except for Marcel's beer, I finished the list before lunch. He tasted the sauce and said: "Brendan, too much lemon!" Otherwise the rest was fine. Then he gave me the next list.

Herman was German, and very proud of the fact. His short hair, trim body, and tanned full face gave him a very healthy look. He was also a Master Chef and taught apprentices at the local vocational school. His office was right next to the range and had windows all round it. From his desk he could actually look into the sauce pans and if he didn't like the look of some dish or the way we were preparing it, he would jump up and shout from the office doorway some order or other in German and the others would react instantly. I learned to react too even though I didn't understand. All the dishes leaving the kitchen for the restaurant passed inspection on a heated table beside his office. No food left the kitchen without his blessing. There was no need to ask who the boss was. His sheer presence made him automatically a leader. He would put the fear of God in me just by looking in my direction. I loved listening to his German accent when he spoke English to me. He could not pronounce English words starting in 'Ch' without putting an 'S' in front, so 'chicken' became 'schicken' and it was hard for me not to laugh. W's became V's, so he 'vos' also in London for a while. If I laughed it would be the end of me. No one wanted to see Herman upset. I often saw him shouting at the apprentices: they would shiver in his presence. As far as I could understand he never said much good about them. One of them told me, much later, he never felt appreciated and so never made an effort.

There were two telephones in the kitchen, one on the wall beside the "passe" – the heated table where food was passed out to the waiters – and one in the chef's office. No one was allowed to answer the phone except the chef, even if it rang constantly when he was not available. If he was working in the kitchen when it rang he would run to the wall phone and slide with his clogs the last six to ten feet right up to the phone, pick it up and greet the caller with a loud, "CHEF." Every caller was expected to realize that this was the ultimate power of authority answering. The four-letter introduction was intended to convey that message. If by some unfortunate lack of hearing the other person did not understand the greeting, they would be subjected to another growl of "CHEF" until they came to their senses and realized that it was actually 'himself' on the line.

Despite his accent and his domineering role, he was an excellent chef. All the chef de parties (section chefs) understood the clear hierarchy in the kitchen and looked up to him with respect. I was soon told where I fitted in and when and where I was to be seen and heard. According to the brigade, I was just an Irish boy over here to learn cooking the right way because if English cooking was anything to judge by, then Irish cooking could not be any better. Any cooking I would learn here would surely be an improvement on what I had already experienced. So I was basically to shut up, do my work and learn to cook the Swiss way. As far as they were concerned, Ireland was just another part of England.

This kitchen setup was very different to the hotels in Limerick and Dublin. There, I could talk to all the chefs and not have to feel inferior except for my lack of culinary knowledge. We would have a pint together after work and talk about this and that. Now I was learning a very different level of cooking and began thinking that maybe one day I would become a Master Chef like Herman. Maybe I could teach as well and answer the phone as "Chef" and when people did not understand me I'd tell them this was the Irish boy who went to Switzerland and did they not realize who they were talking to? Then I would stop daydreaming, come down off my high horse and get on with chopping the parsley for lunch, keeping my audacious dreams of becoming a Master Chef to myself.

I had left my home country where everyone spoke the same language and now to find myself here in Switzerland, confronted with not one but four national languages, was a difficult transition. The pot washer was Turkish, the bellboy Spanish, the maitre d'hôtel French and except the chef, Mr. Lee, and myself, everyone in the kitchen was Swiss. Which language should I concentrate on? Who could guide me? I was the only monolingual employee. Slowly as I started to meet other employees, they all thought because I spoke English that I was English. What a consolation! I began to educate the hotel staff on Ireland and how we also were a bilingual country. I counseled them in the history of our small country, and how we almost lost our native language, Gaeilge. And I told them that it was thanks to our great writers and poets that we made better use of a foreign language imposed upon us than the imposers themselves.

I took consolation when I discovered that the Swiss language does not really exist at all and for that reason no one speaks 'Swiss'. Instead, the people of the land have adapted the languages of their neighbors and developed them into dialects: French to the southwest, German to the north and Italian to the southeast. In the northeast they speak Romanch, which is a mixture of French, Italian, and a little German. This was anything but simple. As a result there are four different lingual regions in the country. Biel, the town in which I was working, was right on the border of two regions, making it bilingual in German and French. As in many countries, populations in certain regions consider themselves better than others. In this respect the Swiss were no different. The Swiss Germans thought the Swiss French were generally lazy and the Swiss French disliked the Germanic style of dominance. The Swiss French compare the Swiss German language to a throat irritation because of its very guttural tone and the Swiss Germans do not really care because there are more of them in the country anyway so they can keep on with their "Ya ya! So so! Und, ach so?"

Marcel was Swiss German and also spoke French: we had great fun every day at work. We would tell each other stories while we worked. His English improved day by day and I began to pick up some French. We talked about London and the type of life he had there. He understood what I was going through by living in a foreign country. He would meet other Swiss people living in London, and reminisce about the homeland. He talked about wandering the streets not knowing much of what people were saying and lacking any sense of belonging. He only went there to learn English and was happy to return home. He loved the pubs, the singing and the 'craic' – fun, because pubs were great places to meet people, much better than the "Bistros" – as the Swiss call their cafés – where everyone sits at their own table and wouldn't ask you if you had a tongue in your head.

He couldn't understand my reason for coming to Switzerland. I told him I didn't come here to learn any language, I came for the cooking. I spoke a language that half the world speaks and the other half wanted to learn. I wanted to learn how to cook different foods, foods other than the standard Irish fare of steaks and fish and chips with fried mushrooms. I wanted to know how to make a good sauce and poach fish without knocking all the good out of it. I wanted to make pates and terrines that up until now I had only read about. "And you tell me you went to London to learn English?" I asked him. You went to a country with a lower standard of living than here and it's no wonder you wanted to come home. I left a country with a lower standard of living than here and I'm not so sure now that I want to return. Everything works here: everyone has money, a job and a good life. At home, it's different. Some people live on the dole all their lives and can only dream hopelessly for a better life.

We talked about many things as we worked and it was nice to learn a little bit about the country from him. After work I could watch television but not understand much of it. The newspapers were all foreign to me. It didn't matter if they were French or German, I still couldn't read anything significant.

I also worked with Urs, the cold kitchen chef. He allowed me to bone out pork loins when it was quiet and no food orders were coming in from the restaurant. One day Herman arrived and shouted at me for touching the expensive meat, reserved only for experienced chefs. "Vot is ze Irish boy doing with ze meat?" he bellowed. But Urs explained that I was doing a good job. Realizing I was not ruining "ze meat" he asked: "Vere did you learn how to do zis?" I told him about my training in hotel school and could see the surprise on his face. The next day he called me to his office and told me I would be promoted from Stagiaire to "Commis Chef". He was not aware I had attended a cooking school. It felt great to get a little recognition and to be promoted to Commis Saucier after so little time at the Elite. It was then I realized that during my visa application my position had been changed from commis chef to Stagiaire – intern – so Herman had no way of knowing I had completed any training and I did not know what a Stagiaire was and really did not care. I had a job, and that was enough for me.

Now with my promotion, Marcel would let me grill Dover sole, sauté the expensive meats, finish sauces for the restaurant, and eventually he let me put the finishing touches to dishes before bringing them to Herman for his blessing. On a very busy night, my very first grilled sole stuck to the grill. Marcel, looking at the bits of fish all over the hot plate, got upset because now the sole was wasted and the order delayed. "Brendan, I told you the grill has to be very hot!" he shouted. I made sure the grill was properly heated for subsequent sole and got the markings lined up the right way. To do this I placed the seasoned and buttered sole on the hot grill at a forty five degree angle to the grill bars. After a few minutes, using a flat metal spatula, I moved the sole in the opposite direction also at forty five degrees. Then when I turned the sole over it had the classic diamond grill marks well proportioned all over the sole. Now, Marcel was happy looking at every sole as they all looked the same, like twins, and I became comfortable with the grilling process. Every time Herman called out a table order, the entire brigade responded with a loud "OUI CHEF!" to let him know we heard the order. So I also began crying out "OUI

CHEF!" but I still depended on Marcel to translate the order for me.

After two months two new commis arrived. Jean-Daniel was Swiss French, and Robert, Swiss German. I did not speak any German so with Robert I communicated by hand signals and pointing to different foods. I would be in the walk-in fridge getting ingredients for Marcel. Robert would come in looking for a particular food and I could not help him because of my lack of German and he, not speaking English, could not help me either. I had a few words of French by now and got along well with Jean-Daniel. He was the Commis Entremetier – the vegetable section – and a few years older than me. He had a girlfriend; she lived with her parents and worked in an office in the town. She would visit him in his staff room every morning before work and they'd do the business. He invited me to his parent's house up in the hinterland, not far from the lake. They had a restaurant on a farm and were so welcoming. I felt at home right away, helped them with the hay and the animals, and they wanted to pay me for a day's work when they saw how useful I was on a farm.

Fresh saltwater fish was highly appreciated in Switzerland due to the distance from the coast. A delivery of expensive fresh Dover sole arrived every week. Since my promotion, I was allowed to trim and skin it and lay it on ice. First I took off the head with a sharp chopping knife then dipped the tip of the tail in boiling water which loosened the skin. I would peel back the first inch of skin with my fingers, then using a towel, pulled off the skin from tail to head on both sides. It was like unwrapping a present, exposing this delicious, slightly tinted flesh that once cooked, would provide incredible dining pleasure. Using a fish scissors, I trimmed the fins and washed out the guts. Now the fish was ready for cooking. I asked Urs where he wanted me to put the fish guts and trimmings. He had a very different temperament to Herman, and so with a big smile he said in French that I could shove them in a particular part of my anatomy! And everyone started laughing. By now I had enough French to understand what he said. Then I devised a plan with Jean-Daniel to get back at him.

We kept the bones for making fish stock, then wrapped up the fish guts, the heads, and skin in "La Suisse", the daily newspaper, made a nice parcel, and sent it in the post to Urs's wife whom we addressed as Madame Urs. Five days later he came to work carrying the parcel that by now had developed an interesting 'parfum' and told us Madame was not amused to have received such a smelly parcel in the post. That morning, everyone on the bus he took to work was looking around to find the source of the smell. Herman thought the joke was priceless or "terreeble" as he would say. He stood in his office doorway and called out: "Urs, the Irish boy knows how to give back a yoke, ya?"

Desserts were simple but flavorful. 'The colonel' was made with lemon sherbet and vodka and served in a brandy snifter. One perfectly round scoop of lemon sherbet was placed exactly in the center of the glass, then a shot of vodka was poured in and it was served immediately. A similar but creamier dessert was 'Le Ballon Rose', the pink balloon, served in a larger burgundy wine glass. If I let the sauce touch the side of the glass, it could not be served and Herman would shout at me to take it back saying: "Irish boy, make another von."

On Marcel's day off, Herman showed me many dishes and helped me refine the fundamentals of cooking. To poach turbot, he sautéed some finely chopped shallots in a little butter, the finer the cut the more the flavor emerged. I tasted flavor I never knew existed in a shallot. Then he deglazed it with white wine. This process released any caramelized sugars on the pan and transferred them to the liquid, intensifying the flavor. Now he arranged the turbot neatly in the pan, sprinkled it with salt and white pepper powder, covered it with a little greaseproof paper and set the sauteuse just over the tiny gas flame that was the pilot light for the big burners. The turbot cooked so slowly that it did not shrink much in size; it turned opaque, then to snow white when fully cooked. "A fish is like a voman," he said. "Treat it wery gently and just give it ze right amount of heat to bring out ze goodness and ze flavor." As we waited for the turbot to cook, he went to see Urs in the cold kitchen and I moved the turbot off the heat thinking it was the correct thing to do. When he came back, he went ballistic. "Vot are you doing? Stupid Irish boy! If I leave ze fish on ze pilot light it is because I know how long it vill take to cook!" He was a perfectionist. Then we strained the liquid, which by now had absorbed a little of the fish flavor. It was thickened with a roux – a mixture of butter and flour – then seasoned with salt and white pepper powder and finished with a little cream and the inevitable spoonful of hollandaise sauce. Then he showed me his secret for adding even more extra flavor. He added a tiny pinch of cayenne pepper to the sauce and that made all the difference: not spicy … just highly seasoned, and the sauce came alive. There was a reason he was a Master Chef.

Venison was put on the menu in September, just after I had arrived. This was my first time tasting this meat. It was sweeter than beef, lower in fat and packed with flavor. The saddle, revered, was the most expensive dish on the menu and usually served for either two, four or six people. Medallions were cut from the muscle in the leg, like the top round; the rest was used for "Civet" – jugged venison. Venison was marinated for two weeks in a mixture of red wine, brandy and port with a mirepoix and additional herbs such as rosemary, bay leaf and juniper berries and kept in a large container in the walk-in fridge. Marinating removed some of the strong game flavor and tenderized the meat. A separate specials menu was written with only venison dishes. Customers came to the restaurant purposely for the venison. Game season, prevalent all over Switzerland, would last from September until Christmas.

Marcel showed me how to make venison demi-glace which would be the basis for all venison sauces on this new menu. I roasted chopped venison bones in a gas fired tilting stockpot located in a corner of the kitchen near the chef's dining room. The secret was to roast them slowly in order to get an even brown color and develop intense flavor. If they became black it would introduce bitterness to the demi-glace and influence the taste of every sauce made with that base. Then I added a mirepoix (rough cut vegetables) and tomato paste, then roasted them also to extract more flavor. Finally I deglazed the lot three times with red wine, and then three times with water, each time letting the liquid evaporate, which intensified the flavor even further. The process up to that point took about two hours. Then the bones were covered with water and allowed to simmer for six hours. After that I strained the liquid and set it on the range to reduce further and concentrate the flavor, then strained it one more time, cooled it and stored it in the fridge. This was a base from which we made many different game sauces.

Game season was my first time cooking with blood, other than the black pudding I made with my mother. I learned to thicken the jugged dishes with pig's blood which was kept in a bottle in the walk-in. I would heat up the previously cooked pieces of jugged venison to order in the game demi-glaze. Once it was hot enough I poured in a few spoonfuls of blood while stirring constantly. It coagulated instantly which gave the sauce a creamy consistency. It was important not to let the sauce boil as it would curdle and become un-servable. This dish was usually garnished with sautéed lardons – cubed smoked bacon – chanterelles, pearl onions, and chopped parsley. Despite that it was a heavy dish, it tasted delicious and was a popular menu item.

On another day Herman was seasoning "Haricots Vertes" to be served with steaks for a table of four. He sautéed a few of my finely chopped shallots in butter on low heat, added the blanched French beans, and tossed them in the sauteuse with a flick of his wrist. As I watched, he sprinkled some salt and white pepper powder, checked the taste, determined if they needed more, then turned to the seasoning rack and between his thumb and forefinger took a precise amount of seasoning and gracefully sprinkled it on the beans and walked away telling me to toss them one more time and that they were good to serve. I asked him if he wanted to taste them again after I had tossed them. He looked at me and said: "Irish boy, I know how zey taste; I do not need to taste zem again." It was incredible for me to see how he could taste a dish, determine how much seasoning it needed, then pick up that exact amount between two fingers, add it to the dish and know it was perfect without ever tasting it again – he could see the flavor. It took me years to develop that ability.

Marcel gave me a small bag of dried morel mushrooms to make morel mushroom sauce. They had a very strong aroma. I had picked mushrooms many mornings in the field-below-the-road on our farm when I would collect the cows for early morning milking and my mother would fry them for the lodger's breakfast, but these mushrooms were different. Smaller, wrinkled and hollow, almost like a tiny tube, morels are an elite mushroom that give off a strong earthy taste. They are usually delivered dried, although some mushroom pickers delight in finding them fresh in the forest and delivering them to hotels and restaurants for cash. Morels are expensive so the more devious pickers would insert tiny stones in the hollow part to add weight to their find. I soaked them overnight, then strained off the water and kept it. I washed the morels several times to remove the fine sand, then cut them in half lengthwise, washed them again and stored them in the fridge. To make the sauce, I would first reduce the water they were soaked in by two thirds. This concentrated the morel flavor. Then I sautéed a few chopped shallots and chopped garlic in butter on low heat, added the washed morels, sautéed them and flamed the lot with brandy. Flaming burns off the alcohol but leaves the flavor. Then I added some demi-glace and finally a little cream to give the sauce a smooth finish. The addition of salt, black pepper mill, basil, thyme, and parsley gave the sauce a soul and hence life. Morel sauce was usually served with veal escallops or roast veal saddle accompanied by fettuccine or rice.

The hotel also had a Chinese restaurant. The chef – Monsieur Lee – was Hong Kong Chinese and prepared all the Chinese food for the menu on his station at the end of the island stove, furthest away from Herman's office. He would ask me to carry the finished plates of food to the little elevator for transport to the restaurant one floor above the kitchen. It was a pleasure to see him cook. The wok and ladle were extensions of his hands. Gently moving the wok over the flame while the ladle danced over the different bowls of ingredients, dipping for a little garlic here then back to the wok for a stir, then reaching out again for ginger, and so the dance went until the dish was complete and was poured on to a Chinese platter. It was like watching a conductor guiding an orchestra through their music. With his steady smile, he was a stately figure at the end of the island range preparing one flavorful dish after another. On quiet nights Monsieur Lee would take the wooden wine crates and use them for karate practice in a small room behind the kitchen. It was fascinating to see him kick each wooden crate with his bare feet and turn it into smithereens without ever cutting or hurting his feet. The hotel owner always complained because there was a deposit on each crate and told Lee it was costing him money. Monsieur Lee responded that he should concentrate on getting more customers to order Chinese food to pay for it.

When a trout dish was ordered, it was fished from the tank, killed, gutted, and seasoned in a matter of minutes. It took me a while to get the knack of killing the fish. We prepared trout in two ways: Meuniere (pan-fried with butter) and 'au bleu' (poached). It was important to keep the slime on the fish for poaching as the slime turned light blue during cooking giving the fish a very appetizing color. So I had to kill and gut the trout without using a towel which often meant the fish would slip out of my hands and into the large sink we had for that purpose and Marcel would shout: "Hurry up Brendan." The poaching liquid called a 'court bouillon' consisted of water, white wine, bouquet garni, white peppercorns, salt, parsley stems and lemon. The trout was placed in a 'fish kettle' containing the simmering liquid and brought to the table in that container. It was served with vegetables, steamed turned potatoes and melted butter. The fish kettle had a perfect fitting cover with a decorative handle resembling a fish.

By now I was picking up some French and was eager to begin speaking more with everyone in the kitchen. I had not yet understood the formal and informal application of the language and used the informal one day to greet the owner's wife as she came into the kitchen. The next day the owner asked Herman to speak with me about this major linguistic faux pas. I apologized to her the next day and found out she spoke English. She was very nice to me after that and we spoke often in English. It was around that time that Urs told me I should also be addressing Herman in the formal. So using "vous" instead of "tu" in French, I began to change the way I spoke with him. The informal is used with friends and family, the formal for everyone else except when addressing children. I also practiced my French with the receptionist as much as possible. She was very understanding and did not laugh when I made mistakes – as I often did. During one of our conversations at the reception, the owner walked by and gave us a nasty stare. That evening Herman told me I was not to be seen in public areas of the hotel wearing my chef's jacket. Chefs were meant to be in the back of the house.

Unlike in Ireland, I never went out after work with the senior members of the brigade. Then one evening after work Herman invited some of the brigade for a drink, and he included me, which was unusual because we never met outside of work hours. He ordered a bottle of red wine – a Cote du Rhone. It was interesting for me, coming from a beer and whiskey background, to see how he tasted the wine. The waitress showed him the wine label to verify it was what he ordered, opened the bottle at the table, and poured a little in his glass to taste. He swirled it in the glass, put it up to his nose, swirled again and tasted it, swirling it around in his mouth and sucking in air, making gestures and sounds akin to brushing teeth. He nodded to the waitress. "C'est bon." She began to pour for everyone, serving him last. This was a new experience for me, so I asked him how he knew the wine was good. He replied that when tasting he compares the wine to the last good wine he tasted. That was the first time I learned about taste memories. He told me that when customers order a dish they also compare the flavor to that of the last time they ate that dish. Taste memories are practically stored forever and can be retrieved in an instant, triggered simply by a familiar taste, aroma, or memory of a particular dish. Some of the strongest taste memories are from our childhood. As I write this, taste memories come back to me of the many foods I cooked with my mother years ago in our kitchen, triggered often just by the memory of her teaching me and retrieved faster than any computer.

Accidents were common in kitchens, but are never the less surprising when they happen. I was helping Jean Daniel with a large stock pot of boiling water in which we were blanching bones for a stock. Bones destined for making white stock are blanched to remove impurities, this helps provide a clear stock. This is done by placing them in cold water, bringing them to the boil, rinsing them off, and then setting them up again in cold water to make the stock. Using the tilting mechanism we poured the boiling liquid into large two-handled tubs on the floor so we could carry it to a large sink across the kitchen. When we lifted the tub with one of us on each side, Jean Daniel slipped and fell, and his shoulder and back were scalded badly. Work stopped and everyone came to help. He was screaming in pain. Herman jumped into action taking a scissors and cutting off his jacket and trousers before the skin stuck to them. Monsieur Lee came over and poured salt on his shoulder saying Chinese medicine recommended salt to prevent infection. We covered him with a table cloth while we waited for the ambulance. When I visited Jean Daniel later in hospital he was swearing at Monsieur Lee as by now large blisters had burst on his shoulder letting the salt into his wounds, causing incredible pain. He was away from work for one month. I felt so bad for him.

The Maitre d'hôtel, an opulent man with a mop of greasy hair combed to the side, always dressed in the same black suit with a white shirt, and seldom came into the kitchen. When he did, he would only speak with Herman. He never said hello to the kitchen brigade so everyone considered him an arrogant bastard. There was a young, petite, French speaking waitress that sometimes sat at the staff table behind the kitchen. I often practiced speaking French with her during her break. Urs told me: "Be careful, she is the Maître's girlfriend. He gets very jealous when other men speak to her." So I kept my distance but not before noticing that she ate raw potatoes like apples, saying she preferred them raw. I thought she would feel right at home in an Irish potato field: no need for boiling water for this girl to get a meal ready!

Marcel also taught me how to make good beef consommé. We first prepared a clear flavorful beef stock. To this we added ground beef mixed with egg whites, ground vegetables, ice cubes, pepper corns and bay leaves. As the stock came to a slow boil, the beef and egg whites coagulated and formed a layer which rose to the surface trapping impurities and clarifying the consommé. We then added a half onion which was browned in a cast iron pan. This added the classical golden color. To taste it Marcel took some in a ladle, poured it on a coffee saucer and sipped from it. Then he poured one for me. I thought this was a smart way to taste food.

I was approaching the end of my one year contract at the Elite and was not sure what I would do for my next job. I had begun to fall in love with Switzerland. The food, the scenery, the organized life style and the cleanliness all made major impressions on me. I was not sure I wanted to return to Ireland. I spoke with Marcel about this and he recommended I work a winter season to experience the Alps and learn to ski. He had a hotel in mind if I was interested. He called his friend who was the chef there and got me a job for the winter season in a small family hotel in the Alpine resort of Adelboden in the Bernese Alps. I knew nothing about the region. All I knew was that I had a job for the winter season with a staff room in the hotel and meals provided. I would figure out the rest when I got there. Marcel brought a map from his home and showed me where the resort was, and even told me which trains I could take to get there. I began to plan for my move to the Alps. My contract would begin one week before Christmas and run until Easter Monday when the hotel closed at the end of the season. I was sad to leave everyone at the Elite behind me. They had been very good to me and despite the hard work I learned many methods that refined my cooking skills and above all, I learned the importance of flavor.

I took the alpine bus from Frutigen which travelled up a winding road around numerous hairpin bends until we reached the bus station in Adelboden. I was used to the double-decker buses in Dublin, but this bus had three levels. I had to admire the bus driver's skill as he negotiated the narrow roads that sometimes dropped off in incredibly steep declines. Even more impressive were the hairpin bends and the steep turns. The wall of snow on the roadside had already begun to build up and it was not yet Christmas.

It was my first trip into the Swiss Alps – a perfect winter wonderland setting. The resort was beautiful! The main street was lined with chalet style buildings all with snow capped roofs and Christmas lights hanging from the eves. Each chalet contained a shop at street level with apartments and large balconies overhead. It was unbelievable that I would be living and working in such a beautiful setting. Comparing the scenery, architecture and mood of the people from Bienne to here, I could not believe I was still in the same country. It was getting dark as I walked from the bus station to the hotel. I could hear people greeting each other in French and German and even English – exchanging pleasantries as they moved along the street, some carrying their skis on one shoulder. It reminded me of walking down the main street in Belmullet on a busy shopping day when farmers and neighbors would exchange greetings. Most of these people were just returning from skiing and the atmosphere was very welcoming.

At the hotel I asked for the chef by name at the reception. Hans was a good friend of Marcel's in the Hotel Elite. They worked together previously in many different hotels. The reception area was small and nicely decorated with dried flower arrangements and pictures of Alpine landscapes, piles of brochures and a desk with a smiling receptionist. The windows were lined with lace curtains, mounds of snow visible outside. The entire reception area was dominated by a beautiful stone fireplace with a well stocked fire burning. No turf here, but lots of nice pine wood logs crackling in the flame. The atmosphere was incredibly welcoming with people coming and going and everyone seemingly in a good mood.

Hans arrived and we exchanged greetings. Adelboden is German speaking. I tried to respond with my best German greeting but failed, so we eventually settled on a mixture of English and French. I could understand a little French but when it came to speaking with someone new, I could not get the words together quick enough. As for German, I just knew how to say "hello, how are you," and "goodbye," but even that was challenging when meeting people for the first time. Despite that, we got along very well. Hans was the chef here during the winter and also chef at another hotel on one of the lakes during the summer – a common practice for chefs doing the seasonal circuit. It was a few days before Christmas and the hotel was gearing up for the busy winter season. He told me a hotel of this caliber typically attracted the same families back year after year. They would check in one or two days before Christmas and stay until after the New Year, usually reserving half-board which meant that after breakfast practically all of the guests would be on the slopes for the day, returning only around four or five o'clock. Then they would go to their rooms, change, freshen up, have a drink at the bar and go in to the dining room for a three course dinner. By ten o'clock most guests were in bed in anticipation of another great day on the slopes. Our job was to ensure they were happy with the food.

He showed me the kitchen; it was on the street level with a big window. This was a bonus, the first kitchen I had worked in with a window. I could only imagine the view during the day. The ranges were island style and oil fired which meant they would be very hot. Fridges were off to one side. The kitchen was directly below the restaurant so all food was sent up in a small reach-in elevator. Some people called this contraption a 'dumb waiter' but I thought that's not fair to the many great waiters I know. This took some getting used to because we communicated with the floor above by telephone. The property was built on a slope and fortunately the kitchen was on the side of the building which provided an ideal delivery location and a view of the valley and mountains. After we toured the kitchen Hans showed me my room. Most alpine resort hotels in Switzerland provided staff with rooms and meals. This was partially due to the fact that many staff are foreigners and staying on the property, or close to it, was viewed by management as an extra convenience from a cost perspective and staff could be asked to work at a moment's notice. Rooms were usually in the same building which allowed staff easy access to their accommodation, especially for split shift workers.

My split shift would start at nine o'clock, finishing at two in the afternoon, and again from half five until nine or ten in the evening depending on guest numbers. During the break in the afternoon – L'heure de chambre – I could either sleep or go skiing. Staff dinner was at half five and guests began arriving for dinner at half six. My room was small and the bathroom was at the end of the corridor. My bedroom window provided a view over the main street which looked beautiful in the early evening light. Chalets were so close I could see into comfortable apartments across the street. They looked so cozy in contrast to the cold outside. After admiring this vista, I went to meet Hans in the kitchen for dinner. The hotel was not yet open for guest meals so Hans and I sat at chefs table in the kitchen and had our dinner. As in Hotel Elite, there was a table in the corner of the kitchen for the kitchen staff to eat and have coffee breaks. Other staff was generally not allowed to sit there except by invitation. They usually found a spot to eat in the restaurant. After dinner I left the kitchen, and we agreed to meet at eight o'clock the next morning for my first day of work.

The Alps change dramatically in appearance between night and day. The view from chef's table for breakfast was breathtaking. When the sun rose, I could see between the chalets down to the valley floor and up to the skyline. The snow capped Engstigenalp in the distance captured my attention. Later in the season I took the aerial cable car to the top to admire it up close. Hans had coffee made and fresh croissants ready so we ate breakfast in front of this vista and talked about Marcel and the Hotel Elite. They had worked together in London at the Swiss Center. He then explained how the season would work and what my responsibilities would be. There were just the two of us and a pot washer who also peeled the potatoes, vegetables and washed and prepared all salads. Coffee, tea and breakfast were prepared by the 'Buffet Damen' (pantry girl) although when I met her I realized it was a long time since she was a girl. A plump woman, she was very curt but polite and spoke only German so we had very little conversation.

During our afternoon breaks, Hans taught me to ski. We would take the gondola to the Tschenten Alp, the nearest ski run to the village. At an elevation of two thousand meters it had a dominating view of the valley floor, making the village look like a collection of toy houses dusted with icing sugar. Before I left the Elite, Herman had given me a pair of his old skis and leather boots which attached to the skis with a combination of leather straps and metal clasps. They would have to do as I did not have the money to purchase new ones. In that I could not afford a professional skiing instructor, I soaked up Hans's basic skiing lessons. I began to look at the other ski instructors as they led classes down the slope, imitated what they did, and so with time my skiing improved. On my days off I would take the snow bus to the Hahnenmoos Pass for a day of skiing. It was at the same elevation as the Tschenten Alp but had longer runs. The bus looked like a World War II model with all rear wheels chained for extra grip in the snow. It was a sharp contrast to the modern buses running the Frutigen route.

Breakfast for guests was always continental. The baker delivered the croissants and breakfast breads to us at half six. Occasionally a guest would ask for a fried egg or scrambled eggs. These were mostly English guests being used to a more substantial meal to start the day. I remember Hans showing me how he wanted the scrambled eggs cooked. He started out like any scrambled eggs I have seen by heating a pan with butter, adding the whisked seasoned eggs but then, just before the eggs were completely cooked, he added a few spoonfuls of cream. It made all the difference. They were the creamiest scrambled eggs I had ever tasted. I still use that recipe today. We made English style fruit cakes for afternoon coffee. I offered to make my mother's coffee cake for Hans, thinking he might want to put it on the afternoon coffee menu. He liked it and gave me advice for improving it. He made sugar syrup and flavored it with kirsch brandy, a clear cherry fruit brandy very popular in Switzerland and Germany. Then we brushed this mixture on the sponge cake before assembling it, allowing it to soak in to the centre of the sponge. It really made the cake moist and added another layer of flavor. We called it 'Gateau au Moka' – French for coffee cake. The guests loved it. I wrote to my mother about this and translated the new cake name for her.

He also taught me to make the 'Vacherin Glace.' This is an ice cream and meringue torte, and was a popular dessert at weddings and banquets in Switzerland at the time. He took a metal cake ring, set it on parchment paper and with a pencil drew two circles the size of the ring. Then with the metal ring removed, he piped out the circles with half-inch deep layers of Italian meringue – whipped egg whites with sugar syrup. This was allowed to dry out in a low temperature oven overnight and became crunchy. To assemble the Vacherin, he laid one of the meringue layers on the inside of the cake ring to form the bottom of the Vacherin, added a layer of vanilla ice cream, a layer of chocolate ice cream, then a layer of strawberry ice cream and topped it with the second layer of meringue. After an hour in the freezer he removed the cake ring and decorated the Vacherin with sweetened whipped cream and glazed cherries. It was a simple dessert but wildly popular.

The winter season was nice but not as challenging as my time at the Elite. Menus were simple and did not deviate much. Soups and salads, roast pork loin, braised beef, the odd fish dish, and some alpine specialties. I tasted raclette cheese for the first time and learned to make cheese fondue, two very popular alpine cheese dishes. I also made '*rösti*' which is without doubt one of the most popular potato dishes in Switzerland. It is a potato cake and depending on the region, is made with raw or cooked potatoes. I would make the *rösti* with cooked potatoes: it is rumored that the dish was created to use up leftover boiled potatoes. This is how Hans taught me to make it.

I would grate the peeled cooked potatoes on the large side of the grater. Then heat a little oil in a frying pan, add some chopped smoked bacon and chopped onions, fry them lightly, then add the grated potatoes and mix them together. Many times the potatoes would stick to the cast iron pan and I would have to remove them, clean the pan with salt and 'season' it with fresh oil and start again. Once the potatoes were mixed with the bacon and onions, it was time to press them into a large cake-like shape the size of the pan and add a little butter around the edges for flavor and color. Once the bottom was golden brown the *rösti* had to be flipped over. One of the difficult parts was to flip the entire cake in the air in order to brown the other side. Mine landed many times on the floor before I could master the art of flipping this potato cake and get it to land back in the pan in one piece, exposing a beautiful golden brown crust. Hans was patient with me and put large baking trays on the floor so we could re-use the potatoes.

Outside of work, night life was slow and my lack of German did not help when it came to meeting people. I was still very shy and hesitated when thinking of approaching any girls. After all, how could I talk to them? So I skied most afternoons and worked to learn as much as possible from Hans. Easter was approaching which meant the end of the season. Again I faced the prospect of searching for a job. Hans knew the manager of a busy hotel located on one of the lakes in the canton of Fribourg and could recommend me. He called the manager who asked that I send my Curriculum Vitae to him promptly. He sent me back a contract for a very long summer season, April to October, at the Hotel du Bateau in Morat in the lake district of Switzerland. What was even more surprising was that he offered me the position of 'chef de partie' – in charge of a kitchen section. This was a big step up for me. More responsibility, which meant more would be expected of me. I worried that I would not be able for it, especially as this was a new job and I did not know anyone at the hotel or in the region. Until now I depended on a chef de partie to tell me what to do and to guide me in the kitchen. Now, I was to be the chef de partie telling the commis what they should be doing while still completing my own duties. It would be a major test of my culinary and supervisory abilities.

Le Ballon Rose

A lovely dessert! Be careful or as Herman says, "You'll have to make another von." Mind you, it's so good that you'll want to make more anyway!

Ingredients for 2 portions
2 perfectly round scoops of raspberry ice cream
¼ cup (60 gr.) raspberry puree
½ cup (90 gr.) lightly whipped cream
½ oz. (15 gr.) sugar
2 tablespoons raspberry schnapps –fruit brandy

Assembly
- Place each scoop of ice cream in a large balloon shaped red wine glass.
- Mix the lightly whipped cream with sugar, raspberry puree and the schnapps until it forms a thick pink liquid but still pourable.
- Pour the mixture into the glasses (without it touching the sides) until the ice cream is covered.
- Decorate with fresh raspberries.
- Serve immediately.

Tip
- For a sharper taste replace the cream with natural yoghurt
- This is an ideal dessert for a romantic 'tête-à-tête'.

CHAPTER FOUR

A Turning Point in My Career

In the lake region of Switzerland, ferries carry tourists through canals linking Lake Bienne, Lake Morat and Lake Neuchatel. The Hotel du Bateau, situated next to the ferry landing on Lake Morat, provided the perfect setting for a light lunch, afternoon coffee, or a sunset dinner. On the first floor overlooking the lake was the beautifully appointed restaurant, Lord Nelson. The establishment was named after the British admiral, Lord Horatio Nelson, who defeated the French and Spanish Navy in the 18th century thus preventing Napoleon from invading England.

I met Herr Aebi, the general manager, at the reception. A friendly Swiss German with a neatly trimmed moustache, he spoke fluent English, which was a comfort to me as I was still struggling with conversational German. I learned later he also spoke fluent French and Italian. He drove me to the staff quarters and showed me to my room in a chalet style house overlooking the lake about 10 minutes walking distance from the hotel. We met the next day and over a cup of coffee he explained how the season would run. There would be no Chef de Cuisine – head chef, as such. He decided instead to have two chefs de parties in charge of the entire kitchen, and because of that, paid them a higher salary than other local hotels. The other chef de partie was Austrian and would arrive in two weeks; we would share the responsibility of running the kitchen. In addition there were five commis and two dishwashers. The Lord Nelson, a fine dining restaurant with a lake view, was very popular with the locals. The lake side terrace where we sat with our coffee was a very busy outlet during the season, especially at lunchtime when the ferry arrived laden with hungry tourists. There was also a banquet room for small elegant functions on the first floor.

By now I realized many Swiss viewed foreigners with suspicion. We were often considered second class citizens, despite the fact that the hotel industry depended on thousands of foreign workers, especially in seasonal resorts. Foreign workers were not always welcome in certain parts. As a result many foreigners clustered together as we all had something in common. We were there because the job was of a higher standard and the money was good, better than in most European countries. Nationality didn't matter; we bonded across cultures, religions and languages although certain jobs seemed to attract the same nationalities. Cooks were mostly German, French, or Italian. Waiters were Italian or Spanish. Pot washers were Turkish. Head housekeepers were Swiss and the chambermaids Spanish or Portuguese. So I was very surprised at how Herr Aebi treated me: not at all like a foreigner or a second class citizen. He was genuinely concerned that I get off to a good start for the long summer season. Even much later, and every time I would collect my salary, I would thank him and he would say with a very genuine voice: "No, please! It is I that thanks you!"

The Lord Nelson menu had dishes such as Foie Gras – fattened goose liver – lobster bisque, fresh consommé, veal escalope with morels, flamed veal kidneys, and the ever present Chateaubriand – a grilled double fillet steak with Béarnaise sauce, usually served for two people and carved at the table. In addition, there was a selection of local fish dishes. Trout, pike, perch and char were the main menu attractions for locals and tourists alike. Most fish dishes were served with either rice pilaf or turned steamed parsley potatoes. The perch was a best seller, pan-fried "meunière" with lightly browned butter, or deep fried with tartar sauce and lemon wedges. Both were firm favorites with exceptional demand during the midday rush. A portion of perch meunière consisted of six small fillets, so an order for four took a long time to panfry on both sides, and then prepare the butter sauce in the same pan, deglazing with lemon juice, Worcestershire sauce and chopped parsley. Speed was of the essence lest the butter become brown and ruin the sauce.

Local fishermen delivered the freshly filleted perch every morning. Tiny fillets of the shiny silver skinned fish caught only hours ago in the lake were laid out in perfect lines, and packaged in boxes with ice. I was at ease now, even under pressure, when poaching perch in white wine sauce, remembering what I learned from Marcel and Herman. I added freshly chopped tarragon leaves to the fish sauce which gave it a refreshing tangy bite. Pike is a bottom feeder, an ugly fish with many bones but incredible flesh, ideal for fish mousse, fish stuffing and fluffy quenelles – dumplings. There was also poached turbot in red wine with a cream thickened sauce, served with light rice pilaf. It was unusual to have fish poached in red wine. This classic dish is referred to as 'matelote' – which ironically is French for sailor – and uses red instead of white wine. When the cream is added the sauce takes on a shiny light crimson color that paired well against the snow white color of fish.

I was on my own in the kitchen for the first week. The terrace had not yet opened and hotel occupancy was low. I began setting up the kitchen in a manner that I thought would work best for the season. During my second week Herr Aebi brought in some sausages and asked me to heat them up in water and make a potato salad for 6 people for a private lunch. A pair of pre-poached sausages called "Vienerli", served with potato salad and mustard, was a common dish at the time for a casual meal. I made the potato salad as I learned it from Herman. I boiled the potatoes in the skin, peeled them while still hot and sliced them. I chopped an onion, cooked it in white wine vinegar with salt and white pepper powder, then poured the hot mixture over the sliced potatoes and allowed them to soak up all the liquid. Then I added mayonnaise and that, according to Herman, was real German potato salad! I got so absorbed in making the potato salad that I forgot all about the sausages: they were boiling and had burst! Herr Aebi came to the kitchen and was very upset with me. "You cannot heat up a sausage?" he growled. Then he drove to the butcher shop for more sausages, handed them to me and said, "Don't burst them this time!" I did not realize that cooked sausages would burst if they boiled. Despite the fact that we boiled a lot of food in Ireland, sausages were always pan-fried from their raw state and never burst. Then I remembered the care my mother took in our kitchen at home to not let the black pudding boil. Instead, she simmered it – cooking it just below boiling point. How could I not have thought of it sooner? Applying that simmering cooking principle would have avoided the sausage disaster and the silent message to Herr Aebi that: "The Irish can't cook," a comment I had heard many times since I left my homeland.

A week later the other chef de partie arrived and the season began to pick up. Josef, from Vienna, was very tall with jet black hair combed back in a slick wave. A little older than me, he had worked in Switzerland for a few seasons, had also just finished a winter season in St. Moritz and spoke only German. He was a great cook and I learned many new dishes from him. He taught me how to make Austrian dishes like Tafelspitz, breaded veal escalope Viennoise, and the famous Viennese Sacher Torte. Tafelspitz is a boiled beef recipe with chive sauce, and a horseradish sauce. This cut of beef is usually a triangular shaped muscle located between the end of the sirloin and the top of the rump. Often referred to as 'The cover', it is usually removed before cutting rump steaks. The muscle has one pointed 'spitz' side with gives the dish its name.

The escalope Viennoise was similar to the German schnitzel which we had on the terrace menu and was garnished with a slice of lemon decorated with a rolled fillet of anchovy filled with capers. The schnitzel was generally pork, and had only a lemon wedge for garnish. According to proper menu terminology, Escalope Viennoise should always be made using veal unless otherwise stated on the menu. Some restaurants offered a cheaper version such as 'Escalope de dinde Viennoise' – Turkey Escalope Viennoise – and must mention the word turkey. Joseph also put an Austrian dessert called Kaiserschmarrn on the menu. It was wonderful and simple to make. He took some flour, sugar, a few eggs, raisins, and a little milk, mixed the lot together, added in some meringue and poured the mixture into a buttered hot pan and let it cook slowly on the range. When it was set he cut the omelet-like shape into chunks with a large knife and fork, sprinkled them with sugar and cinnamon and allowed them to brown as he tossed them around in the little pan. He served it with stewed fruit – it was delicious.

May was white asparagus season and we served them poached with Hollandaise sauce. Once the season ended they were no longer offered on the menu. June was strawberry season and we served Coupe Romanoff on the terrace menu. This dessert consisted of two scoops of vanilla ice cream in a large dessert glass covered with marinated strawberries. To marinate them we cut the fruit in quarters after first removing the stem, added strawberry coulis – fruit sauce, and flavored it with vodka and sugar. We placed a few spoons of the mixture on the ice cream and topped it with whipped cream and a wafer. I served thousands of 'Romanoff's' while the strawberry season lasted. It was common for customers to come to the terrace in the afternoon for 'café crème' – large espresso style coffee, and order a dessert from the menu. Romanoff's were popular, but my favorite was Café Glace – coffee ice cream topped with whipped cream and sprinkled with chocolate coffee beans and served with a pencil wafer.

Each day at twelve o'clock the tourist-laden ferry docked, filling the terrace instantly. We had to be ready in the kitchen; otherwise chaos would ensue for the entire lunch service. Two hundred a la carte orders came in almost at the same time. Perch meunière, deep fried perch, steamed parsley potatoes, side salads, and tartar sauce, with a slew of dessert orders toward the end. Then orders from the Lord Nelson would begin to trickle in: veal with Morel sauce, pike dumplings in tarragon sauce with steamed potatoes, and many grilled Chateaubriands, which took a long time to cook. Josef took care of these dishes while I concentrated on the fish dishes. The commis did the cold kitchen dishes and desserts for the terrace. Other than the perch meunière which was only cooked a la minute – to order – we had some of the deep-fried fish partially prepared half an hour before service began, in anticipation of the rush. I would "blanch" several portions of deep fried perch in advance. There are many ways and many different reasons to blanch food. Raw Pommes Frites can be blanched in oil at a lower temperature, and then be finished very quickly at a higher oil temperature which allows them to develop the classical golden color. The same principle applies to deep fried fish. I would season the fillets with salt and white pepper powder, lemon juice and Worcestershire sauce. Then sprinkled with flour and dipped in a frying batter they were blanched – pre-cooked in the deep fryer. When an order for deep fried perch came in it was simple to put six fillets back in the hot deep fryer where they would turn golden brown and become crisp in two minutes without any loss of quality. Everyone was busy; there was no time to talk other than calling food orders. Two to three hours of non-stop service, then the ferry came back, picked up the guests, and the terrace emptied. Josef was tremendous at working under pressure and never lost his cool no matter how many table orders were on his station. If a waiter annoyed him at the height of the service he'd look over his shoulder at him, and without getting upset just shout in German: "Arschloch' – asshole!" Then turn around and keep working. As a result, waiters kept their distance. This pace continued for seven months. Every day was another challenge. Some days, service did not go so well. Customers complained that food took too long to serve, and we got angry, mostly with ourselves, for not preparing correctly. Other days it rained: the terrace was closed and we sat around.

The Maître d'hôtel in the Lord Nelson was French. Most head waiters in Switzerland at the time were either French or Italian. They had flair and graciousness, terrific customer skills, and guests loved them! He spoke English and we often chatted during quiet times, although Josef did not like the Maître because he often asked me why I wasted time speaking with him. I found 'Le Maître' – as most staff referred to him – to be much friendlier than the Maître at the Elite. This particular day he was elated and came to see me. "Brendan, J'ai des très bonnes nouvelles – I have great news !" His son just had an eye operation in Paris and it was a success. He was over the moon and so happy. I asked him what type of operation he had. It seemed his son had a rare dimension missing from his eyesight which provided depth perception to objects, rendering everything he saw flat. When he called his father the morning after the operation, he said the first thing he noticed was the bread roll on this breakfast tray was round and not flat as it had been for the last twenty years. I was happy for him. Like me, Le Maître was a foreigner, working the seasonal circuit, and he could not take the time off to be with his son. Asking for extra time off during the busy season was not something foreigners did. The job was too important and might not be there upon his return.

We seldom saw the hotel owner so it was unusual when he came into the kitchen one day to discuss a dinner he was having in the Lord Nelson for twelve people. He was friendly, impeccably dressed, and had a constant smile. Josef and I wrote a menu for him, and he agreed to our suggestions. When he left, we began planning the details. Then Josef told me the owner liked men and that the dinner was for his boyfriend. This was my first encounter with this kind of relationship. I decided to keep my distance. Sex education was not a part of the Irish National School curriculum, and no one asked questions in that regard when I was in school. I had enough on my plate trying to figure out how things worked with the women, never mind two men. Josef said the boyfriend went to get his hair styled every day at the local hairdresser and wasn't that a waste of money because all he had to do was comb his hair in the morning like he did – pointing to his slick black mop of hair – and it wouldn't cost him any money at all.

It was late September and the season was coming to an end, a time when the hotel would close for the winter. I realized I had learned a great deal of German from Josef. I could now have a basic conversation without looking or sounding too foolish. I was cooking better food and due to the busy terrace, had developed the ability to work under pressure. Being a foreigner in Switzerland, I did not yet have a network of contacts in the country and Josef – also a foreigner – could also not recommend any hotels for the upcoming winter season. I got a good reference letter from Herr Aebi and with that I bid farewell to Josef, the rest of the kitchen staff, Herr Aebi and the Hotel du Bateau. I decided I would not work the winter season in Switzerland and left for Ireland to spend Christmas in Belmullet.

The familiarity of my mother's kitchen was comforting. The plum puddings, lined up on the dresser, brought back fond memories. As always, my mother and father were happy to see me home again. The house was decorated and everyone was in good spirits. I helped Mam with the Christmas dinner. This was always a big job for her since I left home, as no one could help her with the details like making breadcrumbs for the bread sauce or peeling vegetables. Using her own recipe, I made the bread sauce for the roast turkey. It was a simple sauce that added tremendous flavor to the meal. I set a small saucepan of milk on a warm part of the range, added a peeled clove-studded onion, a bay leaf, salt and pepper, and left it to infuse for a few hours. Then I removed the onion and bay leaf, added the breadcrumbs and a little butter. The breadcrumbs thickened up the sauce which by now was filling the kitchen with a wonderful clove aroma. I asked my mother to taste it. She looked at me and said; "Aren't you the chef! Why would I taste it?" But I insisted that she taste it and when she did, her reply was, "Add a grain a salt." And I did! We made a great team.

We had a wonderful Christmas. My brothers John and A.J. were also home on holidays. Louis and Fred had not yet left home and with no guests in the house we had the Christmas dinner in the dining room. Although I served many guests in that dining room, this was my first time ever eating there. We had wine with the dinner and Irish coffee with the plum pudding which was served with custard. I flamed the pudding with brandy and everyone thought it was "fancy stuff." To do this, I warmed the brandy in a small saucepan, and switched off the dining room light before pouring the warm liquor on the pudding, then lit it with a match. The blue flame danced over the seasonal dessert. I kept ladling the flaming brandy from the edge of the plate over the top of the pudding. It was lovely to see the liquid flame flowing from the ladle, spreading out over the pudding and lighting up the faces of everyone around the table. I learned to do this in Morat as we had a flamed dessert in the Lord Nelson and it was the waiters who carried the flaming dish to the table.

I had just turned twenty-one, the New Year was approaching, and even though I had no job I left Belmullet for Switzerland. While working at the Hotel Elite I had met Mike, a lad from Enniskillen in County Fermanagh. He was a dentist working in Neuchatel. I had stayed with him before and he would put me up for a few days. I did not have a work visa and the dreaded 'Grenzpolizei' – immigration police – in Geneva were quick to see that. They called me into a side room in Geneva airport and for two hours interrogated me on why I was coming in to Switzerland. In my passport they could see my previous visas and naturally assumed I was returning to work illegally. There are three levels of work permits in Switzerland: Permit A for seasonal workers. Permit B for year-long contracts, and the coveted Permit C which allowed the holder to remain in the country year after year without leaving. Foreigners with the Permit C were admired by other foreigners as it showed a certain level of progress. Foreigners working in Switzerland not in possession of one of these three permits were referred to as 'travaileur au noir' – illegal workers, and if caught were deported. This was what the immigration police believed I was attempting to do and they were right. However they eventually let me enter the country when I gave them the dentist's address in Neuchatel, and showed them I had money to support myself during my holidays.'

There was a pub I used to frequent in Neuchatel during the times I would stay with Mike and knew the barman there. Joe was a heavy set lad with a great smile and a firm welcoming handshake. He was glad to see me again and wished me a happy New Year. I mentioned my job search. "You are very lucky," he said. "The General Manager of the largest hotel in town is downstairs; I will ask him if he is looking for cooks, wait here." He returned a while later and said: "Be at the hotel tomorrow morning at nine o'clock for an interview." I was ecstatic and ordered another pint; things were looking up!

The Eurotel is on the Avenue de la Gare in Neuchatel, which means Banhoffstrasse in German. It seems I was destined to work in hotels located on streets leading to railway stations! Martin, the General Manager, was Swiss German, an affable man with what seemed like a permanent grin – which made it difficult to determine when he was serious or when a laugh was appropriate. I was shown into his office by Beatrice, a very pleasant receptionist. He was looking for a chef de partie. I gave him my references and once he looked them over said he was willing to offer me the position. I would have a room in the staff quarters and meals were provided. He then led me to the kitchen to introduce me to the chef, and I met the man who would have a major impact on my chef's career.

Herbert, the chef de cuisine, was from Germany. He welcomed me in excellent English, introduced me to the staff and showed me around the kitchen. As in many of my previous jobs, the kitchen had very few windows although here a few windows looked out on a parking ramp and provided much appreciated daylight and fresh air. The stove was island style and gas fired with conventional ovens beneath it. The sauce station was on one side with eight burners and a grill. The vegetable station with soups and starches on the other side also had eight burners, with the addition of a deep fryer and a bain-marie at the end of the island for holding hot foods. The cold kitchen was a separate room as was a section for desserts and salad washing. Interestingly the lift for room service opened directly into the kitchen. It was also the lift I took to get to the staff quarters on the third floor. The sous chef was also German and a good friend of Herbert's. The chef garde-manger was French; the chef entremetier was Swiss-French as were several of the commis de cuisine and the two apprentices. The pot washers and dishwashers were Turkish. This kitchen provided food for two restaurants on the same level and banquet seating for four hundred guests on the first floor. I was assigned to the cold kitchen and banquets.

The two restaurants were named 'Pinot Noir' and the 'Carrefour' – crossroads. They were very different in style and consequently attracted a different clientele. The Pinot Noir was a steak house featuring prime steaks such as fillet, rib eye, sirloin, and the most expensive: US beef. The Swiss had just begun to appreciate US beef; it was making its debut in the country. Known for its marbling and tenderness, US beef was sought after by the guests despite its premium price. Marbling is a term for the specks of fat interspersed in the lean part of tender meat cuts. Marbling adds flavor and juiciness provided the meat is cooked correctly. The Pinot Noir also offered escargots in the shell with garlic butter, smoked salmon, Russian caviar, foie gras, and steak tartar – a chopped raw steak seasoned with chopped gherkins, anchovies, capers, mustard, raw egg yolk, cognac, salt and pepper mill and served with toast. For this dish the beef was ground to order using beef fillet. Because of our proximity to the lake we also had fillets of perch, both deep-fried and meunière.

The Carrefour was less formal. The salad bar dominated the center of the restaurant and was very popular, especially at lunch time. A ten seat bar near the kitchen door provided a focal point and was quite common in casual Swiss restaurants and bistros, providing a space for the individual diner and doubled as a coffee bar in the slow periods. The menu was also less formal, with quiche Lorraine, roast chicken, spaghetti bolognaise, and grilled pork chop with mushroom sauce as some of the main menu items. Unique to the Carrefour were two lunch specials, one called the 'Express', the other simply the 'Carrefour', and priced slightly higher. These dishes were intended to be very affordable and served with speed. The Express was always a ready-to-serve-dish such as finely sliced chicken or veal in a mushroom cream sauce, or a Veal Pojarsky – a breaded pan fried chopped veal steak. Customers appreciated the value and the speed at which they could get in and out for lunch. The Carrefour menu items took a little longer. Such dishes might involve a pork steak gratinated with cheese and tomato or a chicken breast cordon bleu.

Herbert showed me how to make terrines and pates. He taught me how to combine the ingredients, keeping the different temperatures in mind to prevent the mixture from curdling, and he showed me how to pass the mixture through a fine sieve to remove any sinew or grizzle so the mixture would have an extra smooth consistency. We added chunks of foie gras and whole peeled pistachios before filling the final product into terrine moulds for cooking. These terrines and pates were very popular on buffet menus for banquets and sometimes even made it to the Express lunch menu during the warmer months, served with a red current sauce flavored with Port wine.

I learned butter sculpting with him. We used a very dry margarine so sculptures held their shape. Herbert showed me the art of preparing cold platters with aspic by pouring a very thin layer of aspic jelly over the platter and allowing it to set before laying out the slices of pate which is the classical cold platter preparation. He would then take some liquid aspic, flavor it with port wine, chill it, cut it into diamond shape pieces and use it to garnish the platters. They were masterpieces when finished. We practiced symmetrical approaches to setting up buffets to enhance guest satisfaction and built up backdrops to offset his beautiful cold platters.

During my first two months I got to know the sous chef very well. He was a smallish man with a full mustache, a slight lisp, and spoke through his nose. Now and again he would go on a drinking spree and I remember one morning after such a spree, we had roast duckling on the lunch menu. He was on his knees at the sauce station looking for a raw duck that had fallen off the table. He was singing to the duck, asking it to come out from where ever it was hiding, and that he had a surprise for it. "Mein liebe Enten, wo bist du? Ich habe ein geschenk fur dich? – My dear duckling, where are you? I have a surprise for you!" Of course the surprise was a hot oven after we helped him find the duck. Despite the odd rendezvous with the bottle, and the very demanding role of sous chef, he was a very organized chef. He cooked great food, kept up the pace when both restaurants were full and several banquets going on upstairs, in addition to motivating the other chefs de parties and supporting Herbert.

The chef garde manger was a trickster and was always joking with the apprentices. On a quiet day we were discussing with Xavier, the French speaking apprentice, the names of classical French chefs and philosophers that he was learning about at school. We talked about Careme, Savarin, Tallyrand, Escoffier and others. All were highly respected chefs in their time. The chef garde-manger was going out with a Dutch girl, so he asked Xavier if he had learned in school about the famous Dutch chef, Fick von Hinten. Xavier did not believe that such a chef existed so we told him to ask Herbert if he had heard about this famous Dutch chef. As he went to see Herbert who was sitting at his desk in the corner of the kitchen, we all left the kitchen as we knew there was no such chef. It was a made up name with sexual connotations – but sounded as if it was real. Herbert went ballistic when he heard the question and shouted at Xavier: "Mein Gott in Himmel, bist du verrückt?! – God in Heaven, are you out of your mind!?" Xavier, mortified for having unknowingly insulted his boss, melted into the floor and turned a very deep shade of red. We were all laughing in the corridor but Herbert was not amused! Apprentices were often the subject of ridicule. I remembered my episode with the spaghetti tree many years ago. Taking a joke was part of the job; it relieved the stress and rarely did any harm.

Herbert taught me a system that never failed for efficiently serving banquets. It involved precise timing. "Brendan," he would say, "have everything ready 30 minutes before it is required. Now you have time to relax before service and check to see if anything was forgotten." I have used that philosophy ever since, and it has served me well. Many of the banquets we served involved roasts, either veal or pork, which were carved inside the banquet room at the last minute providing a fresh juicy slice of meat. Popular side dishes were haricots verts, and Gratin Dauphinois. The latter were simple to make. I would cook slices of peeled raw potatoes in a little milk with nutmeg, chopped garlic, salt and white pepper powder. Just before they were completely cooked I would stir in a 'liaison' consisting of egg yolks and cream which thickened the milk. Then I transferred the mixture to a shallow baking pan, sprinkled it liberally with grated Swiss cheese and baked them in the oven until golden brown. The taste was incredible! Guests loved the flavor of the gratinated cheese combined with the roast meat and fresh mushroom sauce.

I had grown to like Herbert's cooking style as well as his management skills. He in turn gave me added responsibilities, often leaving me to cook entire banquets on my own. My cooking abilities were progressing very well, so I was surprised and disappointed when one day as we were finishing a banquet, he told me he was leaving the Eurotel. He was taking the position of chef garde manger at the Mandarin Oriental Hotel in Manila. This was a major career step for him, moving to a five star luxury hotel half way around the world. He brought brochures of the hotel and the Philippines to the chefs table the next day. All the kitchen staff looked at the pictures of the beaches lined with palm trees, beautiful women in bikinis lying on the sand, and white sailboats leaning into the wind as they glided over turquoise waters. It looked like paradise. We were all jealous and happy for him at the same time. It was so beautiful that I could not blame him for leaving.

Work was not the same without Herbert at the helm. Another German chef arrived and he constantly argued with Martin, discussions that often escalated into a shouting match during service in front of everyone in the kitchen. This made me unhappy. I did not like his domineering style and I was not learning anything new from him so I decided to leave the Eurotel. Martin was disappointed as I had been there for eighteen months and he was happy with my work. I left on good terms and he gave me an excellent letter of recommendation.

I decided to remain in Switzerland and through a contact I was offered a position as chef tournant – replacement chef, at the Hotel Schatzalp in the alpine resort of Davos in the canton of Graubünden. The position was for the upcoming winter season. The tournant position involves replacing every chef de partie, except the pastry chef, on their day off. The pastry chef is excluded from the equation because Pastry is considered a separate profession from cooking, which makes it difficult for a chef to replace the pastry chef for only one day. This meant that I would be cooking in different sections of the kitchen every day. It was a demanding job but I felt that by now I had more confidence and was up for the task. A bonus was that I could ski every day. As my German had improved and Davos was German speaking, I would be less intimidated talking to people. Maybe I would meet a girl that would not mind that I was a foreigner? I felt I was going to have a great winter season!

La Coupe Romanoff

A wonderful recipe with strawberries: I made thousands of these during my summer at the Hotel du Bateau.

Ingredients for one portion
One scoop of vanilla ice cream
5 oz. (150gr.) strawberries
1 oz. (30gr.) strawberry coulis-fruit sauce/topping
2 oz. (60gr.) lightly whipped sweetened vanilla flavored cream
½ ounce (15gr.) sugar
1 tablespoon vodka
1 pencil wafer

Preparation
• Wash strawberries, remove the stems and cut into small segments.
• Mix with the strawberry coulis, vodka and sugar.

Assembly
• Place the ice cream in a large dessert coupe or wine glass. Spoon in the marinated strawberries.
• Decorate with the lightly whipped cream and pencil wafer.
• Serve immediately.

Tip
• For added flavor marinate the fruit one hour in advance.

CHAPTER FIVE

A Five Minute Drink

"Guten Tag Herr Cronin, willkommen zum Schatzalp!"

Upon my arrival at the Schatzalp Hotel in Davos, the chef welcomed me in High German using the formal tone. Herr Koch was a tall thin man with a jet black neatly trimmed mustache, and a firm handshake. He led me from the reception to his office in the kitchen. It was larger than the one in Neuchatel with an oil-fired island range dominating the space. The cold kitchen was one level lower which meant all plated food would be tediously carried by the chefs up a set of stairs before sending it to the dining room. The pastry section was separated by glass windows resting on a four foot high wall located next to Herr Koch's office. In the opposite corner, with a spectacular view of the Strella Alp, was the inevitable chef's private dining room. The biggest advantage was that the main section of the kitchen was above ground with large windows all round. From my work station I could see skiers on the slopes as they navigated the moguls – a real treat.

Like many alpine hotels of the time, the Hotel Schatzalp was a converted sanatorium. Early in the 19th century, the Swiss Alps became a popular destination for patients with respiratory diseases. The clean alpine air, abundant year-round sunshine and healthier diets helped many patients recover. Stories of these tuberculosis patients are described in Thomas Mann's book, "The Magic Mountain." The Schatzalp is the hotel described in his book – at the time when it was one of the most modern sanatoriums in the region. Davos is at an elevation of fifteen hundred meters. The Hotel Schatzalp, located on a plateau three hundred meters above the resort, is accessible in winter by taking a six minute journey on a private cable railway.

After the kitchen tour, I was assigned to a staff room in the cellar with no direct sunlight – it would do for a foreigner. The next day Herr Koch – who was from St Moritz – introduced me to the rest of the chefs. Hans was the saucier/sous chef, a Swiss German from Zurich, Daniel the entremetier was Swiss- French from Neuchatel and Rolf was the garde manger from Berne. We spoke in the informal, which was a first name basis, but always switched to the formal when addressing Herr Koch because of his seniority. My position as 'chef tournant' – revolving chef – involved replacing each one of these chefs on their day off. Each section had a commis who would carry over the details from the previous day and work directly with me. There was a window at my work station with a view of the path that led guests to the famous Schatzalp sled run. It was an attraction in Davos: tourists took the cable railway up to the hotel and made their way along the path behind the hotel, past the kitchen windows, and onward to the sled run – many would wave to me as I cooked.

The hotel had one main dining room, a bar and a terrace which ran the length of the south side of the hotel. It was called the Snow Beach. Because the snow was never cleared it lived up to its name throughout the winter. Guests lay on sun chairs – in the bright sunshine – on packed snow, wrapped in blankets, sipping their drinks and eating from a selection of simple menu items such as 'Croque Monsieur,' club sandwiches, and chef's salad. Later in the warmer spring months the ladies lay in their bikinis tanning in the snow. Food was a major part of every guest's stay so when the skiing was good, guests were generally happy. But when it rained, as sometimes it does above the tree line in winter, guests were house bound, became grumpy and found fault with even the best prepared meals.

It was a week before Christmas and the hotel would open just a few days before the holiday. Similar to the hotel in Adelboden, guests checked in for the ten day holiday period and left on the Sunday after the New Year. This was the busiest period of the season for alpine hotels. All the staff was asked not to go skiing during that time as accidents were frequent which added a burden to all of us if someone broke a leg. We were busy in the kitchen preparing for opening day. The menu was a reduced a la carte with a selection of starters, main courses and desserts. Herr Koch, whom everyone referred to as "Chef", would tell the chef de parties every day the number of portions of each course to prepare ensuring we had enough food for the two hundred and twenty guests. All hot food going out to the dining room was served on silver platters with highly polished covers. There was only one head chef in this kitchen: Chef was in command during service and he made sure the waiters and the kitchen brigade understood that. If a commis waiter had the misfortune to touch any silver platters under the heat lamp without first asking for the table number he would be subjected to a litany of Swiss German swearing emitted in a high pitched voice that, if written out, would surely take up half a page. Herr Koch believed the commis waiters were just messengers and added little value to the meal experience. The flamboyant work was done by the Maître and chefs de rangs in the dining room as they transferred the food to heated dinner plates using highly polished silverware and elegant movements punctuated with a 'Bon Appetit' as they placed the food in front of the guests. Chef once told me of a chef de cuisine from his younger years who always had a three foot stick lying on the food table. It had a two inch nail sticking out of the end and he would swipe it at any commis waiter who annoyed him. They learned to keep their distance.

On my first evening in charge of a station I was covering for Daniel on the vegetable section. I prepared braised endives which were served with Hans's Goulash as one of the main dishes on the menu. Belgian endives are bitter, so to remove the bitterness I blanched them using flour water with added lemon juice which helps preserve their attractive white color. After cooling I dipped them in flour, sautéed them to a light brown color, laid them on a mirepoix in a braising pan and braised them with chicken stock. Braising is a slow cooking method which uses liquid as a heat medium and is ideally suited for tough meats and vegetables, extracting flavor and tenderizing the food.

Chef helped me on the first day and I was amazed at the speed at which he could panfry the endives, removing them from the pan at precisely the right color and lining them up almost in military fashion in the braising pan. It gave me an insight as to the speed he required for service when the dining room filled up. I did not want to be the recipient of his swearing so I knew I'd better do my best to learn his quick methods. The vegetable section was also responsible for preparing all farinaceous dishes so I made Spätzli for the goulash. Spätzli is a pasta style dish common in Switzerland, Germany, and Austria. It resembles a semi-liquid dough made with flour, milk, eggs and seasoning, notably nutmeg. It is then pressed through a grater forming dough droplets that fall directly into boiling salted water. Once cooked, the droplets rise to the surface, are removed and cooled in cold water. Then they are strained and sautéed in butter to a light golden brown color. They are a delicious accompaniment to venison, brown stews, braised meats and the mighty German dish: "Sauerbraten."

After I covered for Daniel, he returned from his day off and then Hans was off so I was working on the sauce section and had to make goulash for one hundred and fifty people. Hans left the recipe for me and the commis was there to help. Goulash is originally Hungarian but it is also a common dish in Austria which makes sense given the close histories of both countries. The dish typically uses cubed beef, sliced onions and lots of sweet paprika. The secret to a good goulash, like any stew, is slow cooking. This method allows the flavors to emerge. The result is a succulent tender dish with a velvety textured sauce bursting with paprika flavor – just like Josef showed me how to make in the Hotel du Bateau. That evening Chef was happy with the goulash, which was gratifying. The next day Hans was back, Rolf was off, and I was downstairs in the cold kitchen preparing starters such as smoked salmon, salads and a warm starter we called Jamaican grapefruit. To make this I cut the grapefruit in half horizontally, separated the sections, sprinkled it with brown sugar and glazed it under the hot salamander – a type of overhead grill – which caramelized the sugar. The guests loved the cold/warm contrast together with the sour sweet flavor combination in addition to the lightness of this dish.

As I was not a pastry chef, I wasn't allowed to replace the pastry chef de partie on his day off. There were two extra commis in that section to help out on off days. The pastry chef was Austrian, the oldest in the kitchen and in poor health. A heavy set man with gray hair, he spoke very little, and had difficulty moving around. Everyone spoke with him in the formal and called him by name, Herr Dorfmeister. In the evening after work, when many of the chefs would chat over a beer in the private dining room, Herr Dorfmeister would bring a small saucepan of hot water to the table and set his beer bottle in it. The thought of warm beer made everyone cringe but he insisted it helped him avoid what he called 'starken nierenschmerzen' – severe kidney pain. By now, and after a few years in Switzerland, I was familiar with chilled draft beer which was the standard way to serve beer in every Swiss restaurant. In Ireland, draft beer was served at room temperature. I only first experienced chilled beer when I came to Switzerland and I liked the added flavor the chilling provided. Despite that, Herr Dorfmeister told me that one cold beer would create such a severe pain in his kidneys that it would prevent him from sleeping during the night.

Every morning at precisely five to eleven, just before our lunch break and no matter how busy we were in the kitchen, I was responsible for serving selected kitchen staff 'l'aperitif' – a traditional pre-meal drink in Switzerland and in many other non-English speaking European countries. During this brief daily moment there was one golden rule – no talk about work. If Herr Koch saw that I was late setting up the drinks, he would call across the kitchen to me: "Herr Cronin, aperitif nicht vergessen!" The timing was so strict as to be almost a religion. Drinks had to poured and ready at precisely five minutes to eleven. If I was even one minute late, the chefs would mention it. As we gathered round the stainless steel table, no one touched the drinks until Herr Koch was present. Then as if on cue, each of us took our drink, looked everyone else directly in the eye while clinking glasses and said "Prost!" Now if that situation took place in Ireland and we had only five minutes for a drink, it would be a cause of national concern; maybe even an amendment to the constitution would be considered given the pressure to finish in such a short time. It wouldn't be worth our time ordering a drink – it took longer than that to pull a proper pint of Guinness. Having a drink in Ireland was a social event – not related, or bound to, time. But here, I suppose it was the Swiss precision in action. Some days the aperitif was just a glass of Swiss white wine. But most days it was a low alcohol drink such as: a Suze, a Vermouth or a Cynar – an artichoke-based bitter, which was the most popular among the chefs. The commis were never invited to this daily ritual – they were usually cooking our lunch during that time. After our five minute drink, and a discussion on the topic of the day, we walked over to the chef's dining room at precisely eleven o'clock where the commis were serving our lunch. Such was the hierarchy.

About half way through the season when all the chef de parties were working and I did not have replacement duty, Herr Koch sent me out to the dining room to flambé the desert with the pastry commis. This was the first time in the season I actually saw the guests. Chefs were not allowed in the dining room, and interaction with guests by 'back of the house' staff was frowned upon. Even Herr Koch did not go 'outside'. As I prepared peach flambé I found it hilarious to see how guests would turn around and go Ooh! and Aah! as the flame lit up the flambé station. The Maître was very helpful; he taught me how to flambé correctly. It is easy to do and makes a great impression. I began by sautéing the peach halves in butter to a light golden color. Normally a dessert flambé begins by caramelizing sugar in a flambé pan, then adding fresh butter and afterwards the food to be flambéed. This takes a lot of time so Herr Dorfmeister had the idea to whip the butter with sugar to almost whipped cream consistency. Not having to wait for the sugar to caramelize meant I could make the flambés much faster as the dining room was full. Once the peaches were a light golden color I tilted the pan to one side and poured in a dash of Cointreau liqueur, keeping my thumb on the top of the bottle to regulate the flow of alcohol. It caught fire instantly and it was the two-foot-high flame, and the hiss of liquid turning to steam, that entertained guests as the alcohol harmlessly burned off, leaving the orange flavor from the liqueur behind. Then I deglazed the pan with some orange juice, let it reduce and served the two half peaches with a scoop of ice cream topped with the sauce from the pan and sprinkled the lot with toasted sliced almonds. Guests loved it. Deglazing is a term chefs use for the process that loosens caramelized food sugars from the cooking utensil – notably a sauté pan. After pan-frying a chicken breast, a steak, or in my case the peaches, and in order to make a sauce in the same pan, chefs deglaze the hot pan with some wine or stock to loosen the caramelized food sugars and transfer their flavor to the sauce. By reducing this liquid, flavor is further concentrated. Flavor created at this level in the cooking process cannot be duplicated later on.

During my free time in Davos, I skied. Days off were spent on the Jacobshorn ski runs located on the opposite side of the valley. A large aerial cable car brought skiers right to the top so rising early was crucial to avoid long wait times at the base station. As my room in the cellar had no direct sunlight, I had no way of looking outside to see what the weather was like before getting dressed. So before I could dress for skiing, I had to make my way down to a basement corridor window to determine if it was a day for skiing or sleeping.

I would be first at the top of the mountain in the morning and the last to close the run. The thrill of fast downhill skiing was intoxicating. I could not give it up. At the end of a great day on the slopes, I often thought how lucky I was to work and live in such pristine surroundings. The blue sky, white capped peaks, and the stillness at the top were all breathtaking. The panorama from the Jacobshorn was incredibly beautiful – snow covered mountains were carved out against a perfect blue sky for as far as the eye could see. And the silence – I could hear the silence! It was such a welcome change from the noise, the stress, and speed of the kitchen. Most work days I had the afternoon off from two until five o'clock. I spent those afternoons skiing on the Strella Alp – a ski run located behind the hotel. It was a two minute walk from the hotel to the chair lift and the run ended at the kitchen door. On this run, a few hundred meters above the hotel, was a small alpine restaurant where I often stopped for a coffee and a Williamine – pear brandy – on the last run before returning to work. So steep was the drop that from the restaurant the hotel looked like a miniature building almost directly beneath us. Maria – the owner, a wonderful lady always wearing a floral apron – made the best apricot open fruit tarts in the region; they were always so tempting that I usually ordered a slice. Herr Koch would often be there with friends, also wrapping up his skiing afternoon with a coffee break before returning to work. I would acknowledge him from across the restaurant with a wave or a nod but seldom joined him as my position in the kitchen did not put me as an equal. He was my chef, period. After this short break I would put on my skis, and then it was literally a vertical drop lasting thirty seconds straight to the kitchen door. I did not even have to move my skis – not unlike a downhill skier racing over the finish line – to experience a natural high before embracing the stress and heat of the kitchen for dinner service.

Seasonal work takes a toll on chefs and we get burnt out very fast. Constantly surrounded by people enjoying themselves, it is difficult to slow down even on days off. Everyone in the streets, on the slopes, in the shops and discos are all at the resort for vacation. We were working six days a week but we also played hard and it was not unusual to have an occasional "nuit blanche" – sleepless night. One evening, as I often did after work, I took the cable railway down to Davos. This particular evening, Francois invited me to Davos Platz for "a few drinks." He didn't speak German and always came over to me in the kitchen to speak French. He was from a small village near Lake Leman. He had come to Davos for the season to try to learn German and drink. He was a nice enough lad, got plastered one night per week, usually on the evening before his day off. Then he slept all day. That night, as we moved from one bar to another, we missed the last train back up to the hotel and with Francois footless drunk, we had no option but to walk up to the hotel. We took the pathway through the forest leading up the steep slope, and every few minutes Francois would lie down in the snow and want to go to sleep. If I left him there in the minus fifteen degree cold, he would be frozen by morning. I would have his death on my conscience and with one less worker; everyone in the kitchen would be upset with me because of the extra work for the remainder of the season – never mind that I let him die. It took several hours of him lying down in the snow to sleep, and I waking him up again and moving a few steps forward, to get him back to his room. I vowed never to go out drinking with him again. As my Uncle A.J. used to say, it is one thing to go out drinking for the night, it's another thing to be able to hold it.

As the end of the season approached, all the chefs began to look for hotels for the summer season. Herr Koch would be back at his regular hotel summer job in St. Moritz, Hans was thinking about staying on at the Schatzalp for the summer, Rolf was returning to Berne and Alex and Francois were fed up listening to Swiss German and were returning to the French speaking part of the country. Herr Koch asked me where I was going to work for the summer. I had not yet thought about it so he proposed that I consider working at the Palace Hotel in Montreux. He would call his friend at the Palace to see if they had a position for me – I was grateful for this offer. We had gotten along very well all season, and I managed to avoid his outbursts, which I have to say were mostly directed at the commis waiters. Unlike Herman at the Hotel Elite, he never shouted at the kitchen staff. He had other ways of getting his point across like the time I was making fresh potato gnocchi for two hundred guests and I was late. Realizing I would not be ready for service time, he did not shout at me but came to my station and began rolling the pieces of gnocchi. This was a tremendous relief for me. He worked so fast that I got his message of what was expected. I thought it was a great management tool for inspiring me to work faster. Potato gnocchi is made with a mixture of flour, eggs, mashed potatoes, and seasoning. They are then rolled by hand into thin strips about a half inch thick and cut into lengths of one inch. This is when they are rolled on a dinner fork which gives them their well recognized markings. Then they are cooked in boiling salted water much like regular pasta.

Two weeks before the end of the season, Herr Koch called me to his office. The chef from the Palace Hotel in Montreux was on the phone and wanted to speak with me. He offered me the position of chef de partie based on Herr Koch's recommendation. I could start as soon as I finished the season in Davos. I was very grateful to the chef for this gesture as it served as a reference. Most hotels in Switzerland automatically issue a letter of recommendation at the end of employment. They are very standard, never the less I was disappointed when I read mine. The general manager, who I never met during the season, wrote the same recommendation for all chefs in the kitchen. Each letter was identical, all that changed was the name. I decided to ask him to rewrite mine. He refused so I tore the letter in half, threw it on his desk and told him it was of no use to me as it did not mention I was a chef tournant – an important fact for me for future positions. I mentioned this to Herr Koch and he asked the manager to write another one which he did, but it was identical to the first! So the chef wrote a personal note, in beautiful handwriting at the bottom of my recommendation and signed it, Hans Koch, Swiss Master Chef. It is one of the most precious recommendation letters I have received in my career.

"Sablé" Biscuits (Butter Biscuits)

We always served Sablé biscuits to accompany every cup of tea and coffee served on the Snow Beach. They literally melted on the tongue.

Ingredients
9 oz. (270gr.) butter
12 oz. (360gr.) flour
2 egg yolks
4 oz. (120gr.) icing sugar (confectioners sugar)
Zest of 1 lemon
Vanilla essence to taste
Pinch of salt

Preparation
- Cream butter and sugar to a light creamy consistency.
- Add egg yolks and flour in stages.
- Add lemon zest, vanilla, and salt.

Assembly
- Using both hands and a little flour roll the mixture on a table top into six inch (15cm) long rolls 1½ inches (3.8cm) in diameter and chill in the refrigerator.
- Cut into ½ inch (1.25cm) slices, sprinkle with sugar and
- lay on a baking tray lined with parchment paper.   Bake at 350F (180C) for 12 minutes.

Tip
- For a different flavor: after baking, dip each biscuit half way in melted dark chocolate.

Makes approximately 80 biscuits (invite some friends). These are the perfect accompaniment to an espresso.

CHAPTER SIX

The Flaming Waiter

The journey by train from Davos to Montreux was beautiful. I had been working in the Alps for almost five months. For all of that time, I never left the resort and only saw snow capped mountains, blue skies, and mingled with people happy to be on vacation who wore big heavy ski clothes, boots and woollen ski caps. Now as the train descended through the numerous valleys, the snow gradually receded. Patches of green punctuated with spring flowers replaced the white. The further down the train went, the greener the landscape became. It was like peeling a vegetable: every layer removed exposed a more beautiful one beneath. In Montreux, spring was in full bloom, and tulips and daffodils lined the lakeside promenade. People walked around in shirts and light clothing. It was warm! It was difficult to believe that just a few hours away the alpine resorts were still snow covered.

Monteux, located on the shores of Lake Leman, is a desirable destination in itself. In summer it hosts a jazz festival which attracts famous musicians from around the world. Some refer to the lake as Lake Geneva. This upsets many locals, believing the lake does not belong to Geneva but to all the cantons that border it – cantons of Vaud, Valais, Geneva and France to the south. I approached the concierge desk at the Palace and a well dressed gentleman led me to meet the chef, Monsieur Durand. An opulent man, wearing a particularly well starched hat, his apron strings tightly hugging his girth, addressed me in formal French: "Bonjour Monsieur Cronin, comment allez vous?" We talked briefly about his friend Herr Koch and then in an excited voice, told me he wanted to show me the new oven. He took a key from his desk and holding it up said: "Voila la clef du four, on y va!" – here is the key to the oven, let's go! I thought this must be some oven if it needs a key to start it. He showed me to a different section of the kitchen and there it was: an eight foot high oven in gleaming stainless steel with a special feature – a window! Sure enough there was a key hole similar to the ignition in a car in which he proudly inserted the key. The oven turned on with a whirring noise, lights came on and it began to heat up. He exclaimed this oven could roast fifty chickens at once! The chickens were laid in trays attached to two revolving chains, one on either side and were visible through the large window. This was the first time I saw an oven with a window. I wasn't sure if it was intended for the chef to look in at the chickens or for the chickens to look out at the chef!

Monsieur Durand then introduced me to Xavier, the sous chef, who gave me very discouraging news. My position was not to be with the Palace but with a smaller hotel managed by the Palace and located directly across the road on the edge of the lake. I was very disappointed. I had heard so many great things about the Palace Hotel in Montreux and now I would not be working there but in a smaller unknown hotel called the Lorius. Nevertheless I took the position. Again I was given a room in the cellar, next to Ismail, the dishwasher from Turkey. He played loud Turkish music late into the night. Every morning when he came to the kitchen, I would ask him to turn the music down. He agreed, but the following night it would be at a high volume again. As a result I got very little sleep. Despite the late night noise I was very happy with my room. Because of the slope of the property I could leave my room through French doors leading on to the terrace and walk across the lawn to swim in the lake – even at night, a real privilege.

The food at the Lorius was very good and the service elegant if not a little old fashioned. It suited the clientele which were old and consequently returned in smaller numbers every year. Xavier had dishes on the menu like Osso Buco a la Gremolata – braised veal shank; Mignons de Veau Chasseur – filets of veal in mushroom sauce; Crepes Suzette and Gateau au Vin – wine tart. All food was served on silver platters. Silver teapots and coffee pots adorned the breakfast table and crystal glasses were the norm for wine. Guests had breakfast on the terrace overlooking the lake, took daily walks along the promenade, and dined by candelabra in a beautiful ornate dining room filled with antique furniture, freshly starched tablecloths, and the best china. I was the only foreigner in the kitchen and did not have any contact with guests. I would get their descriptions from the waiters who often were on their tenth, or more, season at the hotel. Each summer the same guests would stay for several weeks, be served by the same waiter, at the same table and order the same wine. That's a lot of same. Still, I learned new dishes and collected more recipes. I thought one in particular was special; Xavier called it Le Gateau au Vin – wine tart. Montreux is located close to one of the Swiss wine regions known as 'Lavaux,' so it was fitting to have a tart made with wine on the menu. Despite my unhappiness, I was expanding my repertoire and developing my taste memories.

On one of my days off from the Lorius, Pascale, a French girl whom I knew from the Eurotel in Neuchatel, came to visit me. We walked along the lakeside promenade and reminisced about our time working together at the Eurotel. She had remained on at the Eurotel after I left. The German chef who replaced Herbert had just left and Martin, the General Manager, was looking for a replacement. She said I should apply because Martin had mentioned my name in the weekly operations meeting as a possible replacement. I wondered if she came all the way to Montreux to tell me this. We had gone out a few times together but that ended when I left Neuchatel. Was this the real reason for her trip to Montreux? To rekindle a past affair?

We had lunch at a lakeside terrace and talked about the many people we knew in common and where they were currently working. Seasonal workers in Switzerland were a strange bunch, mostly foreigners, never staying long in any job, usually moving from the winter resorts to the lake side resorts and back again, always looking out for the next job. No matter what or who we talked about, Pascale kept bringing the conversation back to the chef de cuisine position in Neuchatel. I did not feel I was qualified to apply for such a position. And anyway I was too young in addition to being a foreigner. There were two reasons right there.

This was a position that included managing ten people, two restaurants, and banquet rooms with a seating capacity of up to four hundred. This was a big step and what if I couldn't do the job? I was already thinking of what my next employer would say when they found out I had to leave because I was not up to the job. Applying for any other position in Switzerland would be difficult after that kind of failure. But eventually, Pascale convinced me to apply for the position. I called Martin the next day and set up an interview on my next day off. So now there was no backing out.

The following week I met Martin in the lobby of the Eurotel and we went to the Carrefour for coffee and a chat. I recognized many staff members who had worked here with me when I was a chef de partie. Now he was proposing the top job. Traditionally I would have had to be a sous chef, or second in command, before becoming a chef de cuisine. We went over all the details of the position. He believed I could do it and he would help with whatever he could from correcting grammar on the menus to advice with the food cost. So with that support in place, I accepted the job and became the youngest chef de cuisine in the Eurotel hotel group. The salary was much more than what I was earning at the Lorius, but a lot less than if he hired a Swiss.

Despite my short stay, I left the Lorius on good terms and moved to Neuchatel. I was given a room in the staff quarters and took over the kitchen on the first of June 1977 after being in Switzerland just under four years. I was thrilled and frightened at the same time. I wrote to my mother telling her what I believed was good news. After all she was the one who got me "cheffin'" in the first place. She wrote back saying how proud she was of me and it gave me renewed courage to tackle the job.

Work was not easy to begin with. The staff tested me in every way: my cooking skills, menu writing, my French – which was improving but I still made mistakes on the menu. I was tested in purchasing, staff scheduling and my ability to supervise. I was a foreigner so I had to work even harder to earn their respect and hope that would get me through my first few months. I had to get along with every member of the staff if I was going to survive.

Although I made many decisions, it took me time to make them and they were not always right. My responsibilities grew and the diversity of the position of chef de cuisine slowly began to emerge. The hotel had about one hundred rooms and guests were a mixture of what we call "Frequent Individual Travelers," business men, and holiday makers. Neuchatel – a big watch making town, attracted businessmen from all over the world.

In my previous position here, I was the grill chef for a while, so I had a little experience as to how this kitchen would work. The Carrefour, much like a brasserie, was still a popular restaurant. Most restaurants in Switzerland serve food only during meal times so lunch service would begin at half eleven and end at two o'clock. Then most of the staff would go home for the afternoon break, returning at dinner time. We usually had a small menu available in the Carrefour in the afternoon with sandwiches and desserts.

In Switzerland, practically everything except public toilets closes for lunch from twelve to two o'clock. Lunch break was a big affair in most people's work day. Some workers went home to eat and some would have lunch in a restaurant. So every day regular customers came in at exactly twelve o'clock and ordered either the 'Express' or the 'Carrefour'. During lunch, we guaranteed that the Express lunch could be served in three minutes, the Carrefour lunch in seven. Waiters would bring in the order to me, then serve guests a drink, bread and butter, and we would have the Express under the heating lamp ready to go within three minutes. It was that fast! Dishes for the Express were always ready-to-serve, but freshly cooked that morning. We might have a slice of quiche Lorraine with a salad or a chicken curry with rice, or a white pork or veal stew with buttered noodles. Not only did it have to be fast, it also had to be cheap. This menu was designed to bring regular customers every day for lunch which meant I had to vary the menu every three weeks to avoid repetition. The Carrefour special took a little longer to prepare and cost a few francs more. This could be a grilled slice of turkey breast or chicken with a mushroom sauce and noodles with a small side salad, or a four ounce steak with a vegetable and potatoes. Sautéed horse steak with burgundy sauce was a popular option. Horse was cheaper than beef, a little sweeter, not always as tender, but the Swiss liked it. With Ireland's strong history of thoroughbreds, I could only imagine the outrage if I put horse steak on the menu in Jury's Hotel in Dublin.

In addition to the two restaurants we had several banquet rooms. Food for these banquets came from the same kitchen. We would serve three course plated meals, sometimes a buffet or a cocktail reception. Never the less it had to be planned and prepared. I had to cost out menus, calculate selling prices, order food, schedule staff, and then ensure the food was prepared and served. So it was stressful when the first floor had one or two banquets going, the Pinot Noir was full, and the Carrefour was busy. People's tempers sometime flared and chefs got upset if a little thing did not work out or God forbid, a waiter made a sly remark about the speed of dishes coming from the kitchen. Voices would be raised, vulgar names called and insults would fly. I would have to step in and calm everyone down.

One particularly busy night I was at the pass calling out the table orders as they came in and supervising food going out when a waiter brought me a fondue heating set to refill with lighter fuel. Seeing that there was no flame in the container I began to pour the liquid fuel into the burner, but there was a tiny flame inside that I could not see. The fuel ignited and the burner shot out a flame which sent burning fuel right on to the sleeve of the waiter's jacket. So now I had a waiter with lighter fuel in flames on his sleeve and him screaming, "I'm on fire, I'm burning!" The atmosphere in the kitchen changed instantly! All eyes were on the waiter who was Italian so the whole episode was in French with an Italian accent. Je Brule! – I'm burning! The commotion brought other waiters in from both restaurants. When they saw the waiter with flame on his sleeve they too began to get hot and bothered. I took a jug of cold water from the service station and poured it on his sleeve to put the flame out. He was badly shaken, but not hurt. He immediately accused me of trying to kill him and that I should have known there was a flame in the fondue set and it was a very stupid thing to do.

I took off his jacket with the burn mark on the sleeve, threw it in the dishwashers sink, and told him to get right back to work. Then I shouted at him in my best French: "You have no burn marks; it was only the sleeve of your jacket. So don't make a big fecking deal out of a little flame on your jacket!" There was silence in the kitchen. The brigade had never heard me raise my voice before. Then I looked over at them and everyone got back to work. When the service was over, I bought the waiter a drink and we sat at a corner table in the Pinot Noir. We both realized we had over reacted and apologized to each other. We had to work together again tomorrow. It was common to get flare ups like that. The heat of the kitchen and high stress levels, the non-stop speed of service, the customers' expectations, and the waiters shouting for their tables all added to the mix. Sometimes all it took was a comment taken out of context to start a war.

It is a popular belief that a chef needs only to know how to cook, no additional skills required. It should be said that the term chef in French, German and Italian means the top person in a managerial role. The term is not necessarily unique to cooking. Hence the term chef d'entreprise, head of the factory, or chef de chantier, head of the construction site, and chef de cuisine, head of the kitchen. By now I was discovering the wide array of responsibilities I had to assume, in addition to cooking. I had to schedule staff, including dishwashers. Write and price menus for functions and daily specials. Ensure cleanliness, rotate stocks, check food quality, attend management meetings and generally keep everyone working together so that I had a kitchen to be head of. I quickly discovered that if I solved all the little problems people brought to my attention, they could get back to cooking. This meant that I was solving more problems and doing less cooking, but if that was what it took to keep my first position as head chef from going down the drain, then so be it.

After a few months we began to settle in to a routine and everybody got used to the Irish chef. I was learning as I went and as with most chefs, I learned a great deal from the other chefs in the kitchen and they in turn learned from me; it was a huge team effort. We had two apprentices, three chefs de parties, four commis chefs, and two dishwashers completed the team. The Food and Beverage cost controller was an Austrian lad who worked in a small office behind the kitchen and helped me with inventory, menu costing, purchasing and keeping my monthly food cost percentage in line. We spoke a mixture of French, English and his native German. The great thing about figures is they transcend linguistic differences.

One chef de partie was Swiss, the other Austrian and one was French. The commis were a mixed bunch. Some moved on, others were hired and retrained and it was nice when we had a full brigade and everyone worked together. The hotel industry is never static in regards to staff, especially in Switzerland where many workers move with the change of seasons. It was a bigger problem when a chef de partie left because they ran one section of the kitchen, had perfected the recipes and trained staff under them. In Switzerland, in smaller establishments, the chef de partie in charge of the sauce section usually doubled as the sous chef. This is a very demanding position because next to the chef, the saucier usually sets the tone for the rest of the brigade. The sous chef position requires organizational capabilities, physical strength, and excellent interaction with the brigade and the chef – and should, of course be able to cook. When the chef saucier suddenly resigned to leave and work a winter season elsewhere, it meant I would not have a day off until I found and trained his replacement.

We put an ad in the local paper for this position. The kitchens were so male dominated at the time that it was unusual to get applications from women for this position. So when a woman turned up for the interview, the entire kitchen staff turned to stare at her. She was Swiss German, tall, had long blonde hair, and was very attractive. My initial concern was that of the physical requirements of the job. It was not unusual to be leaning over a hot range for three to four hours at a time without a break, being shouted at for food orders, giving orders and still being able to produce good tasting food on time, well presented, and on the correct plates. Never mind putting up with the jokes, the language and the verbal abuse that were common in most kitchens at the time. I mentioned this and she assured me she knew what the job entailed. I hired her with a two week trial period and told her that if things did not work out we would mutually agree to end the job. But that was not necessary; she became one of the strongest chefs in the kitchen, earning the respect of everyone from day one, including me. Her flavors were great and she quickly became part of the team and could tell a joke and drink beer like any of us. It was not easy for her in the beginning but she managed it. She could hold her own with any of the chefs and she gave back as much as she got, so much so that many of the chefs respected her instantly for her ability to tell them to feck off if they were out of line. After two weeks she became the sous-chef and I was able to take my weekly day off again – confidently leaving her in charge.

Mike, the dentist, often came to the Pinot Noir for lunch. I visited his practice a few times for some work on my teeth. He was the best dentist I had ever sat in a chair for. I had a great fear of the numbing injection, but he was so good that I never felt it. He would first numb the gum with a little Novocain on a swab while telling me some interesting story or other. Then when the needle touched the flesh it did not inflect any pain and from there he numbed the gum bit by bit as he inserted the needle so I never felt a thing. This was a big change for me from the dentist who once filled a cavity for me in Limerick when a lot of pain was involved.

On one of his lunch visits, Mike asked if I could cook a 'brochet entier' for him. Brochet – pike – is a popular lake fish, often served as a 'darne' – slice – poached with a butter sauce such as hollandaise. Mike was having his group of friends at the apartment, one of them had caught the fish and would like if I could cook it for them. This group met every Wednesday evening without fail and appropriately referred to themselves as 'L'equipe du Mercredi" – the Wednesday team.

On the day of the meal I prepared the fish by first removing the scales using the back of my chopping knife. Pike are covered in large thick scales which if not removed carefully can create a very unpleasant mouth feel. Next I prepared a court bouillon in a fish kettle – a long narrow container used exclusively for poaching fish. This court bouillon consisted of water, white wine, leeks, onions, celeriac, carrots, bay leaf, black peppercorns, lemon, parsley stems, and some salt. The fish kettle was the length of his cooker so I could use two gas burners to bring it to a boil and let it simmer to infuse the flavors.

When it was time to place the fish in its final bath, all the lads came in to see this spectacle. Mike introduced me to all of them. They were very friendly and came from all walks of life. I remember one man in particular, he was smoking a pipe – he had so many v's and w's in his long, almost unpronounceable, German name that the lads just called him 'Volkswagen' for simplicity. He did not seem to mind. The fish still had the head on – its two eyes staring at us from a sad looking face as if to say; "Do I really have to do this?"

There was a big cheer as I put the fish in the kettle and placed the lid on top. The lads went back to their gin and tonics and waited for the call to table. Once cooked, I removed the fish and portioned it out, its snow white flesh a beautiful contrast to the sautéed spinach and the rich yellow hollandaise sauce. Steamed parsley potatoes rounded out the dish and everyone was happy with the 'brochet du lac', saying it was "fameux!" Such evenings were a welcome break from the fast pace of the kitchen.

Hassan the hotel dishwasher was Turkish, a tall man with a weather beaten face which told of an outdoor workers past, perhaps construction or farming. He had left his wife and children in Turkey to come to Switzerland to offer them a better life with the money he sent home every month. He lived a meager life at the hotel and longed for the time when he could go home to see his family. This was no strange issue to me. Growing up we were surrounded by farmers who worked in London and Scotland, seldom saw their families, and also sent money home. They would go home for a few weeks' holidays to see their families, visit relatives, and then leave again.

Hassan would ask me if there was pork in the staff meals. I asked him why and he told me that his religion forbid him from eating pork. Up until then I only had experience with the Catholic religion. According to the fiery sermons at mass in Ireland and from our teachers in the national school, we were all damned anyway no matter what we did or what we ate. "A bunch of sinners," they said. The minute you were born, you were a sinner. You got up in the morning you were a sinner, you went to bed at night you were a sinner. When I left Ireland I did not know anything about other religions or whether they were sinners too? As far as my national school education went, we were all Catholics in Ireland, went to mass on Sunday morning, ate fish on Fridays, believed in God, no other religion was ever discussed....and we were still sinners! No getting away from the sinners. As I travelled I learned about other religions. I learned about how the Jews also could not eat pork, and I thought maybe that accounted for why there was only bread and wine at the Last Supper. I never understood that at school – having a supper with only bread and wine and no spuds – we never asked because who knows what kind of reaction the teacher would have. She might get the bamboo stick out at us for asking a stupid question. So every day I made sure that Hassan got some meat that was not pork and he was happy with that. I never asked him whether he was a sinner or not. My father gave me one word of advice when I was leaving home. Don't discuss politics or religion with strangers because there is no telling what could come out of such a discussion.

I tried to ensure that all the staff had a good meal at least once a day. I remember the hotel operator telling me that after answering the phone for hours she would be looking forward to her lunch break and a nice meal in the cafeteria. It was then I realized how important that meals and breaks are to the staff. I could have anything I wanted to eat in the kitchen and did not realize that many workers sat at a desk and in some cases the highlight of their day was the food they had for lunch. I was constantly surrounded by food and tasty dishes so I never thought much about eating. Food was just there! So we made an even bigger effort to have some nice staff food every day. Leftovers were common but if prepared correctly they were well accepted by all. Good food is not difficult to make but of course there was always something more important to do besides cook for the staff. We wrote a weekly menu for the staff meals which helped tremendously to keep everyone happy. I believe that a well-fed staff is a happy staff and a happy staff is a productive staff. This made my life easier. It helped at the reception when I needed a favor. It helped in engineering when equipment needed to be fixed. All hotel departments I worked with were very cooperative when staff meals were good.

Living by the lake in Neuchatel was a nice experience, especially in the summer. The weather was warm and as the Eurotel was not a lake side property, the work was steady – no tourist laden ferries to overload the lunch service. It was around this time I met Udo. He liked to go for a pint now and again and we would meet in the local Pickwick pub. It was the nearest resemblance to a pub I had ever seen outside of Ireland. The things that make a great pub are the people who drink there and the person behind the bar. Udo was a marine engine mechanic who ran a small garage with Walter, on the outskirts of the town. Udo serviced and repaired marine engines and outboard motors for boat owners on the lake. So on my days off I would go with him to various inlets and harbors around the lake to service engines. This was a great convenience for owners to have their boat serviced during the week. In many cases he had keys and would take it for a spin after the service – just to be sure it was working fine. I would often come with him and we would pull in for a drink at some lakeside restaurant before returning the boat to its mooring. He was the neatest mechanic I had ever met. It was a pleasure to watch him working. When he took the engine apart he would lay out the parts in the order they would be required when he would put them all back together again.

Udo introduced me to scuba diving. We began diving in the shallow part of the lake to see if I would like it. After a few times in the wet suit and getting a glimpse of the underwater world, which fascinated me, he introduced me to a diving club and I began training for my diver's license. We trained in a club near Lake Morat where I had worked a few summers previously. One day during training the instructor gave our class an exercise. We were in the lake and had to dive in pairs to a depth of ten meters, stay for three minutes and come up to three meters to decompress for three minutes and then back to the surface. This was twice the depth I had ever been to previously. So we began our dive. I did not know my diving buddy that well so when we got to ten meters we just floated there waiting for the three minute interval to pass. He signaled to me that we should practice buddy breathing so without thinking I removed my mouth piece. Now I was the only one in the class that had a two-corrugated-hose regulator leading to the tanks on my back, so when I wanted to put it back in my mouth I had to hold it up over my head which would allow the air to push all the water out and then I could bring it down to my mouth and breathe.

The other divers had modern single hose regulators with a purge button that forced air through the tube, clearing the water so they could breathe again. It was a very simple method perfected by Frenchman Jacques Cousteau. So I watched my buddy take the regulator out of his mouth, purge it and put it back in again but when I tried to do the same, I forgot that I needed to hold it up over my head so I had a tube full of water when I put it in my mouth. I tried a second time to clear it but I was already beginning to panic. The third time I tried to clear it my lungs were bursting for air; I had swallowed a lot of water and was 30 feet from the surface. Dark thoughts began to cross my mind. Was this the way people felt when they were drowning? I began swimming to the surface which we were taught was not the right thing to do for fear of getting 'the bends.' Nevertheless, I kept kicking to the surface. Then my buddy put his hands around my flippers to try to drag me down again. This made me panic even more and I started using my arms to propel me faster.

By now I was sure I would never make it to the surface. Even though I could see the light, it looked so far above me. I kept kicking my feet and with my mouth closed I managed to free myself from my buddy and got to the surface just before I passed out. My buddy turned me on my back, used his regulator to get some air into me, and at the same time swam to the shore bringing me along with him. It took me a while to recover and to realize that I was sitting on the rocks and not on a cloud with a harp. That had to be to the closest I ever came to dying. The instructor surfaced, and when he heard what happened, shouted at us. "Why did you decide to practice buddy breathing when my orders were to dive to ten meters, wait three minutes and resurface?" No one answered him. Then he told me to suit up again. He was taking me down again to ten meters, I was not sure if I wanted to go back down again. That episode had frightened me, but he said, "Brendan, if you do not do it now, you will never dive again." So we went down to ten meters, no buddy breathing this time. With the mouthpiece firmly clasped between my teeth for fear I would let it fall out, I got my confidence back and gained a new-found respect for Karl-Heinz the instructor.

I finally got my diver's license and began diving in Lake Neuchatel with Udo. Most times the lake was pitch black at a depth of ten meters. But above that depth there was a lot to see. Probably the most thrilling of all was the sense of weightlessness I experienced. Just lying in the water well below the surface with perfectly balanced weights, it was incredible to feel the power of the water keeping me up. We would swim out to where the floor of the lake dropped off into the darkness. Swiss lakes are very deep in spots, so it was mind-blowing to swim out over the edge of an underwater cliff and float there moving up and down ever so slightly with my breathing and know that the bottom – although invisible – was very far down, yet I was not falling. I could see perch and pike, two popular fish on menus around the lake. One perch came right up to my mask. Looking at him, I thought to myself, "I might have pan-fried one of your relatives yesterday," but then he swam away just as quickly as he appeared.

As I was now a department head, Martin decided I should have a small room near the guest elevator and move out of the staff quarters. He felt I deserved some privacy and should not be sharing the shower and bathroom with the staff I supervised. This was a guest room that was too small and noisy for hotel guests and because of its location on the guest floors, I now used the guest entrance to enter and leave the hotel. Since taking the job of chef de cuisine I was working without a work visa which meant if I was caught by the immigration police, I would be deported. A few days after I changed rooms the immigration police made an early morning raid on the staff quarters. Martin was called to the reception to greet them and they insisted he show them to the staff quarters, which he did. Then he immediately came to knock on my door. "Monsieur Cronin, get out of the hotel quickly! The '*Grenzen Polizei*' are checking identity papers, call me later!" This was the moment I had feared: to be deported in the middle of the night. I heard stories from other foreigners of how this happened – the police drove you to a border post and dropped you off on the other side with only your suitcase. You could never enter Switzerland again.

I dressed quickly, took my passport, some money, and left the hotel through the guest entrance. I walked around town for most of the day, cringing every time I saw a police car. If I had not changed rooms I would be on my way to a border post by now. I had a very narrow escape. I called Martin in the afternoon. The police had left and I could come back to work. They deported some of the room maids and Hassan; I felt for Hassan and wondered how he would fare out as his family now had no way of knowing his whereabouts. So work went on, the restaurant filled up, we continued cooking great food and the hotel promised to get me a work permit.

Martin had a financial interest in a new hotel in the alpine resort of Saas Fee in the canton of Valais. A few months later he asked me to go there for three weeks to help set up the kitchen for the opening. It was an incredibly beautiful hotel with a blend of stone and wood architecture, bold fire places and an inviting '*Swiss Stübli*' – traditional Swiss bistro in addition to the hotel dining room. I put the famous Swiss air dried beef, a local specialty, on the menu. It was also served in the *Stübli*. Raclette was also on the menu, which is made with an alpine cheese – aged especially for melting. It is served with gherkins, pickled pearl onions, small potatoes boiled with the skin, and black pepper from a mill. A raclette grill melts a thin layer of cheese from a large cheese wheel which is then scraped on to a plate using a sharp knife and sent directly to the table. Guests can have multiple portions. I made a small a la carte menu with smoked mountain trout, prawn cocktails, vegetable soup and platters of select air dried meats. Main courses included veal with morels, grilled sole, Chateaubriand, chicken Cordon Bleu and cheese fondue. To make the fondue I would rub the inside of a 'caquelon' – earthenware pot, with a whole clove of garlic and add white wine which I brought to a boil. I then added a mixture of grated cheese, stirring until it melted. I thickened it with a little potato starch diluted in kirsch – cherry brandy – added a few turns of the pepper mill and it was ready to serve. Chef's opinions differ on the types of cheese to use for fondue. I used a mixture of Gruyere, Emmentaler and Vacherin Frigbourgois.

The hotel owner was a farmer turned real estate developer and a great drinker. He would come in to the kitchen to chat with me before the service. I found him to be a pleasant man and we chatted about farming and the differences between what I experienced as a child in Ireland and the challenges he currently had as an alpine farmer. These challenges were very similar. There was little money to be made in farming in both rural communities. Fortunately, Swiss alpine farmers began the transition to tourism as a fall back. The Irish, on the other hand, usually had to emigrate. In the evenings, he would sit on his own at the hotel bar and get drunk and mumble to the guests in his best Swiss German to get the hell out of his hotel, leave him alone, and let him drink in peace. We tried to tell him that guests were putting money in his pocket and to leave them alone, but to no avail. It seemed to us like he had built the hotel for himself and now that guests were enjoying themselves he was almost jealous of them sharing the same space. Once he took a few drinks his personality changed –

the next morning he was the nicest person and had forgotten the episode of the night before.

Since leaving home, most of the communication with my parents and brothers was always by letter so it was very alarming when John called me one day on the kitchen phone. He had terrible news. My brother A.J. had been killed in a car accident. I stood in the kitchen holding the phone in disbelief; memories flying past of a life once lived. It was impossible to think of, yet John gave me the details: AJ died at the scene. I left for Belmullet right away. My father and mother were both in shock as were all of us. I couldn't believe that in the coffin was the lad I used to go drinking with, chasing women after dances, and then courting them in the back seat of his car. It was a devastating time for the whole family. It was the first time I could remember seeing such sadness in our house. The kitchen – still the gathering center of the house – did not resemble the cheery place of my childhood. When my grandparents died and when Aunt Birdie died in Seafield house and even when the Master died, there was sadness in the house, but now it was of a different kind. Funerals were a common affair for my father in the town land – mainly those of older people. After returning from such funerals he always talked about meeting the 'chief mourners'. As a child I believed this was the same group of people whom he met at each funeral and offered his condolences. Now we were the chief mourners to which everyone came to shake our hand, saying: "I'm sorry for your trouble." Even after the funeral visitors kept coming into the house, shaking hands with my parents and paying their respects. Then slowly – after much discussion – neighbors, friends, and extended family left, leaving each one of us to find our own way without AJ. Despite being difficult to leave home after such a family upheaval, I decided to go back to work. Leaving was heartbreaking for me because there was one less hand to shake, one less person to hug and seeing my parents so sad – just tightened the chest. I went back to work at the Eurotel and dealt with my sorrow on my own – as we all did.

Upon my return to Neuchatel, Martin asked me to help out during a busy weekend at a sister hotel in Les Diablerets, a small resort in the Alps. Upon my arrival, I met the manager, Klaus, whom I liked instantly. There is something about charismatic people when you meet them for the first time. Klaus was one of those people who had the ability to make guests feel welcome from across the lobby, before even greeting them. I also met Werner, a very personable German waiter who had been living in the region for many years. He was helping me with the extra functions and we got along well. I was in the kitchen for two full days and then returned to Neuchatel. As I left Klaus asked me: "Brendan, would you like to work here for a season?" I was quite happy with my job in Neuchatel, so I thanked him and said I would keep his offer in mind.

Eight months later after returning from a three day weekend trip to Turin, Milan and the famous St. Bernard Alpine Pass, Beatrice, the receptionist at the Eurotel, called me over as I walked by her desk. She had a telephone message from Belmullet for me. I knew instantly that someone had died in the family because phone calls were only for emergencies. The message read that my father had died three days ago from a heart attack. I had been driving around Italy enjoying myself while the family tried to contact me, doing their best to delay the funeral until I could get home.

I still don't know if it was the sight of my mother grieving or the coffin that would not be opened that touched me the most. After A.J.'s death, my father decided he would retire and give up the dairy cows. After all, it was a lot of work for him with all of us except Fred gone from the farm. He never got over my brother's death and that's what killed him in the end, said my mother. The death of two close family members in the same year was a terrible shock for all of us. My father was very well known in the Barony of Erris and equally well respected in many neighboring town lands, so the funeral was very big. Large crowds gathered at the grave side as the priest prayed and the coffin was lowered beside my brother's grave. With my three surviving brothers, I stood by my mother, two of us with a hand around her for fear she would faint, but she did not; she was a strong woman. Then as the grave diggers began to fill in the grave, the crowds began to push their way forward so each could shake her hand and offer their respects. The crowd was so large that with time we had to guide our mother to the car so she could rest. As was the custom, many neighbors and friends came to our house afterwards to offer condolences. They were offered tea or a drink and as with my brother's funeral they slowly drifted off, leaving us to face the reality of the sadness alone.

The house would not be the same without the Boss around. Memories of him were everywhere. From the animals that he loved, to the fields where I saved hay with him, to the empty armchair by the fire and the absence of his pipe tobacco aroma, there were voids which would never be filled. How would my mother manage without him? Fred was still at home but not old enough to take on the task of running the farm. He was also interested in going to college. It was then I made the decision to leave Switzerland, move back to Belmullet and work the farm, at least until my mother could decide what to do with it. So after my father's funeral, I went back to Switzerland to resign from my job, pack my bags, and return home.

Martin was very understanding when I told him. On my first day back at the hotel, I walked in to the kitchen and to my surprise Hassan was back at his dishwashing job. I went over to see him, welcomed him back and asked what happened? I wanted to know how he got back into Switzerland. By now I was working legally, and no longer afraid of deportation. I was not so sure about him. He told me the immigration police brought him to the border with just the belongings he could put in a suitcase. He was homeless for a few days but luckily found a job in a kitchen so he could eat and earn some money. Then he came back into Switzerland by walking through the railway tunnel under the Alps. I could not believe he actually did it. But he described it in such detail that it had to be true. So desperate was he to get back to his job that he risked his life rather than go back to his family a failure. He described how he walked along the wall inside the tunnel, flattening himself to the ground and holding on to whatever he could when the train came for fear he would be sucked under it, or worse, been seen by the driver who would report him to authorities on the other side. He made the journey at night when very few, if any, trains were running and the cover of darkness helped when exiting the tunnel on the Swiss side. I had a new found respect for Hassan. He had done something I was incapable of. The brigade had a farewell evening for me at the Pickwick pub. Martin came in, Udo showed up with his wife and Mike was there with his wife Mandy. Everyone wished me well and hoped to meet again some time. I was not sure where my future lay, but I knew that helping my mother was important in her time of need.

Back at home, I settled in to one of the guest's bedrooms and quickly got into the rhythm of the farm. Sometime after I had left home, the Boss had a milking machine installed. Fred said the cows liked the soothing rhythm of the machine; its clicking and hissing sounds punctuating the calmness of the byre. He taught me how to use it. The milk was no longer delivered door to door in pint glass bottles. Now I brought it to the local creamery in twenty gallon milk churns. Farm life went on, cows were fed every day, calves were born, and most were sold young as my mother was still not sure how she would manage the farm. So once again, my life revolved around the biological clock of the dairy herd and not around guest's meal times. It was a major mindset change for me and I did not know how long it would last.

Christmas came and went. John and Louis came home for a few days. John was working in Scotland and Louis was working with the Commissioners of Irish Lights as a lighthouse keeper. It was a sad Christmas for each of us. The two empty seats at the Christmas table were a constant reminder of A.J. and my father, both dead in the same year. In January, my mother decided she would sell the cows and the milking machine. It was a decision that tore at her heart. The cows were part of the family. Due to their high milk production, my father decided many years ago to replace all the Jersey and Herford breeds with Friesians. She had watched him build up the herd from the calves of four Friesian cows. He was the first farmer to bring the famed black and white cows to the local town land. And now, selling them was heartbreaking. The auction was set for mid-February. On the day, my mother said she could not bear to go outside the house to see the cows being led away on trailers. She stayed in the kitchen all day. Sadness was in the air all round us, even the local farmers — knowing how much my father cared for all the animals on our farm — were sad as they led away the prizes that they had bought. It also affected me. I was still a boy when some of these cows were born. As young calves, it was my job to feed them. I would put my finger in the calf's mouth so it would begin sucking and then lead it to the bucket of milk.

When the auctioneer let the hammer fall on the sale of the last cow, it was all over. A major part of my father's life's work had just disappeared in the space of a few hours. All that was left were the cow tying chains along the byre wall and the great memories. But selling the cows would lessen the burden on my mother who now just had a few grazing cattle to look after. No more milking twice a day. So with just haymaking in the summer, a few cattle, and the odd guest staying, she could manage. Fred was still in school, and living at home so she was not on her own. That summer I stayed until I had saved all the hay and then left again for Switzerland. I called Klaus to see if he still required a chef and he offered me the chef de cuisine position for a very short summer season at the Eurotel in Les Diablerets — high up in the Alps.

Gâteau au Vin – Wine Tart

When I worked and lived in Montreux – located close to the Swiss wine region of Lavaux – we made "wine tarts" every day. This very special recipe is most appropriate, given the readily available wines.

Ingredients

1.5 cups (3.5dl.) white wine   2 eggs
1 tablespoon (15gr.) corn starch 5 oz. (120gr.) sugar
¾ cup (1.8dl.) heavy cream   2 oz. (60 gr.) butter (cubed)
Pie dough for one pie shell

Optional

Cinnamon for additional flavor

Preparation

- Line a 9 inch (23cm) pie tin with the pie dough and pierce the bottom many times with a fork.
- Whisk eggs, sugar, wine and cream together and heat slowly to just below boiling point while constantly stirring, being careful not to let the eggs curdle.
- Once the mixture coats the back of a wooden spoon
- thicken it further by stirring in the cornstarch diluted with a little water.
- Remove from the heat and whisk in the butter cubes.
- Pour the mixture into the lined pie tin.
- Bake at 350F (180C) for 25 minutes.
- Reduce heat to 300F (150C) and bake for another 10 minutes. Allow to cool completely before cutting into portions. Serve with whipped cream.

Tip

- Use white wine from your favorite regions for a different flavor.

CHAPTER SEVEN

The Bikini Girl in the Cake

Arriving in Les Diablerets was a wonderful experience for me. As the train climbed through narrow gorges, it wound through forests and tunnels, over bridges, and stopping at hamlets along the way. Then just before arriving at the final stop, the valley opened up providing a spectacular view. The train rounded a bend leading into a high flat alpine farming valley about two kilometers wide, which was dominated by the impressive '*Massif des Diablerets*' – The Diablerets Glacier, situated at the opposite end of the valley. The rocky face rose up like a wall eighteen hundred meters above the valley floor. The glacier – visible on top – seemed almost to be sliding over the rock edge, not unlike a spoon of whipped cream on a warm dessert. Its sheer height was breathtaking. It was midsummer and the rock face was adorned with little waterfalls, their white streaks a sharp contrast to the rock, splashing and tumbling as the water cascaded over mini cliff edges, sending it shooting outwards, ending in a misty spray. It was like watching a film with no ending – I could have watched it all day. Adding to this marvelous vista was the background noise of the cow bells. Through the open train windows I could hear the constant jingling as cows munched on the rich alpine grass along the track.

Klaus, originally from Austria, met me in the lobby. He was happy to see me again and introduced me to his wife, Anne, a charming woman with a lovely smile, always eager to please the guests while keeping the staff content, not always an easy balance. It was common in Switzerland to have a couple as managers in resort hotels. Klaus was very much involved in all aspects of the hotel operation. He would appear in every department of the hotel, sometimes two or three times a day. Every evening without fail he was at the reception desk, greeting and chatting with guests on their way to the dining room. Many guests returned year after year in part because of Klaus and the gracious way he treated them during their stay. Then he would come to the kitchen to see if we had everything ready for the dinner service. Once every guest was served, Klaus and Anne would have their dinner at a small table near the dining room entrance. This allowed him to wish each guest a pleasant evening as they left the dining room. The clientele was older and so retired early.

The resort of Les Diablerets had a well balanced mix of locals and tourists, with several hotels, night clubs, and restaurants scattered among the farmland and chalets. The glacier provided some summer skiing but the main summer attraction was hiking. Trails led high up along the mountain slopes offering spectacular views of the village on the valley floor. For tourists less inclined to walk, there was a sports complex in the center of the resort with outdoor swimming pool, indoor tennis, four outdoor clay courts and the popular 'La Potinière' restaurant. No matter where guests were in the resort, the spectacular backdrop of the Glacier was always visible. Even at night, its silhouette stood out against the night sky, a reminder of its size.

We offered full board for that summer which meant that room, breakfast, lunch, and dinner were included in one price. Breakfast was continental with coffee, tea, croissants, butter and a selection of jams, yoghurts, cereals, and fresh fruit. We also offered sliced cold cuts of local smoked ham, cheese and salami. These were served on beautifully varnished two inch thick wooden platters cut diagonally from the trunk of local pine trees. They still had the bark intact giving the presentation of the breakfast buffet a country feel. These platters were usually placed on a buffet where guests could help themselves. Lunch was a light menu with salads, simple dishes such as a grilled veal escalope and perhaps a fruit salad or ice cream for dessert. Dinner menus were more substantial with a choice of starters, a choice of meat and fish for main courses, and Italian cassata or an open fruit tart for dessert. I was there for about six weeks when the season began to wind down. Summer seasons are usually short in the Alps and greatly influenced by the weather. As the end of the season approached, Klaus inquired if I was interested in coming back for the upcoming winter season. By now Mam was managing the farm and the bed and breakfast quite well on her own. Fred was still at home, so she did not need me to help out. I told Klaus I would return for the winter season.

Before we closed for the season, Mam and Fred came to Switzerland for a week and stayed at the hotel. She would sit on the balcony for hours taking in the view and listening to the cow bells. She got along very well with Klaus, admired how he ran the hotel, interacted with guests, and always managed to be in an upbeat mood. She told me: "Klaus is a great man that can do all that every day without fail!" With his ever gallant Austrian formal approach, Klaus always addressed her as "Gnädige Frau Cronin – My dear Mrs. Cronin." He told me she reminded him of his own mother, now elderly and living in Austria, his homeland. Fred and my mother had dinner in the hotel dining room every night with all the other guests and after work we would go out for a drink and talk about home, Switzerland, and the food they just ate. She would ask me how I cooked some of the dishes and was constantly worried I would serve her French snails, even to the point that she suspected I might hide them in her food. One evening I put 'fleurons' on one of the dishes. This is a classical garnish for poached fish dishes – a small half-moon shaped piece of puff pastry is usually placed on top of the sauce accompanying poached fish. She told me afterwards she thought there was a snail inside it and warned Fred not to eat it. They sent it back to the kitchen. We joked about it after dinner.

She was amazed at the height of the mountains, the neatly mowed fields, how the cows balanced themselves on the steep slopes, and even how the calves had little bells around their necks – which had a very different tone to those of the cows. The abundant sunshine was a welcome change for her from the cloudy days at home. I was happy to be able to give her a treat of a few days away from the farm and with Fred along I knew that she would not be alone while I worked. I brought her up to the top of the glacier on the aerial cable car. She was nervous when it swayed over the pylons and would grab my arm saying, "Jesus, Mary and Josef. Brendan, we're going to fall!" And I would reassure her. At three thousand meters we sat on the restaurant terrace and marveled at the view. The glacier was higher than the surrounding mountains, providing an uninterrupted three hundred and sixty degree view of the Alps.

"Wouldn't it be great if Harry was here?" she said. I agreed, but knew he would have never left the farm as he did not like travelling in his later years. I was so happy to see her so content after all she had recently gone through. She deserved a break from the daily routine of the farm. She wrote down the recipe at the end of this chapter before returning to Ireland. As a boy, I remember making brown bread with her many times; she never weighed the ingredients and the bread turned out the same every time. Until now she had never written it down.

I finished the season in October and worked a few small jobs while waiting for the winter season to begin. I did not have a work permit for these short jobs. Employers never asked and I never mentioned it. I got paid in cash every month – everybody was happy. Nevertheless, I was constantly afraid the immigration police might catch me – they were always on the lookout for illegal workers – so I kept a low profile. I avoided getting in a car with the other chefs to go for a night out for if we encountered even a simple traffic checkpoint, the police would ask each passenger for their identity papers. They would see from my passport I had no work permit, take me in for questioning, and deport me. By contrast, there would be no reason to question me if I was just another pedestrian passing by incognito on the side walk. So to minimize the risk of deportation, I frequented places I could walk to, or get to by train or bus, and I grew a moustache to look more like the locals.

I arrived back at the Eurotel one week before Christmas to begin the winter season – with a work permit. It was snowing heavily. The change from summer to winter in the Alps is dramatic. Everything is transformed when the snow arrives. Even the streets are different and many of the small paths and short cuts between the chalets disappear. The glacier changed, the little water falls were gone as the mountain went into hibernation, and ice was everywhere on the rock face. Klaus told me the brigade would arrive over the next few days so I set about getting the kitchen ready and began writing menus and placing food orders.

All the while the snow continued to fall. It fell straight down; the absence of wind was new for me as the west coast of Ireland is a windy place – especially in winter. As a result there were no snow drifts. Swiss chalet design takes advantage of this. The roofs are designed with large overhangs, sometimes as much as two meters. This keeps the snow away from the chalet walls and in summer provides welcome shade, cooling the chalet. However, in the Alps there sometimes is a strong warm wind that blows up the valleys called the 'Foehn'. Storms can get so violent that the Foehn could easily lift the roof from a chalet and snap pine trees like pencils.

Hans was the first to arrive. Born in Austria, he would be the saucier in charge of all meat and fish dishes and all hot sauces. Jürg was from Ostfriesland in northern Germany and would be the entermétier in charge of soups, vegetables, and farinaceous dishes. Jose was Portuguese and managed the cold kitchen. It was his first time in the Alps and he was already complaining of the cold. We also had two local apprentices; both were from families in the resort and so lived at home. The rest of us had staff rooms in the hotel. So other than the two apprentices, the brigade was all foreigners.

On the weekly menu plan I always included fish at least once as a main course. Getting fresh saltwater fish in the Alps was a challenge. The distance from the coast is considerable and freshness was always a concern. Klaus recommended I buy our fish from a reputable supplier in the neighboring resort of Leysin, about 20 minutes away. Most weeks I would drive to Leysin to pick up the fresh cod, salmon, or sole fillets. Sole was mostly poached and some weeks we made paupiettes. To make these we prepared a stuffing with pike by grinding the fish very fine then chopping it almost to a paste in a powerful chopper – which were available only in commercial kitchens at the time. To this we added egg whites, cream and seasoning. As the blades spun at high speed the egg white absorbed minute bubbles of air. The result was a light stuffing which would become even lighter as these air bubbles expanded during the cooking process. To assemble the paupiettes, we laid out the fillet of sole, skin side up, placed a leaf of blanched spinach on top, then piped on a little stuffing, rolled the fillet, and poached it like I learned from Herman. The thin spinach leaf provided a spiral of green when guests cut into the cooked fillet. The velvet texture of the stuffing added terrific mouth feel and the sauce provided the silkiness. I used cayenne … just like Herman showed me. Not spicy, just highly seasoned!

On one such visit to Leysin to collect fish for the week Monsieur Zulauf, the owner, called me into his office. He was from the German speaking region and moved to Leysin to open his comestible shop many years ago. He spoke excellent French with a very strong German accent. On this particular visit, he called me aside. "Vous avez une moment Monsieur Cronin, s'il vous plait?– do you have a moment please?" Trying to think what might be on his mind, I began wondering if all of the previous bills had been paid. When we sat down in his office, he turned to me. "Monsieur Cronin," he said. "Have you given any thought to getting married?" I was very surprised he would ask such a personal question. I didn't know him that well even though I saw him weekly when I collected fish and we chatted, but it was mostly small talk. "Now," he continued, "there is a lovely young woman in the next village. The only daughter of an innkeeper, she would make the perfect wife for you. She will inherit the Inn from her parents, and with you being a chef, you would have a readymade business and a family all in one. What do you think Monsieur? Would you like to meet her?" I thanked him for thinking of me but I was not yet ready to get married and left with my fish. I was amused at the whole story and told Anne that evening. She mentioned that Monsieur Zulauf thought of himself as the local matchmaker and he was always trying to get single people connected. She even told me the name of the Inn and the name of the daughter in question. I sent Jose to collect the fish for the remainder of the season.

Werner, whom I had met on my weekend to the hotel during the previous summer, was working again at the Eurotel as a part time waiter. He invited me to Gstaad one evening to sample some of the cuisine there. One of the frustrating things about Switzerland for monolinguals is that by driving just a short distance the language changes. Just when you spend years perfecting a language, then move a few kilometers, you have to start all over again. German speaking Gstaad is a twenty minute drive over the Pillon Pass going from French speaking Diablerets. This was not just any German but Bernese German, a very particular Swiss German dialect which the Bernese are very proud of. The difference in affluence between the two resorts was evident. In Gstaad upscale boutiques such as Cartier, Gucci, and Hermes lined the streets. And of course The Palace Hotel perched high above the village, its turrets jutting towards the sky, set the tone for elegance.

Werner told me the beautiful American actress Elizabeth Taylor had a chalet in the village as well as Roger Moore and many other famous people. Les Diablerets did not have this type of clientele. It attracted more families and business seminars. We ate at the bistro in the Hotel Olden. It was a memorable meal. Not for its upscale gastronomy, but for its simplicity: Raclette cheese made in the valley, local potatoes, pickles, black pepper and a bottle of 'Aigle les Murailles' white wine from the Swiss Chablais region, and great conversation with Werner.

The season at the Eurotel quickly became a routine. I would rise early and with the brigade, prepare all the dishes for the evening meal, ski in the afternoon and then head back from the slopes for the service rush of two-hundred and twenty guests eating a three course meal in two and a half hours. Klaus decided to offer only half board this season, so breakfast and dinner were part of an all inclusive price. With no lunch to prepare, this allowed the kitchen brigade to finish our 'mise-en-place' – preparation – by twelve o' clock so we could all go skiing until the runs closed at four in the afternoon

Klaus did a lot of marketing for the hotel. He tried to have groups check in during the traditional slow periods in the season to increase revenue. He told me he had booked a conference group for a week in March. They would have breakfast, lunch and dinner for four days during their conference and a gala dinner on the last night. I prepared the menus and discussed them with him. He wanted a surprise for groups' dinner on their last night at the hotel. He loved surprising the guests. It was a big thing with him. Often times in the winter he would organize an afternoon walk in the snow covered forest for the guests.

He would lead them on a predetermined loop in the forest behind the hotel for about one hour. Guests would get bundled up in ski jackets and big boots and Klaus would lead the way, holding a big St Bernard dog on a leash, to a small forest close by. Once out of sight of the hotel, he would come to an old farm chalet and there behind the chalet I would be waiting with Jurg and big containers of 'Gluhwein' – mulled wine, ready to pour the hot beverage and hand out pastries to each guest. Every time we did this, it was gratifying to see the surprised look on guests' faces as the Gluhwein was not mentioned when they signed up for the walk. It was timed perfectly so guests could catch a glimpse of the last rays of sunshine reflecting off the top of the glacier. It was a simple event that had a major impact on guests' stay.

Now we had to come up with a solution for the group's gala dinner surprise. Klaus had an idea! We should make a big cake, get the organizer to cut it and as he begins to cut the first slice, a girl jumps out of the cake and kisses him. One thing about Klaus was when he got an idea he did not change his mind easily, so I knew I would have to make this work. I talked it over with the brigade to see how we could accomplish this feat. How long could the girl be inside the cake? Would she have enough air? Would she get hurt when the organizer cut the first slice? All these thoughts were going through our minds as we went from one idea to the next trying to figure out a solution. Finally we made some progress. The girl would have to be put inside the cake in the kitchen, and then we would bring the cake out to the dining room. Jurg asked, "Will she be a heavy girl? Will we be able to lift her and the cake?" "I don't know," I replied. "It depends on the girl!" We decided we should plan to have the cake on a trolley so we could wheel it out. Then it would not matter how heavy she was. We decided to use a laundry trolley, build the cake around it, and leave a door for the girl. I went to Klaus and told him we had a plan and he said he found the girl. One of the dancers from the casino in Montreux agreed to do it. So for the next few weeks we prepared the shell for the cake. The trolley was two meters high, and a meter square. The maintenance department covered the outside of it with light plywood and installed two small doors for the girl to get in and out.

The cake would be a vacherin glacé, a frozen ice cream torte, in three flavors with meringue, vanilla, chocolate and strawberry, just like I learned to make in Adelboden. The plywood would be completely covered with meringue shells – attached with royal icing. It took a week to make all the meringues and bake them dry. Then it took another two days to stick them to the trolley using royal icing. When it was finished the trolley resembled a cake two meters high and was hollow – leaving room for the girl. The real cake was in the freezer garnished with fresh whipped cream and glazed cherries.

On the evening of the event, the girl arrived with her agent and both came in to the kitchen. Now it was time for her to get in the cake. She took off her long winter coat revealing a skimpy bikini with frills – which left very little to the imagination – and very high heeled shoes. She handed her coat to the agent and stepped into the cake. I closed the doors and continued talking to her as we wheeled the trolley to the dining room because I was afraid she would fall inside the trolley and ruin the surprise.

Klaus had the music turned up and once we arrived at a predetermined spot in the dining room, he lowered the volume and called the organizer over to cut the cake. It was priceless to see the surprise on the organizer's face as he approached the cake with a large knife and the girl opened the doors and jumped into his arms

– especially as his wife was also at the table. As the commotion was at its height and everyone was watching the dancer that had literally jumped out of the cake, I removed the knife from the organizer's hand – lest he accidently stab the girl – and the waiters discreetly served the real Vacherin through a side door as the trolley disappeared back to the kitchen. Everyone was thrilled. The entire group was on their feet clapping and cheering. After he finished kissing the girl, the organizer came to Klaus and congratulated him on a great conference and said, "We are coming back again next year, Ja?" Klaus was beaming. It was a good night; our long hours had paid off!

The season was coming to an end and I was on the move again. Klaus wanted me to stay for the summer season but my mother had no one except Fred to help her with the hay. I declined his offer. I had a farewell evening with the brigade; it was Easter Monday, all the guests checked out that morning which allowed Klaus to lock the hotel front doors until the next season. We were each going our own way, the ski runs were closing, another chapter in the resort's history was coming to an end and I returned to Ireland.

My Mother's Irish Brown Soda Bread

I made the following recipe with my mother many times as a boy. Until recently, she had never written it down. I share it with you as a very fond memory.

Ingredients

2 teaspoon baking soda   1 teaspoon baking powder
1 teaspoon salt   2 oz. (60gr.) butter
1.6 cups (3.8dl.) buttermilk or sour milk
8 oz. (240gr.) white bread flour (high gluten)
8 oz. (240gr.) whole wheat flour or bran (bran adds density – and fiber – to the baked loaf)

Optional

4 oz. (120gr.) raisins or 1 teaspoon caraway seeds

Directions

- Heat the oven to 350F (180C) degrees.
- In a bowl, combine the dry ingredients.
- Rub in the butter with the tips of the fingers until the mixture resembles fine breadcrumbs.
- Stir in the buttermilk to form a dough.
- Turn the dough onto a floured surface, knead very briefly and shape into a round flat loaf about two inches (4cm) thick.
- Cut an "X" in the top with a sharp knife, sprinkle with a little flour and bake on a floured baking sheet for approximately 50 minutes.
- Makes one 9 inch (23cm) round loaf.

Tip

- To check if the loaf was baked my mother would lift the hot bread off the baking sheet and knock on the bottom of the loaf with her knuckles.
- A hollow sound indicated it was baked.
- A dull sound meant it required further baking.

CHAPTER EIGHT

The Hairdresser

Work on the farm was less complicated now that the cows were gone. Most of the haymaking was done by machine. Nevertheless moving back to the farm was a big change for me from the twenty four hour non-stop bustle of hotels. My mother did the cooking; I saved the hay and my brother Fred helped after school. She made her now famous spaghetti meat sauce recipe for the three of us. It was a meat and tomato sauce, very similar to the meat sauce I used to make in Switzerland. She served it with spaghetti, toasted garlic bread and grated cheese – it was delicious. She was very proud showing me this new dish since it was very different from the food she cooked when I was growing up – we never had spaghetti then.

Fred had just finished secondary school and was ready to leave for college. So, driving the Boss's car, the three of us made the long trip to the town of Tralee in County Kerry to get him settled in his digs and his new school. The trip was bittersweet for my mother: the last son was leaving home, but like all of us, he was leaving for a better future. She was very sad all the way home and spoke very little. A few weeks later, having almost finished the hay, I got a call from Werner. He was working at the Park Hotel in Gstaad. The head chef left unexpectedly in mid-season, and he asked if I would come to Gstaad and take over the kitchen. This put me in a difficult position. The hay was not finished and I did not want to leave my mother with that burden. I had finished baling the hay in the hill field, and the three fields in Pickle Point and the Curragh field; however the hay in the big field above the house had still to be baled. Despite that, Mam told me to go; she would get the neighbors to finish the little bit of hay that was left. She said she could not have it on her conscience that I turned down a job to stay and help her out. "You have to leave now," she said. "Take the job; I will be fine here on my own." So I called Werner back and accepted his offer.

The change from driving a baling machine to cooking in a luxury hotel in an elite resort was difficult to adjust to because of the speed at which it took place. One day I was on the tractor at home, the next I was at the Park Hotel in Gstaad in time for the height of the summer season. From Montreux, I took the small train called the 'Montreux-Berner Oberland' to reach the resort. From traveling through vineyards with panoramic views of Lake Leman, to lush pasture land, and finally through Alpine meadows, the train journey from Montreux to Gstaad is one of the most scenic in Switzerland. As I approached the hotel, a path led through beautifully manicured lawns and up to the main entrance, guarded by a well dressed doorman with a peaked hat whom I later got to know as Josef. He led me inside and introduced me to the receptionist and she called Werner.

The Park was typical of the hotels that began catering to foreign travelers in Switzerland during the middle of 19th century. It had not changed much since. The reception area was spacious with antique furniture giving it a lived in look, and fresh mountain flower arrangements added to the personal touch – an element often missing in hotels. The Park was old but beautiful, situated on a hill overlooking the resort, surrounded by landscaped gardens dotted with flowerbeds and majestic pine trees sheltering secluded benches where guests sat reading – some dozing in the afternoon sun.

I met Werner and we reminisced about our last season at the Eurotel. He was in great shape and looking forward to working with me. The former chef, Willy, had left two weeks earlier under mysterious circumstances; I did not want to know more. The kitchen brigade was all Swiss for a change. They were happy to see someone take over the organization of the kitchen and plan their schedules, order food and write menus. Emil, the chef saucier, was an avid hunter and was in the process of getting his hunter's license. He later showed me his collection of mounted deer skulls and antlers, explaining in detail how he had the antlers cleaned to avoid any putrid smell. He could describe all the wild mountain animals and the exact dates of the hunting season for each category. It reminded me of my father who also hunted, but mostly for wild duck, snipe, pheasant, and grouse. Over the next few weeks I settled into the split shift cycle and life took on a sense of regularity.

One evening shortly after I arrived, while walking through the restaurant, I met a very nice American couple. They lived in New York City where they owned a jewelry store. Every summer they came to the Park for a few weeks – the pure alpine air and cooler weather was a welcome relief from the city summer heat. When they found out I was Irish they were eager to speak English and chatted incessantly. Later, Werner told me the entire story. This couple would not let anyone except their own driver chauffeur them around. Their chauffeur would drive them to the airport in New York, fly with them to Zurich and drive them to the Park hotel – a four hour drive. Once the chauffeur brought their bags to the room he drove to Zurich and flew back to New York. At the end of their summer stay in Gstaad, he would repeat the trip and pick them up at the Park. I thought this was a nice way to see the world, with your own personal driver. They were very pleasant people, neither fastidious nor pretentious. I remember meeting them several times during the summer and telling them about my aunts, Kathleen and Grace O'Malley, who both worked at the Waldorf Astoria Hotel. They said they had been to that hotel many times and that it was highly regarded in New York.

This couple liked lamb and often asked me to prepare roast rack of lamb Provençale. For this dish I would take a rack of local mountain lamb, trim off the fat and the silver skin which lies between the meat and the fat. The silver skin – sinew – is very tough so removing it provides a more tender bite. I exposed two inches of the tips of the rib bones by removing all the fat between the bones. This procedure – sometimes referred to as 'frenched' – was mostly done for better presentation of the rack when it came time to plate it. Then I seasoned it and browned it all over in the frying pan using a little olive oil. This process of caramelizing the outer layer of protein in the meat creates tremendous flavor. I then brushed it with Dijon mustard and covered it with a layer of Provençale mix. The mustard provided extra flavor and allowed the mix to remain on the meat. To make the Provençale mix I sautéed very finely chopped shallots and garlic in butter on low heat until they became transparent, added breadcrumbs, and seasoned them with salt, pepper mill and the famous 'Herbes de Provence' which is a classical mix of rosemary, thyme, sage, basil, and parsley – quite common in the Provence region in the south of France. I put this mixture on the meat side of the rack over the mustard and roasted it in a moderately hot oven until the interior was 'rose' – pink.

I served the lamb sliced in one-inch thick chop-like cutlets – each with a bone – with a light demi-glace, sautéed Lyonnaise potatoes, and buttered French beans. As I sliced it the aroma of roasted garlic, caramelized meat protein, and the Provençale herbs filled the kitchen prompting the waiters to ask for a slice. It is a good idea to let the meat 'rest' a few minutes before carving. This allows meat juices to distribute evenly in the meat so when it is carved the juice remains in the meat adding tremendously to both flavor and juiciness. After their meal, the jeweler and his wife would seek me out to offer their thanks. It was gratifying to get a compliment and even better to get it directly from the guest. This was the first hotel where I had any meaningful contact with guests. It made them real in my eyes, not just some incognito person the waiter brought food to in a room the other side of the swinging kitchen doors.

One of the highlights of the summer season at the Park was Swiss National Day. The Swiss Confederation was established on August 1,[st] 1291 so on that date, every year, the Swiss National Day is highly celebrated all over the country. There was a lot of planning at the Park leading up to this day. The hotel's public areas and large sections of the gardens were decorated with lanterns and small Swiss flags. Guests sat outside enjoying the warm evening air and mountain views while listening to a Swiss folk band and yodelers playing in a small courtyard at the end of the garden. The

Park's owner sat with friends at a secluded table under the pine trees, sipping white wine. They talked of National Days in years gone by, debating the atmosphere in any given year. Even the weather was discussed. One man was adamant it rained in 1943 and the fireworks were cancelled, another insisted that no, the festivities were cancelled because of the war. And so their conversation went on to talk about people who had died since the last celebration and other events of the village and the valley. Crops were discussed, new chalet construction debated, and families that had moved away were reminisced. This conversation took place as we were setting up the outdoor buffets. It sounded to me like a conversation that could have easily taken place between two farmers at the Belmullet monthly fair. These people were no different – very in tune with the local news and goings on.

For this particular Swiss National Day we created a buffet dinner with many local and national food specialties. The owner, an elderly gentleman whom I had not met since my arrival, insisted we include the traditional poached trout served cold with a cherry in its mouth. This was a dish he had served at the Park every August 1st for many years. Werner showed me a picture from last year of how it should look. Each trout was poached beautifully, had a marinated red cherry in its mouth, and was presented on a silver platter with its head curled back to its tail. The trout were small enough to serve one per person. To prepare this platter, I began by fishing fifty trout from the fish tank in the kitchen, gutting them and tying the mouth to the tail. Then I placed them in the court bouillon for fifteen minutes to cook, allowing them to turn a classic blue color. The next step was to cool them and coat them with aspic – a savory jelly – and insert the cherry into each mouth. Finally they were presented on an aspic coated silver platter. It took me a half day to get all the trout poached without the flesh and skin splitting. Despite this intensive preparation, I thought the presentation did not look that great, but the owner insisted they be on the buffet.

The buffet began with a variety of salads and homemade dressings. We usually made our own bread rolls for these evenings, so for a different presentation we placed the raw rolls closer together on the baking sheet and as they proved they fused together. When removed from the oven the bread looked similar to a bunch of grapes complete with leaves – also made from dough. Guests could then remove a roll at the buffet, as if they were picking a single grape, which had a great effect of freshness. Smoked baked ham on the bone was another favorite. I cooked the ham by simmering it for many hours, removed the skin and some of the fat, then wrapped the entire ham in brioche dough, brushed it with a mixture of egg yolk and cream and baked it. The egg yolk and cream gave the brioche a golden brown sheen during the baking process. When we began carving the ham at the buffet, steam rose from it and the aroma of hot smoked ham and brioche wafted through the dining room. I served this with mild Swiss mustard, 'Gratin Dauphinois' – gratinated potatoes, and buttered French beans. Guests loved those buttered French beans.

Desserts were always popular. We served a choice of open fruit tarts (predominantly apple, pear, and apricot), two kinds of chocolate mousse (dark and milk), ice cream and crème caramel. Crème brulée was also a popular item. To make this I would add a trickle of freshly caramelized sugar to the vanilla cream turning it a darker color. This was piped into tall wine glasses and served with a pencil wafer. For the open fruit tarts, I sprinkled a layer of ground hazelnuts on the pastry before laying in the sliced apples, pears, or apricots. As the tarts baked, the hazelnuts absorbed the juices, adding greatly to the flavor. For better presentation, once the tarts were removed from the oven I brushed them with apricot glaze to add sheen. This was usually a good quality apricot jam, heated and diluted with a little water – a presentation trick I learned from Herr Dorfmeister in Davos. Guests always appreciated the choice we offered on the buffets and the fact that most of the food was local. The evening concluded with the traditional bonfire in the garden while other bonfires could be seen at strategic locations on the surrounding mountain tops, shining and twinkling like stars in the night sky.

One evening after work, Werner and I drove over the Pillon pass to see Klaus at the Eurotel. He was surprised to see me back in Switzerland and disappointed to hear I was at the Park – and not working with him. I mentioned the circumstances but he was obviously not pleased with me. I could understand his reasoning; I had told him at the end of the winter I could not work the summer season with him, but nevertheless ended up at the Park Hotel – 30 minutes away, halfway into the season. Surprisingly, he asked me if I would come back for the next winter season. I agreed. By now the end of summer was drawing near. It was time to close up the Park hotel. It would lie dormant for a few months to awaken again a few days before Christmas with mostly the same staff. Closing the hotel at the end of the season was a lot of work for everyone. The entire kitchen had to be thoroughly cleaned, including refrigerators, ranges and ovens. Inventory had to be conducted and perishable food used up. Then when the last guest checked out, we could leave.

By the following Christmas I was back at the Eurotel in Les Diablerets. The brigade was a mixture of different nationalities, some French, some Swiss and one Italian. Before the hotel opened, I thought we should get to know one another better, so I suggested the entire brigade build a big snowman on the traffic island just outside the main entrance to welcome our guests as they arrived for the festive season. This team building concept was something I learned from Herr Koch in Davos. At the Schatzalp, the entire brigade went bowling once a week. It helped us to connect outside the work place and we got to know each other better, an aspect that helped the atmosphere in the kitchen, especially on busy nights when stress levels were high – and working even closer together became extremely important.

The brigade had been busy preparing mise-en-place all day. Stocks were simmering, demi glace was reducing, stores were arranged, compound butters – whipped flavored butters – were made and now it was time to take a break for the evening. It was minus 10 degrees Celsius and everyone was feeling the cold as we shoveled snow to make the snowman. I asked the assistant manager if he could make an exception and issue a bottle of vodka to generate some 'internal heat.' After much pleading he agreed, especially when I told him he could transfer the cost to the kitchen. It is incredible how a little drink allows people to loosen the tongue. People who did not know each other until two days ago were telling jokes and laughing. Now the brigade was really coming together. Sometimes I had to translate jokes from German to French or vice versa. It was like being in an outdoor pub. We finished the snowman … and the vodka! So rather than let the energy fizzle by going back into the hotel, I invited everyone to La Potinière restaurant across the street for a coffee.

We had a long hardworking winter season ahead of us; each had to pull their weight so it was important to get acquainted. As we chatted and laughed, I was happy to see everyone getting along. Then I noticed a girl at the bar. She was with an older man and they were both chatting and laughing with the barman. When the older man left I went over to her and invited her – in my best French – to join us in celebrating the beginning of our season. She responded with a polite, "non merci." Disappointed, I went back to join the brigade. The next day I asked Anne if she knew who this girl might be. After I described her, Anne thought she must be the local hairdresser. I made a point to get my hair cut.

Now on my second winter season at the hotel I was getting to know the locals a little better as they often came to the hotel bar in the evenings. Monsieur Urweider was one such person: a petit man with a thin face who always wore a small hat – even indoors. He owned a farm not far from the hotel. One evening as he was sipping his wine at the bar he asked me if I would buy 'un petit veau' – a little calf – from him. Thinking it would be nice to have local milk-fed veal on the menu, I agreed, and made plans to meet him at his farm the next day to inspect the calf. The animal was in a stall next to Monsieur Urweider's horse. He was a former jockey and still kept a horse. I walked up to the calf to see if it had any meat on its bones. I had seen how my father and the cattle jobbers did this at the monthly fairs in Belmullet many years ago. I ran my hand along its back feeling for the muscles, then down its neck for the same reason and then put my thumb and index finger in its nostrils so I could open its mouth to determine its age by its number of teeth. I decided the calf was well 'filled out' – a term we often used at home on the farm when a young animal began to put on muscle. We agreed on a price. Monsieur Urweider would deliver the butchered animal to the hotel and promised me the cured calfskin for my apartment. For the next two weeks, it was the talk of the village as he told everyone he met how the chef at the Eurotel bought his "favorite calf," at times mentioning he regretted selling it, and that he missed his calf so much he should have kept it as his pet. He even told people I forced him to sell it. On many evenings after the sale, he would come into the bar and lament with me how he still regretted selling his 'darling little calf.'

Milk-fed veal is prized by chefs and guests alike for its tenderness and delicate flavor. A calf destined to be sold as veal must only be fed on milk or milk formula to qualify as veal. In essence, the animal is anemic – because milk contains very little iron – hence the sought after light color of the meat. If it did not have a thick skin to camouflage the paleness, it would look like a pale faced person. This light color is a quality factor chefs look for during purchasing. As I could not tell if Monsieur Urvieder's calf was pale, I had to inspect its mouth to see how many teeth it had. I was looking for only milk teeth – the presence of permanent teeth indicated an older animal. Once the calf goes out to pasture, the nutrients – especially iron – in the green grass convert the meat from pale pink to bright red in a few short weeks. Now it is beef – sometimes referred to as 'baby beef' for its first few weeks in pasture.

We used every part of the calf on the menu. The top of the shoulders contain very tasty meat. I added a stuffing to the boned out shoulder to make great flavored roasts. With the belly and lower shoulders we made 'blanquette de veau.' This is a classic white veal stew thickened with a roux and garnished with pearl onions and button mushrooms. We split the saddle in half and cut tender veal chops from it. The top round cut from the legs made great escalopes which when bread crumbed were pan-fried to become 'Escalope Viennoise.' The silverside and eye of the round were excellent for glazing – a more gentle form of braising – typically reserved for larger cuts of white meats. There were four shanks left, and we cut them in 2 inch pieces and made Osso buco with them. This is a braised veal shank, a dish of Italian origin in a succulent sauce – although the calf does not have to be Italian to make this dish. Many customers would eat the exposed bone marrow in the Osso buco using an espresso spoon. For additional flavor we made the classic Gremolata mixture of finely chopped garlic, chopped parsley and grated lemon rind. We served a teaspoon of this mixture on top of every bone. It enhanced the presentation by covering the marrow, and guests loved the added flavor. The pan-fried calf's liver provided a great staff meal and Klaus and Anne ate the kidneys – flambéed with Dijon mustard. Lastly, all the bones were used to make white stock and some demi-glace. It was a very profitable purchase despite the many hours we spent dissecting the carcass. I never got the calf skin despite many visits back to his farm; Monsieur Urweider never came through on his promise.

As the brigade settled into the season, we developed a daily routine which allowed me to ski every afternoon during the split shift. This was a great stress reliever for me. I loved the speed of downhill skiing and the silence on the chair lift going back up. It was such a welcome change from the noise of the kitchen. On my way back to the hotel from the slopes I often stopped for a coffee and pastry at the local 'Patisserie' and it was on one of those days that I met the girl I saw at the bar before Christmas. She was sitting on her own at a small table. I sat down at the next table. Realizing it was the vodka that gave me the courage to approach her the first time, and now without any vodka, I puckered up the courage, leaned over and said: "Bonjour, when would be a good time to come in and get my hair cut?" She looked at me, and in a determined voice said: "I am not a hairdresser so I wouldn't know." That took the wind out of my sails and I left none the wiser as to whom she was. I would have to enlist Anne's assistance once again to find out more about her.

Later that winter Porsche held a car rally on one of the closed mountain passes leading to Villars – a nearby ski resort. All the car drivers stayed at the hotel. We had every imaginable type of Porsche in the parking garage and parked around the traffic island by the entrance. It took the efforts of the entire resort to get the road ready for the race. With multiple hairpin bends the road was ideal for such fast cars. The police helped with traffic, the fire brigade with safety – building up the hairpin bends with snow to prevent accidents, and the ski patrols provided evacuation routes. Porsche had two days of meetings at the hotel, with the race being held on the third day. Every evening they had a special meal in the dining room. One night they had raclette, another evening, a country buffet with the now famous Baked Ham in brioche, and the last evening a sit down gala dinner with an orchestra and singer. On that evening I made Baked Alaska for dessert. To make it I took thin layers of sponge cake, laid them on a silver platter, added layers of vanilla, strawberry and chocolate ice cream sprinkled with candied peel, then covered the lot with another thin layer of sponge cake and sprinkled it with Grand Marnier liqueur. On this I piped a one inch deep coating of Italian meringue – egg whites whipped with hot sugar syrup. On top I placed a few empty half egg shells and sunk them in the meringue so they were practically invisible to the guest. Now the platters – which were about 15 portions each – were placed in a very hot oven for a few minutes to brown the meringue, but not melt the ice cream, then we stored them in the freezer. When the time came to serve the dessert, I filled each egg shell with warmed brandy and set them alight. Klaus turned down the dining room lights, signaled the orchestra for music, and five chefs walked through the dining room each holding a flaming platter over their heads. With this show the guests began clapping and all stood up and cheered us on. We then served the dessert from a buffet at the end of the room while the music continued. Although the dessert was simple, such presentation made it a spectacular event. The group had a great experience and we were very happy with their stay – which suited us as we wanted them to return next year.

To celebrate the end of the successful Porche rally, I went out after work to La Potinière restaurant. The girl whom I now knew was not a hairdresser was sitting on her own at the bar chatting with the barman. I asked if I could join her for a drink. She agreed. She lived in Villeneuve, a town on the lake next to Montreux and came up to Les Diablerets only on weekends. The older man I saw her with the first time was her father. It was Friday evening; she had just come up for the weekend and was having a glass of wine. I told her about the flamed Baked Alaska, she thought it was a nice idea but asked if it was not dangerous with the flames as we weaved in and out between tables. Her name was Christine and she agreed to go skiing with me the next day. Things were looking up. I had finally met someone who agreed to ski with me.

The next day, we met at the restaurant at the top of the Isenau run. We skied all the trails, and I discovered that she knew everyone from the ticket punchers, the lift attendants, and the restaurant staff. She was an excellent skier, not thinking twice before taking the steepest runs, overtaking other skiers and getting to the bottom well before me. I struggled to keep up with her. On our way back through the village we stopped for coffee in the same restaurant where she basically told to me to jump in the lake for calling her a hairdresser. But now we both laughed about it. She was studying to be a teacher at a college in Lausanne and was scheduled to complete her degree in the spring.

One afternoon much later in the season, unbeknownst to me, she was skiing some distance behind me with her mother who was eager to see who this 'chef de cuisine' was that her daughter was talking about. She cautioned Christine about going out with a seasonal worker and a foreigner at that, and told her: "He probably has a girl in every resort he worked in," although she admitted to Christine, "he is not a bad skier…for a foreigner!"

In February I spoke to Klaus about doing a ten day Irish food promotion for the following month, in time for St. Patrick's

Day. He thought it was a great idea and we began planning the menu. I was able to get Aer Lingus – our Irish Airline – to sponsor part of the promotion. I had gotten to know the Aer Lingus station manager in Geneva, Brian Scanlon. He was a tremendous help with procurement. He donated menu covers from their first class menus and provided green and white paper with the airline logo for printing the menu. The menu had a beautiful gold cover with a graphic of 'Murphy's Five Pounder' – a trout, specially created for Aer Lingus by Rai Uhlemann.

I put some Irish classics on that menu. I had smoked salmon flown in from a little factory in Geesala, a town not far from my home in County Mayo. It was dry, a characteristic of good Irish smoked salmon. Guests loved that texture and flavor. I also had lobster cocktail, Irish oysters on the half shell, chicken liver pate, deep fried plaice, cod meuniere, Irish lamb cutlets, and Irish stew. We also had spareribs with cabbage, Irish black pudding, brown lamb stew and lamb steaks. These were cut from the leg, grilled with the bone still intact, which kept the juiciness. For potato dishes I made 'boxty', a typical pan-fried Irish country potato cake using raw potatoes, eggs and a little flour. I also made a potato cake with cooked potatoes and scallions which has a very different flavor. For desserts, I made simple apple tarts like my mother used to. But the most popular dessert was the Irish Mist frozen soufflé. I served it sprinkled with coco powder and using a "Parisienne scoop" – a metal spoon commonly used to make melon balls. I removed a tiny scoop of the soufflé and filled the hole with Irish Mist Liqueur.

Through an importer in Basel, I was able to bring in Paddy's Irish whiskey, Guinness stout, Irish Mist Liqueur, and Tullamore Dew whiskey, all of which were delivered directly to the hotel. It took me some time to explain Irish Mist Liqueur to the girl at the importer's office. "Mist' in German means liquid cows' manure, so she had trouble understanding that the Irish were not bottling this most abundant of liquids but rather a much more appetizing and soothing beverage. "Do you mean to tell me that the Irish are bottling cows' piss?" she asked me in German on the phone. After a few minutes explaining and listing the ingredients, she finally understood what I wanted to import.

The promotion was a great success. We filled the dining room every evening for the ten days. Brian came up from Geneva with his wife Callie. Mike came from Neuchatel with his wife Mandy and some of the lads from "L'equipe du Mercredi" and many of the locals I knew came to see what this 'Irish food' was about. It was great to get such support from everyone. Most liked it. Anne was pregnant at this time and their third child was born during the Irish promotion. I suggested they name the boy Paddy but they declined. Christine brought her parents in for dinner and I met them briefly for the first time. They liked the food and called me 'Monsieur'. Over all I was very pleased with the outcome. It gave me a chance to introduce guests to a selection of Irish food, which would hopefully change preconceived negative impressions in Switzerland about our national dishes and the ever present implication: 'The Irish can't cook.'

By now I had been working in Switzerland for seven years, sometimes legally sometimes not, and another season was coming to an end. I felt I had done the resort circuit, summers here, winters there. I had learned a tremendous amount of classical cooking. I could cook some Italian, French, Austrian, and German dishes. My cooking techniques had improved dramatically since leaving Ireland; I now had a good understanding of how to make guests happy at the table. I still felt there were many more dishes and ingredients I could learn about if I wanted to become as good a chef as Herman, Herbert, or Herr Koch − or even become a Master Chef like them − so I decided to leave Switzerland and find work in another country to expand my repertoire.

Until now in my professional career, other than at the Eurotel in Neuchatel, I had never applied for a job. I was always fortunate to have been recommended to my next position, but now, that was about to change. For the first time ever, I applied to an international job placement agency for a position outside Switzerland, with no particular country in mind. I spoke French and German and felt that should help me to travel further afield.

The agency responded they would contact me as soon as they found a suitable position which matched my qualifications. In the meantime I would travel to Belmullet.

Before I left Klaus had a big party for the staff at the end of the season. The guests had left; we sat in the main dining room and he served beer to everyone. We had a small buffet to use up the last of the food. Christine came and joined us. She surprised me as she mentioned she was going to Ireland that summer with her school friend to celebrate their graduation. They had planned this trip before we met and now that they knew someone in Ireland they wanted to visit my home town. That was something to look forward to because depending on what offer the agency sent me, I did not know if I would see her again.

The next day Klaus and Anne surprised me with an invitation to eat at 'Le Pont du Brent' restaurant. This was a highly renowned restaurant in the village of Brent, near Montreux, overlooking Lake Leman. The chef, Gerard Rabbet, provided an amazing evening of dining pleasure and came to the table very briefly at the end of the meal. I was very grateful to Klaus and Anne for this wonderful epicurean evening and the great conversation we had on so many different topics. I left for Belmullet the next day to make hay and wait for the agency's response.

When I got home I told my mother about Christine, and that she would be visiting with a friend. She said they could stay in one of the guest rooms. A few weeks later I picked them up at the train station; when we got out of the car at home my mother walked up to Christine and welcomed her by name. I had no idea how she knew which one of the girls was Christine. I suppose it is a mother's intuition. The next day the agency called. They had an offer of a position for me in a beach resort hotel in West Africa, was I interested? I was. Could I be in Paris for an interview in two days? I agreed – despite the awful timing. I would have to leave Christine and her friend with my mother while I went to Paris for the interview. I flew to Paris on a one day return ticket. The interview was in the Hotel Royale right off the Champs Elysees not far from the Arc de Triomphe; the interviewer was the resident manager of the hotel which was located in Lomé, the capital of Togo in West Africa. He introduced himself as "Monsieur Dufour,' a very distinguished looking gentleman with well combed slightly graying hair, wearing a tailored suit. He welcomed me and we began the interview right away over a light lunch. When lunch was over he offered me the position with a start date in one month. I accepted. He had reserved a room for me at the Royale and invited me to join him for dinner that evening. I told him I had to be back in Belmullet that evening to help my mother with the farm and my flight was leaving in two hours. He sounded surprised, almost disappointed, but nevertheless would send me a contract. Needless to say the Algerian taxi driver drove like hell to get me to the airport on time and complained from the minute I got in the car until we arrived at the airport. He knew so much about the running of the country and what was being done wrong by the government that I suggested he become a Politician. He did not agree. I got back home the same evening just in time to invite the girls for a drink in McDonnell's pub to celebrate my new job.

Christine also had good news. While I was in Paris, she received news from the school superintendent informing her that she had been appointed to a teaching position in the small village of Veytaux, on the outskirts of Montreux. She was very happy about that – but not so happy to hear I was leaving for Africa. Neither was my mother. She said: "Africa is the white man's grave, not every white man who goes there comes back." She reminded me of the story about my uncle, Father Brendan O'Malley, when he was in the missions in Africa and nearly got captured by the rebels and how my grandmother pleaded with him not to return there. He agreed – and he never went back. After a few days both girls left to continue their trip around Ireland, and I got back to hay making.

It was around this time my brother Louis decided to move back home and run the farm while still staying on as a light keeper. It was a two week rotation on various lighthouses around the three thousand mile Irish coast line. He bought cows and introduced a very well managed grazing system which maximized every square inch of meadow land by moving the cows through various pastures. This made my departure for Africa easier as I knew my mother would not be on her own. I could now plan my move to Togo – grave or no grave.

Fillets of Sole in White Wine Sauce with Herbs

I served this dish throughout the season using the sole I purchased from the "matchmaker".

Ingredients for 4 people
12 fillets of sole
½ oz. (15gr.) finely chopped shallots
½ oz. (15gr.) butter
¾ cup (1.8dl.) white wine
¾ cup (1.8dl.) fish stock
½ cup (1.2dl.) heavy cream
1 teaspoon each: finely chopped chives, parsley, dill
Salt and white pepper powder to taste
Roux, (2 tspn melted butter mixed with 3 tspn flour)
Pinch of cayenne pepper to taste (should not be spicy)

Procedure
- In a stainless steel pan gently sauté the shallots in butter on low heat until they become transparent, remove pan from the heat.
- Fold each fillet of sole in half, skin-side inwards; lay them in a single layer on top of the sautéed shallots.
- Season with salt and white pepper powder.
- Pour in the wine and stock – being careful not to remove the seasoning from the fish, cover with parchment paper and poach very gently on the stove top.
- The liquid should not boil.
- This takes about 7-10 minutes.
- When cooked the fish should be firm and have turned a white color.
- Remove the fish, being careful not to let the fillets break, and keep warm.
- Through boiling, reduce the liquid by half and whisk in the roux until it thickens, cook for 5 minutes.
- Add in the cream, season and strain. (You may also choose to blend the sauce which adds more flavor).
- Finally add the herbs and a pinch of cayenne and taste one more time.
- Pour the sauce over the fish and serve with a rice pilaf or boiled or steamed peeled potatoes, and – a glass (or two) of your favorite white wine.

Tip

- I often stir in a tablespoon of hollandaise sauce at the last minute to increase richness and pleasure the taste buds.

CHAPTER NINE

"Yovo, Yovo, Bonsoir!

As I exited the terminal at Lomé International Airport in Togo two things happened at once. The intense heat hit me and before I had time to adjust, two taxi drivers each literally grabbed my suitcases leading me to different taxis. Wondering first at their intent, I realized they each wanted the fare, and bargaining was expected. This was a new phenomenon for me: first I did not know how to bargain very well – prices in Switzerland were set in stone, bargaining was not a part of Swiss culture. Secondly I did not know the distance from the airport to the hotel and what the fare might cost. So I left the two taxis drivers haggling over who would drive the 'Yovo' – white foreigner – and sat into the back seat of the third taxi in the line. The driver spoke French. I told him to bring me to the hotel and to ask the other two taxi drivers to put my cases in his car. After a few minutes with lots of raised angry voices and stares in my direction, they obliged by throwing my luggage in the car and off we went to find the hotel.

The trip was eventful to say the least. The road was bumpy. It had many potholes – some as big as small craters, loud African music on the radio and the dust blowing in through the open windows added to the tropical atmosphere that was so different to the one I had just left. There were people everywhere, some walking on the road, some on bicycles weaving between cars, others – mostly women with baskets on their heads and babies strapped across their backs supported in swaths of beautiful fabric – were walking in the sand by the roadside. I was trying to take it all in. There was so much to see. One woman, rather than put down her heavy load, just lifted her clothes and while standing up, relieved herself in the sand as we drove by. No one except me took any notice. This was an incredible change from the highly structured society I had become accustomed to in Switzerland.

We finally arrived at the hotel. I paid the driver what I was told later was a small fortune for such a short trip. He had done a detour to run up the meter. The hotel was breathtaking, located in its own compound about 100 meters from the beach and surrounded with beautifully landscaped gardens, flood lit coconut trees, a pool, tennis courts and the open air 'Mono' restaurant and bar. Across the road just meters from the waves was the Coco Beach outdoor restaurant with tables nestled under thatched umbrellas and lines of deck chairs waiting in the sun for their temporary owners. The white crested waves were a beautiful contrast between the golden sand and the turquoise blue ocean. The beach went on for miles in both directions.

The chef was French. This was my first time working with a French chef and although I cooked many French dishes in Switzerland, it was not the same as cooking with a French chef so I was worried my cooking skills would not be up to his standard. Despite my initial fears, Jean-Pierre was very pleasant, gave me advice when needed, and was especially helpful when it came to solving problems with the local chefs. He was very confident, almost arrogant at times, but the African chefs loved him. He had earned their respect over the two years he spent at the hotel. He assigned me to work with Ame, the African Sous chef. Ame was a large man, constantly wiping the sweat from his forehead with a white handkerchief that he kept in his trouser pocket. When he calmly issued an order, the other chefs jumped into action. Having seen this I realized that if I earned his respect, the rest of the brigade would follow. From a supervisory standpoint we were on the same level, both of us reported to Jean-Pierre. Ame was in charge of the Mono restaurant and the Coco Beach. I was supervising the French restaurant in the hotel.

I learned to cook many French regional dishes with Jean-Pierre such as frog's legs with fines herbs, veal sweetbreads with lemon, scallops with porcini and veal escalope Valley d'Auge. This was a sautéed veal escalope with sliced apples lightly tossed in butter and served with a cream demi glace. The menu also included barracuda in a red French wine sauce, Iranian and Russian Caviar, Foie gras, roast quail, and flamed veal kidneys. Desserts were very French. We served Pear Richelieu, Tarte Tatin – an upside down apple tart – and the very funny 'Pets de Nones' – nun farts. These are a traditional French fritter made with choux pastry. It was really the name that made them special, their origin stemming from a convent. The story behind the name really meant that nuns also farted – just like everyone else.

A local specialty was the Agouti cooked in tomato sauce with palm oil. This dish – a type of stew – was made using the meat of a rodent called a cane rat, similar in size to a large rabbit. It was a local delicacy and was constantly on the menu. It was served with 'ablo' – a steamed fermented corn based dumpling extremely popular in the country. Many of the cooks would prepare ablo for themselves for lunch. A favorite meal for them was ablo with palm oil or a green chili sauce thickened with okra – ladies fingers – which gave the sauce a slimy consistency. As they dipped the light colored ablo in the sauce it took on a green tinge as if the dumpling was coated in green slime. Despite its unappetizing appearance it was high in carbohydrates and filled the stomach, a major advantage for people living below the poverty line. I also noticed during staff meals that they did not eat much animal protein. One day there was meat for the staff lunch and one of the chefs took more than his share. He put it back when the sauce chef laid his chopping knife against his throat, saying, "We have to share evenly." The knife appeared out of nowhere – and disappeared just as fast. Jean Pierre told me not to get involved. He said, "Let them sort it out between themselves."

The brigade in the main kitchen which served the French restaurant, room service and banquets, consisted of ten African chefs. Ame supervised the Mono with another six chefs. There were three non-African chefs – Jean Pierre, myself, and a Swiss pastry chef who arrived on the same day with me. We ate all our meals in a tiny private dining room behind the kitchen. Oegy, the commis saucier, cooked for us every day. We ordered from the menu. It was Jean-Pierre's way of checking Oegy's flavors. I learned a great deal from Jean-Pierre during our meals together. He was a recipient of the 'Meilleur Ouvrier de France' – a prestigious French award given to candidates who pass a rigorous exam in their chose profession – and is presented by the French President during an elaborate ceremony. Like all of us 'expats' Jean Pierre lived in a villa on the compound with his French wife and two children. He was nearing the end of his two year contract and was thinking about immigrating to Canada. This did not please me as I got along well with him; the prospect of another French chef coming in was upsetting.

Since his arrival, the pastry chef was having a difficult time adjusting to work, the African life style, and the pastry staff. It was apparent he was not getting their support or respect. He could not get the pastry staff to make the desserts his way, which prevented him from putting his ideas on the menu. This defeated the purpose of bringing in an expatriate chef from Europe. The three of us talked about this during our meals. Jean-Pierre gave him advice on how to get the Africans on his side, but every day he came back saying it wasn't working out with them. I felt bad for him because the same could happen to me which would have made my professional time there unbearable. I was doing my best to get along with the staff, helping when I could, trying to understand the tremendous cultural differences, giving advice on flavor and presentation, and standing back when necessary – like the episode with the knife.

Every Sunday was Jean Pierre's day off. Most times he would have a barbeque at his villa; some kitchen staff would grill the food and do some simple serving for which he paid them. One Sunday he invited a group of expatriate friends for his daughter's birthday. She was about fifteen or sixteen years old so he ordered a special cake from the pastry department. This was a typical French family meal around a large table in the garden of his villa, the type of meal the French are notorious for – that goes on forever. The pastry chef decided he would personally make the cake, a three layered Genoise – sponge cake – with a chocolate raspberry filling coated with vanilla flavored whipped fresh cream. The cake arrived at the table with lit candles and happy birthday lettering, everyone sung, his daughter blew out the candles, and then Jean-Pierre ceremoniously stood up to portion the cake. As he sliced through the cake the knife met resistance and he found that he could not cut through it, try as he might.

It turned out that while the pastry chef was assembling the cake, his pastry staff took a cleaning sponge with green metal backing from the dishwashing area and inserted it between the cake layers when he was not looking. Jean Pierre extracted the cleaning sponge in disbelief; everyone applauded the joke and called for the real cake to be brought out – there was no real cake. The pastry chef was on the evening flight to Zurich the next day. The African pastry staff had decided they were going to get rid of their new 'Yovo' pastry chef and had devised a plan. I thought their plan was ingenious and realized they could – without hesitation – easily do the same to me. Without ever saying a word or having an argument they managed to have their boss fired. The staff never mentioned his name again – and I learned a very valuable lesson in intercultural communication.

In the following weeks I made every effort to get along with the kitchen staff so I could help them in their work. It was difficult to see them preparing foods when I knew I had a better, faster way to achieve the same result. But it was not about me. This was their livelihood and from their point of view, I was the outsider who did not understand. I could suggest and demonstrate, which most times did the trick and they adapted the procedure or recipe. Shouting rarely worked.

But there were also times outside of work when I had the chance to get to know the staff better. One day the entermétier told me: "Chef, I saw your car in my neighborhood yesterday; you did not stop to visit my house." I answered: "I did not know that you lived there. I will come to visit you next week on my day off." He was ecstatic. I consulted Jean Pierre on the proper protocol for this visit and he recommended I bring a case of beer as a welcome gift. The next week I turned up at a determined time and his entire family was there to meet me. He introduced me to everyone; some spoke French, some only Togolese, but all were welcoming. I met his wife and children. They greeted me, "Bonjour *Mesieur.*" We finished the beer and had a great time. He was so happy I had visited his house and met his family. But during my visit I had noticed one of his little boys, was obviously sick. He lay in bed in the corner of the main room and did not move throughout my entire time there.

Three weeks later the entremétier came to work and told Jean Pierre that his little boy was dead. I could not believe it. Just a short time ago when I met his family, they looked so happy. But Jean Pierre told me that infant mortality was high in many parts of Africa. I felt so bad for this man who just lost one of his children. Yet he came to work because he needed the money. The guests he cooked for would never learn of his hardship.

Jean Pierre taught me to prepare frogs legs and the revered Escargots Bourguignonne – snails in garlic butter. Frogs legs were easy to prepare and delicious when served hot with a little rice pilaf. The legs are usually delivered skinless with the bone in. The flesh resembles that of a chicken breast in color but slightly more tender. After seasoning them, I would sauté the legs in a little olive oil and garlic. Once lightly browned, I removed them from the pan, added some butter and chopped shallot, sautéed them to extract flavor, deglazed them with white wine and added fresh tomato concassé – seedless, skinless chopped tomatoes. Next I added thyme and basil, salt and pepper mill and a little demi glace. Then I returned the legs to the sauce to finish the cooking taking care not to let them boil and become tough, and lastly added some freshly chopped parsley. All-in-all it took about 10 minutes to prepare this delicacy. Served with a fluffy rice pilaf, they were a delight to eat accompanied with a glass of crisp white wine.

In addition to the hotel restaurants we also catered in-flight meals for two European Airlines – Air France and KLM. Both flight crews stayed at the hotel. Menus were provided from the respective head offices in Europe as were two ounce jars of Beluga caviar for the first class meals for Air France. We cooked and packaged the meals and delivered them to the planes. One of the dishes for Air France first class passengers was a roast Gigot – leg of lamb. Jean Pierre told me it was imported from France, a specialty from the Normandy region and referred to as *pré-salé*. Because of its unique flavor, *'agneau de pré-salé'* has an *Appelation d'Origine Controlée* (A.O.C.) designation. This means that only lamb that grazes on specific salt marsh areas can be sold as *agneau de pré-salé*. I told Jean Pierre we had a similar lamb in the Barony of Erris where I grew up, but no one knows about it. My Uncle Peter always had sheep grazing on the heather covered cliff tops along the Atlantic; the taste from that Erris lamb is ingrained in my taste memories. Every time I visit Belmullet, the butcher prepared a boned out gigot of Erris lamb for me and I would roast it for my mother. It was delicious. Jean Pierre was surprised to hear that the Irish had a similar lamb.

When we brought these meals to the airport, I would often be inside the plane supervising the delivery and chatting with the hostesses as they began their pre-flight routine for the night flight to Europe. I could borrow the daily French newspaper and magazines which were up to date – most international publications available locally were three weeks old – so it was nice to have recent world news. I also gave the hostesses my letters to Christine to post in Amsterdam or Paris so she would receive them faster. It was almost embarrassing as we prepared Russian Caviar, roast lamb gigot, and served Chateaux Margaux for first class passengers on the evening flight to Paris, while the African chefs preparing it with me had little to eat. The difference in affluence was staggering.

Letters from Christine took up to two weeks to arrive but were so welcome. In one of her letters she told me she had decided to come to Africa for part of her summer holidays. I was ecstatic and began planning things for her to do while I was working. Of course there were always lazy days by the pool she could enjoy. I bought Jean Pierre's car so I had transport to pick Christine up at the airport. She loved Africa and the Africans loved her. The chefs brought her gifts of mangos from their groves. Little children in the marketplace reached up to touch her blonde hair, and to my surprise as we were changing money in the market place, the money handler offered me some camels in exchange for Christine. This offer went on for days as Christine went every day to the market to buy locally made jewelry, yards of dress material, and souvenirs. Needless to say, I declined the camels – much to the money handlers' dismay.

We traveled inland through remote villages and visited the sous chef's family. As the car came to a stop on a sandy spot in the middle of the village square surrounded by thatched huts, the sous chef got out and the entire village came to welcome us. Ame was so proud to bring a 'Yovo' and his 'bonne amie' to meet his family. They gave us warm bottles of Coca Cola which we drank right from the bottle. I remembered Jean Pierre telling me to avoid using ice in drinks and to drink only from a bottle you opened yourself or a bottle you saw being opened. Most people were scantily clad – all were barefoot. Like many of the women selling at the market in Lomé, some village women wore a bra without any outer clothing. A bra was a relatively new item of clothing for these women living remotely; a status symbol for many, it was important to show it off. The incredible poverty was hard to believe. I was living in an air-conditioned bungalow a few hours away in relative luxury in comparison to these people. Yet they seemed happy with their lot, and despite what in my eyes seemed so little, they still shared what they had with us. Why did so many have so little and so few have so much? It seemed an unjust imbalance.

Le Chef du village – village chief – gave us a tour of the village. He was an older man, naked from the waist up, looking very thin and frail, and he smiled when I shook his hand revealing a few white teeth. We saw many thatched huts some with outdoor fires for cooking and despite the flammable thatched roofs, some huts had fires inside. Ame showed us the spiritual areas of the village and their meaning in village life. A simple pile of what looked like broken glass, sticks and animal hair was really a shrine to ward off evil spirits. We were in Voodoo country where many people used witch doctors to protect them from spells, or place a spell or a curse on someone else – a phenomenon I knew of that created some problems at work when a power play was at hand. As we came back to the car I noticed I had a flat tire. Changing the tire was an ordeal because the children wanted to play with the lug nuts. I realized that if they lost them we would be stranded. I ended up putting them in my pocket one at a time to avoid their disappearance. When I took the wheel off I had to put it on the back seat and close the door before taking the spare out of the boot to ensure the children did not roll it away to play with. Even Christine had to hold the wrench lest it disappear as a silver plaything. The Africans loved shiny items.

On my days off we drove out along the coast road toward Benin. The road followed the beach. Mile after mile of beautiful sandy beaches were lined with coconut trees, some leaning down over the water casting their shadows like cut-outs on the bright sand, providing us with welcome shade after our swim. It was a beautiful setting, much like pictures of the beaches in the Philippines that Herbet showed me before he left Neuchatel. We spent many days on those sandy beaches and swam in the rough surf despite a dangerous undertow. We visited Cotonou, capital of Benin and ate a lot of seafood but Christine would never try the Agouti! We went often to the local disco L'abreuvoir – watering trough – and as we pulled up children would surround the car chanting, "Yovo, Yovo, bonsoir! Yovo, Yovo, bonsoir!" It was wonderful to see such joy stemming from so little. I would give them some money to 'keep an eye' on the car.

One evening as we arrived at the disco, an evening when things had not gone very well at the restaurant – customers complained about the food, service was messy, and I was not in a good mood – I shouted at the children: "No money tonight – leave me alone!" When we exited the disco at three in the morning, I had a flat tire; the children were sitting on the ground staring at the car in disbelief: "Yovo Yovo, what happened to your car? Yovo Yovo, what happened to your car?" I got the message and on future evenings I made sure they were paid regardless of my mood – and there was never a problem. After three weeks in the sun, Christine returned to Switzerland. I was sad to see her leave as we both did not know when or if we would meet again. Her departure was a difficult time for me. Everyone around me had a partner they could share the African experience with. When I joined groups or a party, it was like I had two left feet – I felt so out of place. Every time I experienced something new in the African culture, I would describe it in my next letter to Christine. She in turn told me all about her work and the great skiing. We continued to write to each other, a sort of love affair in an envelope – always three weeks late.

Other than the French restaurant, which was located on the first floor of the hotel, most meals were served outdoors except during the monsoon season. It was not unusual to have hundreds of guests for dinner seated around tables in the gardens under the flood lit coconut trees. Table cloths fluttered in the warm evening breeze, candles flickered inside glass shades, and the atmosphere was festive with the African drums and ocean waves competing for attention in the background. After the meal, there usually was a dance troupe performing a variety of local dances, such as limbo dancers and flame throwers. These dancers wore beautiful costumes, their faces often painted with colors specific to the type of dance that evening. Many dances went on for a long time – dancers would be close to collapsing when it ended. It was as if they were in a trance as the drums became louder and louder, urging them on. After this music and dance orgy was over everyone left, and the resort went to sleep. I would meet many of the staff on their way home as I crossed the compound to my villa. Every evening without fail, I would meet the dishwasher from the Mono carrying his plastic bag full of leftovers he collected from guest plates. He was usually the last to leave, carrying tomorrow's meal for his family, a precious gift of nutritious food – he had already eaten his share during work, including any wine or beer left in glasses brought back from the table, hence his slight stagger. On busy nights the stagger was more noticeable. "Bonsoir Chef" he would say without fail, raising his hand in a friendly wave as we passed each other by under the floodlit coconut trees.

One of these outdoor banquets was hosted by the Libyan Embassy and took the entire day to set up. The organizers were very insistent on the location of two portraits of Libyan leader Muammar Gaddafi. I had never seen such large pictures. They were each about two storey's high and were hanging from specially built flood lit platforms making them visible from any vantage point on the hotel grounds. The guest list was diverse: ambassadors from many West African, North African, Middle Eastern and European nations arrived in several shiny chauffeured black Mercedes Benz limousines. The respective country's flag flying on each car were often the sole identifier of their origin.

It was common for Jean Pierre and me to walk through the restaurant so guests could see there were European chefs at work. The guests in turn wanted to know where the 'white chefs' were from. Some businessmen returned every month, some Nigerian, some Ghanaian, and some European. There was a very friendly Italian businessman who had a clothes distribution company. He collected second hand clothes in Italy, had them sorted by size and style, and then shipped them to Togo to be sold by his local distributors. Once every month he came to Togo to collect payment from each distributor. He would spend a few days at the hotel to enjoy the beach and local food specialties – even the Agouti! On the day of his departure he visited each distributor and collected cash in American dollars. Just before leaving for the airport, I would see him at the Mono restaurant, the bulging brief case never far from his chair. He always flew into Zurich, deposited the money in a Swiss bank and drove back to Italy. Then there was the group of Irish construction workers from McAlpine's in Nigeria that would stay at the hotel for a week every few months. It was nice to chat with fellow Irishmen for a change. They told me horror stories of the living and working conditions in Lagos and that I should be thankful I was living in Togo, on such a peaceful and safe compound.

Outside of the hotel, good European food was difficult to find. For expats willing to cook at home, there was a very good European style supermarket in Lomé. I visited it many times. Some days the dairy section would be well stocked but the bread section was empty. On other days it was the opposite. It was seldom that all shelves were fully stocked as they depended on deliveries from Europe or other African countries. I met the butcher, Erik, a nice fellow from Munich. He was a wonderful butcher, so much so that the selection of sausages, mortadella, salamis, smoked hams, and smoked bacon were as good as any I had tasted in Switzerland. His wife Birgit, not being allowed to work locally, sat at our hotel pool every day so I got to know her also. There were many expatriate's wives who came to the hotel pool every day, lay in the sun, and ate lunch at the Mono. It was with this group of people I spent most of my time, as we all felt a bond through our common European heritage.

Many of the tourists staying at the hotel were European, most on their first trip to Africa. The charter plane came every Friday and guests stayed a week or two – many on their honeymoon. We had a standing honeymoon joke in the kitchen every Friday when Bernard – the head receptionist – would come in looking for a late evening snack. When young couples arrived from the airport and felt the relaxed African atmosphere, the warm evening air and the call of the distant waves, some would decide to go to the beach for a night swim. As the beach was completely dark, there was always one couple every week who left their towels …. and swim suits on the beach as they entered the water, only to find them missing when they returned. Now, standing naked on the beach, they had no alternative but to walk to the reception and ask for towels. Bernard, rather than anticipate this every Friday, would say to the naked couple, "One moment please," and take his time rummaging under the desk for towels, allowing the staff to admire the scenery. Afterwards, in the kitchen, with a lot of hand gestures, he would describe the scene at the front desk, the embarrassing facial expressions of the guest, his impressions of the anatomy of the couple and we laughed at the fun of it all.

Fresh fish was abundant but not always easy to get when we needed it. Many evenings when the dining room was about to close, the fishermen's wives would deliver fish to the receiving dock behind the hotel. We never knew in advance when they would turn up, but it was generally after dark. They were mostly from neighboring Ghana and as the corruption at the border post was so prevalent – they were required to pay off the guard – they developed an alternative route to get the fish to us. Under the cover of darkness the fishermen's wives would swim out past the surf with their fish in tow and drift with the current until they were past the border post, then arrange transport to our hotel where they were guaranteed a sale. I would give them a receipt and they got paid from our business office the next day. If we failed to pay they would not come back with future shipments. One fish in particular was a delight to cook. It was the Merou – grouper. This was a delicate fish with wonderful texture. Once properly cooked, its snow white flesh fell apart at the touch of a fork. It did not require any strong sauce to enhance it – actually quite the opposite: very light flavors complemented this fish allowing its true flavor to emerge, highlighting the 'Merou's' place of honor on the menu.

As in any French restaurant, escargots – snails – have a prominent place in the selection of starters, and here was no different. To prepare this delicacy – which is usually delivered canned, with the shells delivered in separate packages – I began by whipping butter to almost whipped cream consistency. This step was important as the more air that gets whipped into the butter, the lighter the dish becomes. To this I added finely chopped garlic, chopped parsley, salt and pepper mill, lemon juice and a dash of Pernod – a French style anise flavored liqueur. I then sautéed the snails in a little of this butter, flamed them with more Pernod and put each one back into a shell and filled the opening with the whipped butter – or compound butter, as is the professional term. To finish the escargot they were baked on special escargot plates of either six or twelve snails, in a hot oven for six to seven minutes, then served – the butter bubbling in the shells – with slices of fresh baguette. The result was always a culinary delight no matter who the guest was.

Erik and Birgit were planning to return to Germany as his contract was over. She would fly home and he was going to drive his friend's jeep across Africa and on to Munich with his dog, a

German Sheppard. My annual holidays would be around the same time, so over a beer we began discussing the possibility of me driving to Europe with him. I thought this would be a great adventure for us and allow me to see more of Africa. We would drive north through Togo, Benin and Niger to Tamanrasset in Algeria and then up to Algiers on the Mediterranean. We would spend a few days windsurfing in Algiers, take the ferry to Marseille, in France and drive to Switzerland, pick up Christine, and go to the Oktoberfest. It would be a great adventure. I began to plan for this and was thrilled at the possibility, not fully realizing the complexities of what such a trip entailed.

Then I met Dietrich, a drifter who drove the Munich - Lomé route quite often. He drove a covered articulated truck loaded with three second hand Mercedes Benz diesel cars and lots of spare parts from Munich to Lomé every month – this brand of diesel car was highly sought after in Africa. On his arrival in Lomé, he sold off the cars, the truck, and spent a week on the beach. Then he flew to Germany with the cash and bought another truck, three more cars and repeated the trip. "It is a very dangerous trip," he told me. "There is a section of road near Tamanrasset where you have to travel in convoys for safety. Will you have a gun?" I did not realize I would need a gun so I asked Erik if I should buy one. He gestured to the dog, "We have the dog and beer, so do not worry about guns." This was not exactly the response I expected and it began to dawn on me that this trip would not be a walk in the park. I asked him about a medical kit and remedies for snake bites. He was uninterested. I realized that with Erik I would have no backup in case of an emergency and decided for safety reasons not to go. He was very disappointed and so was I. I had been planning this trip in my mind for several weeks and the let down was tough to accept. But I did not want to get into a situation where my traveling buddy could not help me out in a case of need. In the back of my mind were my mother's words about the white man's grave. I did not want my grave to be somewhere in the middle of Africa if I could help it. Erik left anyway, himself and his dog. One week later he was back! The driver's door and window of the jeep were all smashed in. He got as far as the Algerian border which was about half way to the Mediterranean. Customs officers would not let him in to the country because the jeep was not registered in his name – a detail he neglected. To enter the country, he decided to ram the border post which was a simple chain stretched across the road. He reversed up and then accelerated to break through the chain only to realize at the last moment that there was a large stone on the end of the chain which as he stretched the chain, swung and hit the driver's window, knocking him to the passengers' side of the jeep. It was a terrific example of African ingenuity. Despite being terribly disappointed, I was glad I had listened to my gut feeling.

Safety and the possibility of illness while working in Africa were always on our minds but not to the point of obsession. The hotel engineer was Dutch and got malaria while I was there. He was jaundiced and extremely weak. We put him in quarantine in his villa; meals were left outside his door so no one really was in contact with him. We could speak with him by phone, and seldom saw him. It took three months for him to get back to some sense of functionality. Even then he looked so thin as to be hardly recognizable. I remember buying a year's supply of quinine tablets before flying there. I took them every day to protect against malaria and after 3 month my eye sight began to get fuzzy and I had headaches. Jean Pierre told me to stop taking them and everything returned to normal. Then his daughter got a parasite infection in the form of a worm that burrows itself in the flesh. She came to show it to us one day, proudly baring her forearm displaying 'le ver" in a small bubble on her arm. "le ver" – worm – was visible as it moved around in the clear liquid under the blister. She was going to have it lanced and removed which would increase her odds of an infection due to poor local health services. Before leaving for Africa I was advised to take out medical flight insurance, which I did. A simple appendix operation at the time in Africa could be a death sentence by infection. My insurance covered the six hour medical jet flight to Switzerland and gave me peace of mind. Fortunately, I never needed it.

I was still planning to take my annual holiday in Switzerland when the most amazing thing happened to me that was to have a major impact on my career. My mother forwarded a letter from Herbert in the Philippines. The letter was posted six weeks earlier in Manila to my home address in Belmullet. Herbert had been appointed Executive Chef for a new hotel and was offering me a position on the opening team of The Royal Orchid Hotel in Bangkok. I would be a sous chef in charge of the signature restaurant and grill. This was an unbelievable offer. It would be great to work with Herbert again so I sent him a telex that I was interested; he telexed back saying a contract would be in the post to me. On his word, I made the decision I would not return to Africa after my annual holidays, but join him in Bangkok instead.

Even though I was ecstatic, this decision did not entirely please me or the management because I had a two year contract and breaking it was not very professional. Despite the sun, sand, constant blue sky and sea, life had become one long routine and living by the beach had become almost boring. The sun rose and set at the same time every day. There was very little ebb and flow in the tide. In essence nothing much changed, not even the seasons, which were reduced to two – wet and dry. The same people came to the restaurant every day and every Friday new tourists arrived for another two week stay while I waited for Christine's letters as my fondness for her grew. My mother used to say: "Absence makes the heart grow fonder," and now that had a new meaning for me. I knew the opportunity to move to South East Asia would not be there in a year's time so I sold my car and any belongings that would not fit in a suitcase and flew to Switzerland to see Christine.

She was teaching at a school in Veytaux, a small village overlooking the idyllic 'Chateau de Chillon' on Lake Leman. She now had her own apartment. We lived in sin for two weeks; at least that is what the neighbors talked about – "The young school teacher has a friend staying...a foreigner, if you don't mind.....speaks French with an accent!" Although everyone was friendly, some residents looked at me with suspicion – as the Swiss do with most foreigners – when I walked through this tiny village. Needless to say Christine was not happy when I told her I was leaving again for Thailand; nevertheless, she suggested I meet her parents. We decided we should invite them to her apartment and by way of introduction I would cook a meal for them.

Her father – grateful for the invitation – insisted he supply the meat: a saddle of venison, his favorite dish. I marinated the meat for two days in red wine, bay leaf, mirepoix, crushed peppercorns, juniper berries and vegetables. This would reduce the strong game flavor and I would use the wine to make a sauce. I had made a demi glace with venison bones the previous day. On the day of the meal, I prepared Brussels sprouts with toasted sliced almonds, and scooped out poached apples which I filled with redcurrant jelly. Then I glazed fresh chestnuts with caramel and prepared homemade Spätzli to serve with the meat – which I roasted medium rare. We served a white wine from Daniel Allaman's winery in Villeneuve – also her father's favorite – with a salad to start the meal. With the venison we chose a strong Swiss red wine – a Dole du Monts from the Robert Gillard winery in the Valais – another of her father's favorites. For dessert I prepared chestnut puree mixed with fresh cream and flavored with Kirsch brandy. I served it with vanilla ice cream and a crunchy meringue. Then I served coffee, liqueur filled chocolates, a selection of fruit brandies, and a Grand Marnier for the ladies. Little did I know that her mother was an accomplished cook and noticed every detail and flavor during the meal.

We had a terrific evening. As they were leaving, Christine's parents suggested I now address them in the informal. I was surprised: Christine even more so as this was only the second time I had met them. In Swiss culture, addressing people by their first name is a big step in breaking down the formality of relationships and is always initiated by the older person. It changes the language used to address people and opens the door to a more informal dialogue. This little cultural initiation is usually conducted over a drink but they decided to do this as they were leaving. People usually shake hands and introduce themselves by first name – no more Monsieur or Madame, so I called them by their first names, Paul and Eliane. They smiled, shook hands and called me Brendan. Elaine gave me a kiss on both cheeks – and so did Paul! Then they left. Now it was time to do the dishes. I had used so many dishes, and kitchen utensils to cook the meal, that it took us forever to wash up and put the small apartment kitchen back together. But it did not matter; Christine was happy because her parents had a good meal cooked by her 'foreigner Irish chef who spoke French with an accent,' and she could see I got along well with them – which was important to her.

The day before I left for Thailand Christine invited me to dinner in one of her favorite restaurants: le Restaurant du Raisin in the village of St. Saphorin. Nestled in the Lavaux wine region, St Saphorin stretches from the water's edge to vineyards high above Lake Leman. It was there I first tasted the much admired St. Saphorin, a light white wine and a perfect accompaniment to fish – so of course I had to have 'fillets de perche meunière' with buttered parsley potatoes. I had cooked so many of these in the Hotel Du Bateau on Lake Morat that I wanted to see if they tasted the same from Lake Leman. Christine ordered the poached 'Omble chevalier' – Char – served with a white wine sauce garnished with pearl onions and capers. It was a special and bittersweet meal; we were both saddened by the prospect that we would probably not see each other again. I was flying thousands of miles away to a new job and she had a teaching position with the state, guaranteed for life. Nevertheless, we agreed to write, our growing affection for each other sealed in more envelopes.

Noisettes D'agneau Aux Gambas
(Lamb Cutlets With Jumbo Shrimp)

This was a popular dish in the French restaurant of the hotel in Africa, "le Grand Soleil".

Ingredients for 4 people
2 oz. (60gr.) butter
1 tablespoon olive oil
1 cup (2.4 dl.) demi glace – brown stock Salt and pepper
12 lamb cutlets approx 3 oz. (100gr.) each – well trimmed
12 pieces of large peeled and deveined shrimp
24 pieces of Parisienne potatoes- small potato balls
16 oz. (480gr.) julienne* of carrots and green beans

Procedure
- Boil or steam the potatoes until partially cooked.
- Pan fry them in olive oil until golden brown, season – keep warm.
- Sauté the julienne in butter until cooked but not soft, season – keep warm.
- Season and sauté the shrimp until firm – keep warm.
- Season and pan fry the lamb to medium – keep warm.

Assembly
- Arrange the julienne in the center of each plate.
- Place three lamb cutlets evenly spaced around the julienne with the bones upright.
- Place the shrimp in between the cutlets.
- Decorate with the potatoes around the outside.
- Drizzle with demi glace.

Tip
- Use the 'touch method' described in Chapter 14 to check the degree of cooking for the lamb.

* Julienne – very fine two inch strips of vegetables.
  Potatoes can be replaced with sautéed potato slices or Fingerling potatoes.

CHAPTER TEN

Thailand

My first view of the Royal Orchid Hotel lobby in Bangkok was as a construction site. The building, rising majestically above the banks of the Chao Prya River, had 28 floors with tower cranes still on the roof. Piles of polished white Italian marble slabs, a crane, and bare concrete winding stairs took up most of the space in the lobby. Looking around, I wasn't able to visualize the 5 star luxury hotel this building would become. It did not look anything like the picture in the brochure Herbert sent me. I met him at the offsite operations office in a nearby office complex and he gave me a tour of the hotel construction site. It was fantastic to see him again after all these years. He had been living and working in the Philippines since we last worked together in Neuchatel and now he was in charge of his first hotel opening. I was so appreciative that he thought enough of my cooking to invite me onto his opening team.

The Royal Orchid Hotel was only a few hundred yards up river from the legendary Mandarin Oriental Hotel in Bangkok. It was the second hotel in the city to be managed by Mandarin Oriental Hotels Limited – a Hong Kong based Hotel Management Company, renowned for the extremely high quality, luxury, design, and operation of its properties. The Royal Orchid had eight hundred guest rooms; a garden lounge restaurant overlooking the lobby; Giorgio's, an Italian restaurant, with river view and a terrace leading to the pool, and then down one level to another very large terrace at the water's edge. There was another restaurant leading off this terrace called the Rim Nam Coffee Shop. The Captain Bush Grillroom, where I would be working, was on the first floor and did not have any windows. However it was beautifully designed, with its own bar and a fourteen seat private dining room. The center of the restaurant had a purpose built buffet made of Italian marble with ceiling high flood lit columns. The walls were decorated with many painting of ships – each in full sail – flood lit with beautifully polished brass lighting fixtures. Seating was very comfortable with upholstered arm chairs and padded table tops to reduce noise. With a thick lush carpet, Thai teak wood paneling and stained glass doors, it was the most luxurious restaurant I had seen so far in my career.

Herbert had assembled a team of European expatriate chefs who would manage these restaurants and the banqueting department which could seat 800 people in the main ballroom on the first floor. The hierarchy was different given the size of the brigade and the diversity of the restaurants, or outlets, as we called them. Each outlet was managed by a sous chef who then reported to an Executive Sous Chef and then to Herbert the Executive Chef. Alphonso was the sous chef for the Italian restaurant and came directly from Italy for this position. He spoke English with a very strong Italian accent and cooked excellent food; I got along very well with him. Freddy was the Executive Sous Chef. He was Swiss German and had just finished his contract with the Regent Hotel in Fiji. Manfred was in charge of the bakery, the pastry, and desserts for each outlet and banqueting. He was Austrian and came from the Holiday Inn in Hong Kong. The sous chef for the Rim Nam Coffee shop was a very pleasant older Thai named TJ. He was the perfect sous chef to complete the team. It was important to have a good balance of local and expatriate chefs, each one drawing on their strengths and as the Rim Nam was the coffee shop serving many local dishes it made sense to have a local sous chef in charge.

We began to write menus and unwrapping equipment which Herbert had ordered from Europe, in preparation for opening day. It was reminiscent of Christmas morning as we unwrapped one beautiful shiny stainless sautéuse after another. Some were for Alphonso to sauté his Linguini con vongole, some large stock pots for the banquet kitchen, and many more for the grill room. Despite that the upper floors and guest rooms were not yet complete, the hotel planned what we called a 'soft opening' which meant some outlets would not be ready and most of the guest rooms would not be finished by opening day. There are many advantages to such a move. The main one is it pleased the owners to have the hotel opened as soon as possible. It also allowed us to identify and correct any operational mistakes before they impacted large numbers of guests, and it tested the staff to operate under pressure. We hired as needed depending on the level of business. Hiring was an interesting process. Thais are a very welcoming people; they smile a lot, so it was difficult for me at first to see past the smile or even to interpret the different types of smiles. Smiles of embarrassment, of happiness, and of insecurity all took time to interpret. As a result, some of the cooks I hired – even though they steadfastly told me they could make such and such a dish during the interview – could not cook, at least not to the level required for a five star luxury hotel. We were the first luxury hotel to open in Bangkok in many years so local chefs at other hotels that were stuck in a position for some time saw The Royal Orchid as an opportunity to move up in their careers. As a result we were flooded with applications and despite the few who lacked culinary skills, we hired some fantastic chefs. I learned so much from them.

For the soft opening we would have the lobby bar, the garden lounge, Rim Nam Coffee Shop, Giorgio's, room service and banquets up and running. The pool, the pool terrace, and the Captain Bush grill would open a little later. In the mean time I helped everywhere. By working with TJ I began learning some of the Thai dishes which were bursting with flavor. Now I was experiencing very different flavors to those I had tasted in Switzerland or even Africa for that matter. Fresh ginger, lemon grass, lemon leaves, Thai basil, Thai parsley – cilantro – were everywhere. Even the aromas in the kitchen were so different to what I had become accustomed to. The combination of spice and lime present in such dishes as the Thai beef salad – and absent in French classical cooking – resulted in an incredible burst of flavor. Yet this was a very simple recipe and only took minutes to prepare. To make this we took a regular rump steak, seasoned it and pan-fried it rare and sliced it into thin strips. Then it was seasoned with freshly chopped chili, lime juice, thinly sliced shallots, Thai parsley and a local fermented fish sauce called 'Nam Pla.' Served warm on a bed of lettuce, it was delicious…and spicy! As the spice hit the taste buds, I reached for a large glass of cold water. TJ laughed and handed me some sliced cucumber and tomato. "Take these instead," he told me. "Let them rest on your tongue and they will absorb the spiciness and cool your mouth." And sure enough they did! What an intelligent use of one food to compliment another. For that reason, Yam Nua salad is served with slices of cucumbers and tomatoes.

By now the lobby had taken on an air of elegance. The piles of marble slabs had become a floor with a sheen which the housekeeping staff enhanced daily. The concrete stairs were transformed into a masterpiece of marble, brass railings, etched glass panels and a plush carpet. Beneath the stairs was a flood lit water feature decorated with plants – fish swimming in and out between them. The transformation in a few short weeks was amazing. Guests could sit on the low marble-coated wall surrounding the water while waiting for an appointment, taking in the busy lobby scene as guests came in, more going out, some walking up the winding stairs and others lounging in chairs reading or just people watching. Hotel lobbies are a wonderful place to people watch.

A few months after the soft opening we opened the Captain Bush grillroom. Captain Sir John Bush was an accomplished British sailor and master navigator. The harbor master of the port of Bangkok for many years, he lived on the site where the hotel now stood so it was fitting to name the restaurant in his honor. Some dishes such as steak and oyster pie, fish pie, and bread and butter pudding were put on the menu to pay homage to his English heritage. There was a grill and roasting spit inside the restaurant, conveniently located next to the kitchen door. I put a few locally raised ducks on the spit each evening that were then carved at the table by the Maître. Among the cold starters were sweet water crayfish, avocado pear with crab meat and king prawn cocktail. Hot starters included a seafood crepe glazed with a light Pernod sauce and eggs Astrakhan which were creamed scrambled eggs flavored with shallots and served in the shell topped with Beluga caviar.

Soups were classics such as lobster bisque flamed with Armagnac, baked French onion soup and the ever popular beef consommé with bone marrow and a poached quail egg. In addition to a great selection of New Zealand and American steaks, we prepared Phuket lobster thermidor, grilled tiger prawns and grilled scallops and oysters. We also had some chef's recommendations such as lamb loin wrapped in Parma ham and baked in puff pastry, and sautéed breast of duckling with a green peppercorn and orange sauce. There were two flambées to choose from: lobster tail in brandy sauce and US tenderloin with a four peppercorn cream sauce. Lobster in general was a spiny lobster, not really a lobster as we would refer to in Europe. These were crayfish, had no claws and had a softer shell.

On my days off I visited the sights of the city. Buddhism is the predominant religion in Thailand and influences many daily rituals, some of which include praying or offering alms in and around some of the beautiful temples that abound in the city. I marveled at the beauty of these buildings and observed the reverence which the Thais displayed when entering and exiting by wearing longer clothing, bowing their heads and observing silence. I visited the other large hotels and got to know the chefs there. The Executive chefs at the Oriental, the Hilton, Regent, Hyatt, Montien and Dusit Thani hotels were all European and well connected in South East Asia. It seemed that among them I was the only newcomer to the region. They would glance at me twice when they found out I was Irish – almost as if they were asking: how did he get in to a five star hotel? Knowing that these European chefs knew that Ireland was not particularly renowned for its food I was content telling them of the hotels I had worked at in Switzerland. That, and my French and German, helped me to be accepted as a peer. Still I strived to get their respect, and remembered what a chef told me years earlier in Jury's Hotel in Dublin: "Learn everything the Swiss can teach you, it will open the doors of the world for you." How right he was. I was now working in a 5 star luxury hotel in a beautiful region of the world, learning yet again a new set of flavors and adapting to another layer of cultural differences, all because of what I had learned – and the people I had met – in Switzerland. What would my life have become if I never left my first job at Jury's hotel in Limerick to pursue a position in Switzerland?

The banqueting department was very big. Bigger than anything I had ever seen previously. Peter, the banquet manager, was from New Zealand and I thought he was very professional and well organized. Having worked previously in the city, he spoke a little Thai and seemed to get along with the Thais very well. We also got along very well and often went out for a beer after work. Peter was always game for a joke. I remember we had a very naïve management trainee from Hong Kong who would believe anything we said. One day Peter was supervising the set up for a large banquet and to test his knowledge, he asked the trainee, "What is the fastest way to count the guests seated in a large room like this?" Guest count was important at large functions as it impacted billing. To get an accurate number, it is easier and faster to count the empty chairs once all guests are seated. "I think..." replied the trainee. But Peter calmly interrupted him in a stern voice saying: "You think, you think? You are not here to think...you are here to know! You have to be sure... not just think! That's what happened to Julius Caesar, he thought he farted but he actually shit in his pants! That's the difference between thinking and knowing – it can get messy!" The trainee didn't know what to do or say after this outburst; he got very red in the face and wandered off. I turned to Peter and said: "Caesar didn't wear pants; he just laid on a couch all day eating grapes. Do grapes make you fart?" We both laughed and the trainee scowled from the other side of the ballroom not knowing what hit him. Trainees were often targeted for a joke.

Despite living in a city of eleven million people, expatriate hotel staff frequented the same bars on evenings out. There was a bar district not far from the river between Suriwong and Silom road. After a busy night in the restaurant, with the stress and the fast pace, most chefs take a while to wind down and finally get to sleep so it was common to go out after work. We moved from one bar to another, but in the end they all looked the same: dimly lit spaces selling cheap beer with bikini clad girls dancing around a pole. In some bars I eventually got to know the owners, usually a familiar sight at the end of the bar. Many were American, some had fought in the Vietnam War and were content to stay in South East Asia, unwilling or unable to re-adapt to the American life style. So they sat in their own bar every evening and counted the money.

My average work week ranged from between sixty to eighty hours depending on hotel occupancy. So a three day weekend was a mini holiday and a welcome break. Peter recommended I visit Phuket in the south of the country so I booked a bungalow at the Patong Beach Hotel. It was a pleasant change, just a two hour flight south of a city with massive pollution, constant noise and smog, but in Phuket I sat in a deck chair on a half moon beach, the only sound being the waves gently caressing the sand. There were only a few people on the beach and in the distance I noticed a person walking and carrying what looked like a cumbersome object. Eventually the person was close enough for me to see it was a woman, her face wrinkled from many years of sun and wind but despite that she was beautiful. She came right up to me and lowered the bamboo pole that supported the weight across her shoulders. She smiled at me as only the Thais can, opened one of the bamboo baskets and out of a container of ice handed me a perfectly carved chilled sliced pineapple wrapped in a plastic bag and ready to eat. After I paid her a few Baht she bowed and left to find another customer. It was the most delicious pineapple I had ever tasted, perfectly ripened, juicy and sliced without any dark spots. The flavor of that fruit on a hot beach in Thailand is still embedded in my taste memories to this day – and often retrieved subconsciously as a benchmark comparison when I eat fresh pineapple. I was sad leaving Phuket and vowed to return again soon.

During my table side visits at the Royal Orchid I met many regular customers who came to the Captain Bush Grillroom. James was a retired American living in the city. He came in every few weeks and always had a drink at the bar before dinner. He would ask for me and depending on the amount of orders in the kitchen, I would briefly go out to greet him because he was a genuinely nice person and always had an interesting story. Generally speaking, customers do not like to see the chef chatting with other customers while still waiting for their meal, so as a rule I would only visit guests at the table during dessert. However there was a back corridor leading from the kitchen to the bar so I did not have to walk through the restaurant. This fellow had just come back from the Gulf of Thailand where he was involved with the American Forces during parachute training. He explained they were training to parachute into water when one soldier – during a briefing – asked him how long it would take for him to hit the water if his parachute did not open. "Well son," he replied, "you'll have the rest of your life!" I thought it was an amusing answer, given the seriousness of the question.

We also had the flamboyant and eccentric Baron staying in the hotel. He would stay for weeks in the presidential suite with his entourage. I never met him but his table was constantly reserved in the Grill room. Even when we were fully booked, his table remained empty – just in case he decided to come down for dinner. The hotel limousine was also always on standby at the Hotel's front entrance – an arrangement of his favorite flowers carefully displayed between the vehicle's front seats. He always ordered room service and sometimes that included items from the grillroom. The room service order taker was instructed to call the Food and Beverage Director when anyone placed a food order from the presidential suite. He would personally supervise the trolley as it was prepared. No one wanted to be responsible for a complaint from the guest staying in the most expensive suite in the hotel. These guests were typically very affluent and expected the best service – the presidential suite exuded affluence and elegance – worthy of a president.

A few months after we opened we were informed by a general memo that the President of the United States would be visiting Bangkok during his trip to South East Asia. A block of four hundred rooms had been booked which were mostly for the press. This group would take up half the hotel rooms and a lot of meeting space as well which was a great boost for business. Special operational meetings began as we counted down the days to the President's arrival. There were rumors he might eat at the grillroom. And then there was talk he might not stay at our hotel. Every day the possibilities changed to the point it was impossible to plan on him coming to the grillroom at all. Shortly before he was scheduled to arrive we received the news that also shocked the world. The President of the United States had been shot. He was expected to recover but his trip to Bangkok was cancelled. It was a major cancellation for us. Four hundred rooms was a lot of revenue. But thankfully President Regan eventually recovered and returned to the White House.

Letters from Christine were a welcome break from the day to day routine in the busy kitchen. I had been in Thailand now for almost a year, and we still wrote to each other every month. Many of my letters to her were posted in Zurich as we had a European airline crew staying at the hotel. In a particular letter Christine mentioned she was thinking of joining me in Bangkok. I was so happy to hear this great news but I found it difficult to believe that it was actually going to happen, that finally we would be together. So a few long weeks later I picked her up at the airport. It was great to see her again and to be in such an unfamiliar country for both of us made her visit even more interesting.

Christine loved the hotel and got along very well with Herbert and all the expats. I showed her what I knew of the city and the night life. On rare long weekends we went to stay at the Royal Cliff Hotel in Pataya where I knew the General Manager – he was a regular in the grillroom during his visits to the city. This hotel was situated on its own beach. We enjoyed breakfast on our balcony looking high out over the gulf of Thailand with the islands in the distance. That balcony was also a great viewing spot hours later for admiring the beautiful sunset: a horizon suddenly filled with a ball of fire slowly being extinguished, as if the sun was ever so slowly lowered into a pool of shining liquid.

We spent afternoons and my days off visiting the palaces and temples of Bangkok. We traveled the canals and backwater by long tail boat where we saw the incredible poverty and hardship of the Thais living in the slums. We ate from the street vendors for whom I had a new-found respect. They could cook a delicious meal in conditions where I could not. On Saturdays Christine would join us at Chef's table for lunch. Herbert had founded a humorous society called BASICO – Beer And Sausage In Chefs Office. We were all members, formally inducted with a certificate. As his office was too small to accommodate everyone we had a large table installed at the end of the pool terrace away from the view of the hotel guests. Despite that it had a beautiful river view. There was only one rule during the meal – there could be no serious discussion. It was all fun and light-hearted, insults would fly and language was often decorative. It helped to release some of the stress. It was harmless. For these meals we prepared special sausages served with a selection of mustards and German potato salad. We were always experimenting with different recipes: veal, pork, chicken and fish sausages – we even made a potato sausage. Although no one had ever heard of a potato sausage it was actually very good.

Sometimes we invited long staying guests to join us; they were very appreciative as I am sure anyone who has stayed for a long time in a hotel would be. One guest in particular came on numerous occasions – language and tone was very different when a hotel guest was present. This particular gentleman took up his sun chair promptly at ten o'clock every morning by the pool and ordered a bottle of white wine in an ice bucket. He then gave the pool attendants strict guidelines not to disturb him until they saw the upturned bottle in the ice bucket. Only then could they approach his chair with a new bottle. He read all day in the sun – while sipping his white wine and admiring the majestic river flowing by.

East/west fusion cooking was a new style of cuisine emerging at the time. This involved blending Asian flavors with classical European dishes. It expanded the range of tastes by combining flavors from both cultures. Examples of this were poached sole with cilantro leaves, grilled chicken with lemon balm, and shiitake mushroom consommé with a puff pastry crust. Later this concept of fusion cooking attracted some well known European chefs to Asia. It was common at the time for luxury hotels in major cities in Asia to consult with renowned French chefs to manage and endorse their signature restaurants. Probably the most revered restaurant in Bangkok at the time was the Normandy Grill located on the top floor of the Mandarin Oriental Hotel. The Oriental constantly worked with French Michelin star chefs to bring the best of French cuisine to the city. At the time Louis Outhier of France was consulting at the Normandy. Typically these chefs would send their top chef de cuisine to manage the kitchen and they flew out a few times a year to introduce a new menu. Herbert talked of Paul Haberlin from L'Auberge de l'Ill in Illhaeusern in France who came to the Mandarin Oriental in Manila to promote his cooking style. He marveled at the dedication and perseverance of these Michelin star chefs which allowed them to be at the tip of the epicurean mountain – and remain there. However, once at the top there is only one direction left to go – the fall is a bitter pill to swallow, sometimes ruining a chef's career.

I met Herve – the chef de cuisine at the Normandy – many times. He was an amazing chef; it was incredible to see how he trained the Thai chefs to be so exact in their cooking. It wasn't that it was impossible; it was just that the daily commitment absorbed so much time, energy and dedication. I had taken Christine to eat there and he prepared a terrific meal for us. Eating at the Normandy was like dining in tropical France – just incredible foods with great tasting wines and, of course, the views of Bangkok. We were surprised one evening when we met Herve out on the town and he introduced us to his boss, Paul Bocuse, who with typical French gallantry turned to Christine and gave her a *'baise main'* – kiss on the back of the hand – saying: *"Bonsoir Madame, enchanté."*

Paul Bocuse from Lyon in France – a world renowned French chef – has done more to elevate the classical culinary profession worldwide than any chef since Auguste Escoffier. I could not believe I was actually meeting this world famous chef in the middle of a city of eleven million people. Christine was over the moon.

Now that the hotel was running smoothly with all of the outlets open, we began planning the official opening ceremony. Their Majesties, the King and Queen of Thailand, were to officially open the hotel. This required a tremendous amount of planning. The Thai Royal Family is highly revered by their subjects. Having their Majesties participate in the official opening ceremony was a tremendous honor for us and a major boost to the employees' pride. Peter told me that during the banquet the Royal Family would be seated on a raised platform so that waiters could approach with food and not be physically any higher than them. It could be a case of lese majeste – insulting royalty – if a waiter found themselves higher than the King and Queen during service. No one can ever be physically higher than the King and Queen as that would denote superiority over them. Even hotel guests were told not to look down from the windows of their guest rooms as the royal family passed by outside. It was best to have the curtains closed.

In addition, no one is allowed to touch members of the royal family. The history books tell of a royal princess in times past who was drowning. All the bystanders stood there and watched her drown for they knew to jump in and save her would be a case of 'lese majeste'. There was also the story of an expat general manager of a local hotel who insisted he personally welcome her Majesty the Queen to his hotel. As the Queen exited her chauffeured car at the front entrance, he mistakenly thought she extended a hand so he reached out to take it. The next day he was no longer the General Manager and instead found himself on a flight out of the country.

We were busy preparing for the royal banquet. Freddy was in charge of the banquet kitchen which would serve the Royal meal. He had the extraordinary ability to prepare large banquets ensuring that food quality and flavor were paramount. This was a very big event so naturally these stories of faux pas at Royal ceremonies made us nervous. A few days before the opening day ceremony, we were informed that his Majesty the King would not attend. On the day of the opening, the press and local television crews were present long before the Queen arrived. There were many royal guards and Royal staff ensuring that the visit went smoothly. We had palace guards in the kitchen tasting the food all day and again just before it was served. They followed us everywhere, stopping short of entering our suite on the seventh floor. Upon her arrival the Queen was scheduled to walk through the lobby and take the elevator to the third floor. There could be no guests leaning on the Mezzanine balconies for fear of upsetting the protocol. A plan was put in place in case Her Majesty decided to take the winding lobby staircase. Nobody could walk before her going up and no one behind her coming down. Christine was highly excited to get a picture of the Queen but had to follow orders from the staff lining the royal route to the third floor ballroom. Her Majesty arrived in the ballroom and the banquet was a success. We served the following menu.

Marinated cured salmon with dill cream

Beef consommé with floating gold leaf

Veal tenderloin medallions with calvados sauce on artichoke
bottoms

Morello cherries marinated in honey with a cinnamon parfait
and white chocolate mousse

Le Mocha
Selection of chocolate pralines

The meal was accompanied with Moët et Chandon, Brut Imperial.

As her Majesty was leaving the ballroom Herbert, Peter, and myself were in the main foyer as she walked by with her entourage. She stopped in front of Herbert, addressed him and held out her hand. Herbert shook her hand and she told him how much she enjoyed the meal and moved on. I could not believe it. Now I was sure we would all be deported and just stood frozen to the spot, fearing I would make a mistake in protocol as she walked in front of me. Later, Peter assured me that if her Majesty extends her hand, it is within the protocol to accept the hand shake.

After the banquet, I returned to my apartment and Christine, extremely excited, told me she met the Queen. I was surprised and so was Christine. She could not believe it! She was waiting on the mezzanine with a guest – an older British lady who also wanted to see the Queen. They walked down a corridor behind the bank of elevators, turned a corner to get a better view and came face to face with Her Majesty! The British lady did a curtsy saying, "Your Majesty." Christine, not knowing what to do, just said, "Hello Your Majesty." The Queen asked her where she was from and when she mentioned her home town on Lake Leman the Queen had more questions. It happened that His Majesty the King went to a private school very near Christine's hometown on the same lake and loved the area. The Queen wished her a pleasant stay and went on her way. Christine was only in the country a few months and had already met The Queen of Thailand!

The next day I had a very important reservation in the private room. The deputy manager of the Hong Kong and Shanghai Bank would be having dinner with ten guests. The menu was simple but because of the client's high profile, everyone was alerted. Khun Opal, the Maître, was in charge of the private room that evening. He delegated the running of the main restaurant to one of his assistants. The party arrived at eight thirty for cocktails and canapés in the bar, and then sat down for dinner at nine o'clock. They had the following menu.

Fresh green asparagus tips with
home smoked duckling breast

Consommé Royale

Beetroot sherbet

Veal tenderloin "en croute" with morel cream sauce
Soufflé potatoes
Bouquet of garden vegetables
Stuffed cherry tomatoes

Amaretto soufflé
With raspberry sauce

Le mocha
Petit fours and pralines selection

The client requested we pour Gewurztraminer white wine all
throughout the meal. Although the menu was not overly
complicated, every detail was thought of. We wanted these guests
to be regulars at the Captain Bush. So things like room
temperature, lighting, floral decoration, linen and table set up
received extra special attention. The private room had its own
phone line so a direct phone number was assigned in case the guest
needed to make a call or needed to be reached during dinner. I
assigned Khun Somkid, one of the grill room chefs, to prepare this
menu with me and the rest of the brigade took care of the main
restaurant. With this system in place we ensured VIP clients were
treated appropriately and would hopefully return.

I had not seen James, the retired American, in the
restaurant for some time so I was surprised one evening when he
sent in his business card with a waiter and asked to see me. Before
every service I would check the reservations book to see who was

dining with us, so I could be prepared to meet them. Depending on the guest, I might offer them a glass of wine or a complimentary dessert. It was a common policy in such restaurants that the Chef and Maître would have a budget for such occasions to use at their discretion. A discreet glass of champagne sent to the table with the compliments of the Chef makes a big impression on guests, making them feel special – which they are! So when I got James's card from the Maitre, I called the barman and asked him to offer the gentleman a drink from me. I then went to see him and without fail he had an exciting story.

While he was gardening he inflicted a little cut on his shin which became infected a week later as he waded through a flooded street – a common occurrence in the city during monsoon season. The infection got worse accompanied with fever so he went to the hospital and eventually became delirious. The next thing he remembers was waking up on the operating table and listening to two surgeons discussing the amputation of his leg – above or below the knee? Fortunately he spoke fluent Thai and told them in his casual Irish-American tone: "They'll be no amputation today lads!" In his opinion he did not have gangrene. "Brendan," he said. "If I did not wake up and if I did not speak Thai to understand their conversation, I would now be a lot lighter. There are other ways to lose weight!" And he laughed, making light of the incident. It was a remarkable story and very believable as I knew what kind of bacteria were in the flood waters that paralyzed parts of the city during the rainy season and the dangers of getting sick in such circumstances.

It was around this time that Freddy told me his girlfriend Jabeen would be arriving from Fiji to stay with him. Jabeen and Christine got along very well. They cooked meals together and Christine developed an affinity for the island flavors. Eventually she cooked the most delicious food for the both of us, always testing a new recipe and flavors she learned from Jabeen. Some evenings it would be a delicious curry with coconut milk, other days it would be a banana pudding and so on.

The restaurant was always busy and as work took up most of my time, it was not unusual for me to be in the hotel for six or seven days at a time. Because of that I usually chose to eat outside the hotel with Christine on my days off. There was a terrific Indian restaurant on New Road called Himali Cha Cha, just a short walk from the Oriental Hotel. It was a dimly lit restaurant with small tables covered with red table cloths and served some the best Indian food in Bangkok. Many flavors resembled those that Jabeen used in her curries. Cha Cha was the owner and often came to the table to chat. He was the personal chef to Lord Mountbatten while the latter was still in India. Then with Indian independence, Cha Cha cooked for various Indian ambassadors abroad, the last being in Laos where he married and opened a restaurant. Later he fled communism in Laos and opened his current restaurant. His curries were excellent and his skill with the Tandoori oven, fresh naan, chapatti, parota, and his chicken with mint, orange or lemon were fantastic. After every meal he would bring over a little metal bowl of roasted fennel seeds. He told us to chew on them after any meal as they aid the digestive system and freshen the breath. We later made this a practice at home after all our meals. I wanted to meet the chefs cooking these delicious foods and asked him if he could show me his kitchen. He led the way through a doorway behind a curtain and there, in the lane behind the restaurant, were a line of young children operating the tandoor and stirring pots of masala and making beautiful dahl – no cooking school needed here! We returned many times but I never again asked to see the kitchen.

As Christine had traveled to Thailand on a three month tourist visa, it was now time to renew it so we decided to visit Penang on the west coast of Malaysia. We were fearful of not getting the visa, and that could mean a major change of plans as Christine would not be allowed back in to Thailand and would have no other choice but to return directly to Switzerland. So we packed with that possibility in mind. Penang was beautiful, its colonial history evident on every street and building façade. The architecture was unmistakably British, and many of the foods offered were reminiscent of Colonial days. We swam on Batu

Feringgi beach and savored delicious Malaysian curries and of course the mighty satay with its fiery peanut sauce. On our last evening, we had a memorable meal – poached salmon dumplings with lobster truffle sauce and fillets of red snapper with Noilly Prat sauce and red caviar – at the Feringgi Grill in the Rasa Sayang Hotel. It was a brief two day rest. We got the visa with little trouble as it happened, and returned to the bustle of Bangkok and the kitchen routine.

Despite having all outlets open, many banquets running, and the pool deck full every day, the hotel was not doing as well as expected. Business was not picking up. Marketing was expanded, menus were changed, and room rates modified, but all to no avail. Finally, Buddhist monks were consulted. They visited the hotel and after an extensive tour of the property determined that the spirit house was in the wrong location and that was the reason our business was not thriving.

Many private houses and businesses in Thailand have a spirit house. This is a miniature house often with elaborate decorations and provides shelter for the spirit of the place. Its location is paramount to the success and happiness of tenants and is determined by consulting with Buddhist monks. Employees make offerings to the spirit house on their way to and from work. Garlands are often hung on it and some people light incense and pray to the spirit. I remember one day seeing a roasted pig's head left as an offering. I often admired this little house and how the employees and locals approached it – with great reverence – to offer their respects and perhaps ask a request. The hotel's spirit house was located near the front entrance and now had to be moved. I learned that a spirit house's positioning must not allow the shadow of the hotel building to fall on it. During an elaborate predawn ceremony with monks in saffron colored robes leading the way, the house was moved to a better location and as predicted, business improved, room occupancy increased, the outlets began to thrive, and it did wonders for the employees morale – the spirits were appeased!

It was at the Royal Orchid that – as a chef – I had my first encounter with the press. As the Captain Bush grill room was the first fine dining room to open in a major city hotel in the past ten years, it automatically attracted food writers and food critics. I counted on the Maître to know when a food writer or critic came in so we could accommodate them – after all he knew the local scene better than me. But sometimes, for a variety of reasons, that was not possible. Now that the restaurant was getting busier, food reviews were expected. *Living in Thailand* was a widely published magazine in the city and contacted us to do a feature on the Captain Bush restaurant – they had already eaten from the menu and made their review.

Now they wanted pictures and to speak with the chef. This was my first restaurant review, I was very nervous. The reporter and cameraman came to the restaurant early in the morning. The reporter chatted as I prepared dishes for the camera. He wanted descriptions of each dish, particularly the ones the reviewers tasted on their clandestine visit because the Maître had not recognized them: Roast rack of lamb, crayfish tails with broccoli mousse, breast of pigeon salad and the supreme of red snapper with watercress vermouth sauce. Manfred prepared a dessert trolley and a selection of his wonderful breads, and of course the much sought after Captain Bush chocolate cake.

When the review came out it was very positive. The restaurant décor was very well described; the flavors and food presentation were equally descriptive as was the predominantly French wine list, and the article even mentioned that the 'affable' chef was Irish from County Mayo. In addition, there was a two-page picture spread of the restaurant with all the dishes mentioned in the review presented on a table in the foreground, as well as Manfred's dessert trolley – with me standing in the center wearing my hat. Everyone in the food and beverage department was overjoyed for us to get such recognition. Herbert was happy; Manfred wanted a picture and I bought copies of the magazine for all the kitchen staff. The long hours paid off. Needless to say the restaurant became even busier after the review was published.

The Portuguese Embassy was located next to the hotel set amid its own gardens which led down to the river's edge. The Portuguese ambassador came to the grill room quite often. He would ask to see me and insisted we spoke French, regardless of anyone at his table. He was a gourmet – the man just loved good food and wine. One day he called from the Embassy to speak with me. The call came to Herbert's office and the ambassador asked to speak with the chef. Herbert responded that he is the chef. The ambassador said, "No, I want to speak with the Irish chef. He is the only one who can prepare my sturgeon at the embassy." Herbert handed me the phone saying, "It looks like you got a promotion!" I was embarrassed to say the least.

In any case, the ambassador asked me to come over to the embassy and prepare a platter of smoked sturgeon that he had received from a friend. In his opinion I was the only one who could do this properly. I had first learned to slice smoked salmon in The Great Southern Hotel in County Donegal many years before and I did the same for the ambassador – the slices of sturgeon were so thin that the plate was visible through it. Smoked fish – as with all cured meats and fish – release flavor best when sliced paper thin. He stayed with me in his kitchen chatting incessantly as I carved. The servants looked on in amusement at seeing a 'Farang' – foreigner – cooking in their kitchen with their boss. Farangs were normally guests at the Embassy – only servants worked in the kitchen. The ambassador was delighted to speak French and afterwards invited me to his study and poured glasses of port for both of us. He was a great conversationalist, and we chatted on several topics as we admired the great river – a veritable city artery – flowing by. Upon my return to the Captain Bush kitchen I apologized to Herbert lest he think I was promoting myself to a higher position. He laughed and said, "Forget about it, buy me a beer tonight."

Every time the Ambassador came back to the grillroom he would keep telling his guests about the Irish chef who spoke French and could slice smoked Sturgeon so thin that it melted on the tongue. He regularly ordered the baked crabmeat with chili and chives. To make this, I sautéed some crabmeat in butter with finely chopped garlic and freshly chopped chili, flamed it with Cognac and added some breadcrumbs and chives. Then the mixture was filled into a cleaned crab shell, coated with Hollandaise sauce and gratinated. The ambassador loved it. Later when he met Christine and found out she spoke French, he invited her to lunch once every month to the Embassy so he could practice his French.

We had a few visiting chefs during my stay at the Royal Orchid. Most were European. This was a common occurrence in Asia to attract business while providing authentic dishes. Guenther arrived from Vienna with his wife for a two week Austrian promotion. She was the hostess in the restaurant, spoke with the guests and explained the menu and their cultural heritage. Guenther was the chef and prepared dishes such as Tyrolean Ham with creamy horseradish, vegetable strudel, pork fillet with beer mousse and the famous Tafelspitz. Desserts included the popular pancakes with apricot cream and Kaiserschmarrn with stewed plums, very similar to the one Josef taught me to make at the Hotel du Bateau in Morat years previously. These two-week promotions usually placed six months apart were highly anticipated by the regular customers and allowed them also to meet new chefs and taste different dishes. When we had a visiting chef I remained in the kitchen to ensure they got all the help they required and let them go to each table after the meal.

The renowned English chef Prue Leith of London sponsored a two week food festival at the grill room and promoted her restaurant and catering business. She sent one of her sous chefs, who was a delight to work with, and I learned so much from him. Like Guenther he brought many ingredients with him and supervised every step of the preparation, presentation and managed public relations, press and internal promotions with ease. He prepared dishes such as potted shrimp with walnut salad, lambs tongue with watercress sauce, beef wellington with port sauce and scalloped potatoes with cream. Desserts like blackcurrant fool, hazelnut meringue cake, and brown bread ice cream with caramel sauce were extremely popular. Manfred helped him to make all of these with his pastry crew. We had a great two weeks in the kitchen. He met many of the regular guests and was featured in the press. Before he left he presented me with a copy of Ms. Leith's book *The Best of Prue Leith*.

Where to Eat, a dining and entertainment guide for the city, did a review on the restaurant. The guide featured us as 'The restaurant of the Month,' with me on the cover page next to the picture of the Captain and a selection of dishes with Manfred's chocolate cake in the center. It was a very positive four page review of all aspects of the food, wine, and service punctuated with color pictures of the 'luxurious' restaurant. After extensive descriptions of food and flavors – among which they highlighted the Beluga Malossol Caviar and its spectacular presentation on individual ice sculptures illuminated from underneath, the following paragraph appeared at the end which I found amusing as it highlighted my constant struggle as an Irish chef for recognition outside the mainstream nationalities common to the profession.

> *"And who is our Captain Bush Grill chef? A globetrotting Frenchman? Austrian? German or Swiss? Why no other than another good looking 29 year old expatriate bachelor master chef in Bangkok, this one from Ireland. Brendan Cronin who is cooking up quite a reputation for himself for his antics in the kitchen (correction: master-pieces in the Grill room.) Befittingly, in our illustrious chef's honor, we ordered Irish coffee (amidst choices of Darjeeling, Ceylon or Earl Grey teas); Espresso or Café Brulot. It was the perfect crowning of a brilliant meal; Brendan's art is a tribute to the Grill's namesake sailor-harbor master, Captain Bush."*

It was time again to renew Christine's three month tourist visa. We decided to take a longer trip, visit Malaysia and Singapore and get the visa at the Thai Embassy there. Since arriving in Bangkok, I had heard so many great things about Singapore and how different it was to Bangkok and even other Asian cities. The train journey to

Singapore took seventy two hours and we had a cabin to ourselves. To break the journey we stayed two days in Kuala Lumpur – the capital of Malaysia. This was our first visit – other than the two days in Penang – to a Muslim country. This only became evident on the second morning at the train's breakfast table when the waiter mentioned that they did not have bacon or sausages. During breakfast the previous day we had bacon, eggs, sausages, tea, toast, and coffee as the train was still traveling in Thailand and now on the second day there was no bacon because we had crossed the border during the night while we slept.

We fell in love with Singapore at first sight. There were so many similarities to Switzerland. It was clean, organized, and safe to walk around at any time of the day or night. A bonus was the tropical climate and its proximity to the ocean. We visited Arab Street, a narrow street jam-packed with every type of vendor and a magnet and must see area for tourists. One of the highlights of our trip was a meal at the Movenpick restaurant. Movenpick operated many of the highway restaurants in Switzerland so I was familiar with their concept and food selection. We ordered Swiss wines, Quiche Lorraine, and the popular Swiss dish 'Emincé de Veau' – shredded veal with mushroom in a cream sauce served with rösti. Christine enjoyed the meal so much that she felt she was back in Switzerland – transported by her food memories. Movenpick is world famous for its ice cream and we made sure to round off our meal with generous helpings of their Caramelita flavor. We realized how much we missed Swiss food as it was not that prevalent in Bangkok.

We returned to Thailand by bus via the east coast of Malaysia. This was the first time I saw a television in a bus. It was located at the front and angled so the driver could also watch. After all he was also on the bus. So for the entire trip we watched the driver as he moved his eyes back and forth between the road and the television. Programs were in Malay so we did not understand. We were just worried the driver would forget to occasionally move his eyes back to the road. Our first stop was Kuantan, and there was a beautiful Hyatt hotel with its own beach, cobalt blue swimming pool, two restaurants, a bar and a rack rate that was far above our budget. Though I was working in luxury hotels, it did not mean I could afford to stay in them – a common phenomenon for many hotel employees. Directly across the road from the Hyatt was a locally run hotel with about ten rooms and we asked to see one. It was simple, clean and the price was right despite the fact that it had an air conditioner in the window which emitted decibels louder than a small jumbo jet. We had a wonderful meal of satay with peanut sauce and white rice from a street vendor and managed to find a beer. The relish served with the satay was a combination of sliced shallots, cucumber and red chili marinated in vinegar with a little sugar. The sweet sour taste combined with the peanut sauce added the final touch to a wonderful classical Asian dish. After dinner we plucked up our courage, walked across the street into the Hyatt, collected two towels from the pool terrace and had a wonderful swim. Attendants naturally thought these two white tourists must be hotel guests and greeted us warmly. After our swim, we thanked them and walked back to our little hotel.

The next morning we were woken by a tapping on our window. As we were on the second floor I assumed it was a bird, but lo and behold it was a little monkey swinging on a tree branch. He did not move away as I approached and thought what a great natural wakeup call system this is. He stayed at the window until we checked out – maybe he was on staff?

We continued our trip north to Kota Baru, a town famous for Malaysian Batik – hand dyed cotton fabric. We stayed at a small hotel in the town center and spent our time in the markets selecting Batik of which we bought enough to open a shop in Bangkok. The predawn Islamic call to prayer greeted us on our last day in Malaysia. The loud speakers on the nearby minaret blared out the muezzin's message as throngs of people filled the streets on their walk to the mosque. We took an early morning taxi to Sungai Golok, a remote border crossing town on the Malay Thai border and from there took the train to Had Yai. At the border crossing we had to explain to the guard that Christine's passport was a real one for he had never seen a Swiss passport before. For a while he refused to believe it was actually a travel document. With its bright red with a white cross, it is often mistaken for the Red Cross. As we talked, hundreds of people were just crossing into Thailand without showing any documents. Some were on foot, some on motorcycles laden with basket of vegetables, some were herding animals along, and some with heavy baskets balanced on a bamboo pole resting across their shoulders, yet Christine's passport was of great interest to him. With my few words of Thai I managed to convince him it was actually a real passport. Then when he asked for mine, he just glanced at it, nodded, looked at me as he handed it back, as if to say, "Ah! Of course, an Irish passport, I see these here all the time. You'd be surprised how many Irish people cross this border every morning at five o'clock. Fire away Brendan, good lad, and have a great trip!"

From Had Yai we flew to Phuket and I brought Christine to see Patong beach. I was disappointed; it had changed enormously since my first visit. Real estate developers had finally discovered Phuket and construction had increased. Building sites were everywhere. It was amazing to see the changes that took place in just over one year. There were new hotels, and it was more expensive. At the airport, construction was also underway to lengthen the runaway which would allow jumbo jets from Europe to land, thus avoiding the current stopover in Bangkok. "Beach attendants" now charged for the deck chairs and umbrellas. There were many German restaurants serving typical German fare. It seemed strange to be eating such heavy food in the tropical heat, yet many tourists wanted their favorite food when they traveled half way round the world. So schnitzel with potato salad and Black Forest cake were served en masse with larger steins of beer. I preferred the Larb Gai and a helping of mango with sticky rice.

Larb Gai is a spicy chicken salad. It is made with ground raw chicken which is then sautéed and seasoned with lime juice, salt and pepper, sliced shallots, Thai chili and Thai parsley. Much like the Yam Nua, it is served with slices of cucumber and tomatoes which cool the palate. By now Christine was used to spicy food and actually could eat spicier than me. So when the waiter asked if she liked tourist spicy or local spicy, she ordered the latter. For dessert we ordered mango and sticky rice which is a popular dessert in Thailand. It is made using special glutinous rice which becomes very sticky when cooked. Combined with coconut milk and palm sugar and served with slices – or cubes – of ripe mango, it is a delight to eat. Later that evening Christine's lips erupted in blisters as if she had touched a hot iron. It seems the food in the south of the country was spicier than in Bangkok – or maybe the chef was heavier handed with the chili. I found out it was not the latter. Our ten day trip was coming to an end; we had discovered beautiful parts of South East Asia, many of which were off the beaten track, met wonderful people and tasted delicious foods along the way. The next day we bid farewell to Phuket's golden beaches, flew to Bangkok and I got back to work as I had a VIP reservation coming up in the Grillroom.

The Confrérie de la Chaîne des Rôtisseurs, an international gastronomic society, reserved the private room for a special dinner. I was familiar with this society as Jean Pierre initiated my membership while I was in Togo. I had since then let my membership lapse. This was a very important banquet for the hotel and the restaurant was also open for regular guests so Herbert and Manfred came to help out. We served the following menu.

Marinated salmon trout with coriander and Sherry flavored ratatouille

Consommé and watercress cream soup in demi-tasse

Cassoulet of veal sweetbread and prawns

Tamarind sherbet

Breast of duckling with cherries and cinnamon sabayon

Belgian Endives with truffle vinaigrette

Baked Chauvignole cheese in puff pastry

Rendez-vous of fresh fruit with clove ice cream and champagne
sauce

Espresso
Assorted chocolate truffles

Wines
Apperitif – Kir Royal
Pouilly Fuisse 1979
Chateauneuf-du-Pape 1979
Champagne Lanson Black Label

Martel Cordon Bleu
or
Napoleon Mandarine Liqueur

This menu demanded the utmost attention as all guests had an extensive background in food and wine. The banquet was a success – even though it took hours to prepare, which was a given. Despite the long hours, a chef's ultimate gratification is to know the guest is satisfied with the food, wine and service – whatever it takes. I am no different.

Shortly after this dinner we had the Mandarin Oriental's Food and Beverage Managers Seminar. This was an annual seminar for all Food and Beverage managers in the group so managers from Mandarin Oriental Hotels around the world were staying at the hotel. On the last day of the seminar they would have their gala dinner in the Grillroom. Cooking for such a distinguished group was a daunting task. With Herbert – who knew many of the managers – we wrote the menu and we cooked it together with the Grillroom kitchen staff. The following menu was engraved on a metal plaque for each guest to take home as a souvenir.

Home cured duck breast with marinated fruits

Consommé and watercress cream soup in
demi tasse

Grilled scallops with green asparagus and Port-flavored truffle
essence

Pink champagne granite

Panfried lamb "noisettes" with garlic cloves
Potato and zucchini tart
Timbale of pureed vegetables

Cheese platter with fig puree

Tamarind frozen parfait with honey glazed cherries
and three chocolate flavored mousse

Blue Mountain coffee
Darjeeling
Chocolate coated confied fruits

When we wrote the menu, I thought it was unusual to have garlic cloves as a garnish. After cutting them in half, Herbert showed me how to remove and discard the center stem inside each clove. Then he blanched the cloves in milk and caramelized them in butter to serve with the lamb. He said, "Now the guest will not have a strong smell of garlic off their breath." The milk absorbs much of the flavor. Manfred baked a selection of European breads and the pantry girls made dishes of butter roses for each table. These were made by first whipping the butter to a light consistency. Then using a piping bag with a specially fitted piping nozzle, the butter was piped in the shape of a rose onto a tooth pick and left to set in ice water. Once cold, the tooth pick was easily removed. The roses were served in chilled silver butter dishes decorated with a fresh pink orchid – guests marveled at the artistic flair of the presentation. After the meal the managers were given a tour of the kitchen and I met many of them. They were extremely pleased with the meal, and I was grateful to Herbert and Manfred for helping me. It was important that as the newest Mandarin Oriental Hotel we offered a high quality event – we were under scrutiny. These managers would return to their respective hotels in Hong Kong, Manila, Jakarta, Macau, and many other locations, and during their morning operations meeting would describe the quality of their stay, so this was our opportunity to send a message that the newest hotel in the group could hold its own – and we did.

We had a large convention for IBM which dominated most of the banquet space and reserved many guest rooms for four days. On the final evening we created a market style event on the terraces by the river. We selected some street vendors to set up their stalls and cook authentic dishes a la minute. Guests strolled from vendor to vendor, literally tasting the foods of Bangkok. There were dishes such as Rock lobster, Tiger prawns, white snapper, and fried noodles with pork, chicken or seafood. Also offered were tenderloin steaks, satays, grilled squid, fried rice and many desserts and ice cream.

Our pantry girls set up fruit carving stations on raised bamboo platforms. Dressed in elaborately woven traditional silk Thai dresses, they sat amid piles of beautifully arranged fruit, their legs folded behind them in elegant fashion. Using small razor sharp fruit knives they carved intricate designs in papaya, water melon, mangos, and opened rambutans, and jackfruit. They also arranged segments of the revered and despised Durian fruit. This fruit is perceived in much the same way as French red-smear cheese such as a Munster or a Livarot – you have to get past the strong aroma to experience the incredible flavor. There was an elephant at the end of the terrace, its Mahout proudly explaining to guests the great importance of the elephant's role in Thai culture. Then there was the monkey show with a few very small monkeys dancing as their master guided them along. Seen from the upper level terrace this 'street scene' was a fair duplication of the real thing found on many of the city streets. The guests loved it.

During my afternoon breaks, I would often take the ferry down river to the Oriental Hotel with Christine and have afternoon tea in the authors' lounge. This was one of the most historic hotel outlets in Bangkok. Earl Gray and Darjeeling teas were served with cucumber sandwiches on fine china as we sat on white rattan furniture admiring the history of famous writers such as Joseph Conrad and Ernest Hemingway who stayed and wrote there in times past. I knew the Executive Chef at the Oriental; he was of Italian background, a long time resident of Thailand and highly respected by every chef in the city. He had been at the helm of the Oriental kitchen for many years and spoke, read, and wrote fluent Thai – a terrific accomplishment in my eyes. I would leave our table and pop in to the kitchen for a few minutes to say hello, he was always happy to see me. A visit to Bangkok for any chef was not complete without a visit to his office, an espresso, and a chat.

I also knew the Executive Sous Chef at the Oriental and met him many times on such visits. He often came for dinner to the Grill room with his girl friend. A tall blond haired man with a pleasant smile, he was also well respected by all the entire kitchen staff at the Oriental. On one of our afternoon visits to the authors' lounge, he joined us at our table for afternoon tea. It was there he told me that after many years at the Oriental he was planning to join a new opening team for a hotel in Singapore. What he said next took me completely by surprise and influenced my relationship with Christine. He asked if I was interested to be on the team with him and lead the opening of the signature restaurant at this new hotel. This was astonishing news. Here I was having afternoon tea with my girlfriend in one of the most famous hotels in the world, surrounded by the history of writing geniuses who left major legacies to the literary world, and this chef – whom I knew for only just over a year – was offering me an extraordinary opportunity in Singapore. Like me, Christine was speechless; we just looked at each other. He mentioned that the hotel was still under construction and the position would be available in about a year. I was ecstatic because that coincided with the end of my contract at the Royal Orchid.

This news and offer of a three year contract in Singapore made us both think about our relationship and where it would lead. Staying in South East Asia for another four years required that we think about our living arrangement. It was only a matter of time until the Thai Embassy would refuse Christine another sequential tourist visa. There was a simple solution: we both agreed we should get married. Christine would then be automatically included on my work visa and could stay in Thailand as long as I did. It wasn't a formal request for marriage; we just both thought of it at the same time and came to the conclusion that it would be a sensible solution allowing us to remain together.

The next day we went to see the personnel manager, Khun Prasert, to get his advice about where we could get married in Bangkok. He said, "I can bring you to the registry and will act as your translator." We thought this was perfect. "But," he added, "for a 'small fee' the registry could come to the hotel and marry you there." This was even better. We asked him to arrange it. The hotel marketing manager – a former British Hong Kong policeman – agreed to be our witness and we were married two months later in our apartment on the seventh floor of the hotel overlooking the graceful Chao Prya River. Christine had a beautiful low-waist, nineteen twenties 'flapper' style silk dress made for the wedding and I had a suit tailored – both were ready in about a week with only one fitting. We bought bunches of pink orchids in the market place and ordered Champagne from room service. Three 'officials' came from the registry and Khun Prasert translated. We greeted them with the traditional 'wai' – both hands with palms together and raised to the face while bowing slightly. The higher they are raised the more senior the greeting. When all signatures were complete each official received their plain white envelopes – containing the 'small fee' – and left. We celebrated with Champagne and went to dinner at the Dusit Thani hotel.

Afterwards we went to the Toby Jug pub – and told all the chefs we knew there. Even the dancing girls were happy for us and brought Christine flowers for her hair and orchid leis for me. A few weeks later we received our official marriage license. It was written in Thai and signed in the year 2527 of the Buddhist calendar – it looked like we had gotten married five hundred and forty three years in the future as it was 1984 in the Gregorian calendar. We had it translated to English at the Swiss embassy before we could understand it, but the year remained the same – George Orwell would have been very confused. We sent a copy to my mother and Christine's parents, and promised them a wedding in Europe.

We decided to get married in the small church in Les Diablerets. Christine began the preparations for the wedding many months in advance. Paul and Eliane would manage the details for us and we would arrive from Bangkok two days before the wedding. The dinner would be held at the Eurotel. I wrote to Klaus and told him we wanted the 'country buffet' with the smoked ham in brioche. We left the details to him. Paul arranged a local Swiss folk band and I provided an Irish band from Dublin through a contact with Brian Scanlon. Mike from Neuchatel agreed to be the best man. Finally, months later, all the details were covered and we arrived in Switzerland with flowers for the entire wedding – pink and white orchids, which Christine had pre-ordered from the girl she bought her weekly flowers from in the street market.

Mam and Fred came over for the wedding. John was working on an oil platform in the North Sea and could not get the time off. Louis was on the Fastnet Rock Lighthouse off the coast of County Cork and could also not get away. Mike was the perfect best man and Brian offered to play the fiddle in the church. He played 'The Coolin' – a beautiful Irish ballad that made even the Swiss cry. Outside the church, Christine's cousins played the alphorn and younger ones rang cow bells. The Swiss have a nice tradition at weddings; they don't necessarily invite all guests to the dinner. Instead an invitation to a type of short cocktail reception immediately following the ceremony would be extended to everyone in the church. Then the immediate family and a 'few friends' get invited to the dinner. We did the same.

When we arrived at the Eurotel it was obvious that Klaus and Anne had not disappointed. They had done a spectacular job. The dining room where I had cooked so many meals in times past was now set up and beautifully decorated just for us. We were the guests today. The buffet was wonderful; platters of air dried meats, Gruyere from the local cheese maker, poached whole salmon with lime mousseline, and a selection of bread that would feed a battalion, hot fish and meat dishes in silver chafing dishes, the famous ham in brioche and of course, a selection of desserts that went on forever. The Swiss and Irish musicians were already playing. Then the wine began to flow.

Mam sat beside me at the head table and enjoyed herself, even dancing with me later in the evening. Fred also sat with us and enjoyed himself despite the language difference, although many people spoke English. Mike read out all the telegrams and gave a speech, jokingly highlighting my 'wild lifestyle' before I met Christine. Brian played the fiddle with the Irish band and the evening progressed very well. Normally weddings like this would fizzle out around midnight as the Swiss were not great late night partiers, unlike the Irish who would sail through the night. I anticipated this and asked Klaus to bring out the box of 'tongue looseners'. I had delivered this to him the previous day and asked him to wait for my signal before serving it. After the coffee was served, I opened the box and put a bottle of Irish whiskey with new glasses on each table giving precise instructions on how to drink it. Such instructions if given in Ireland would indeed be an insult, but the Swiss – and many other nationalities – had a nasty habit of putting ice – and water – in this most precious and respectful beverage, which changed the taste. It actually eliminated the dusky taste of the wonderful Irish whiskey, and in my mind is an insult to the great distillers who craft this majestic beverage. If Irish whiskey was meant to be served with ice, Ireland would probably be located in Scandinavia. I wanted each one to appreciate the delicate nature of one of our national beverages. I even had bottles of Irish Mist and Baileys Irish Cream for Christine's older aunts, the latter beverage however does support the use of ice quite well.

The tongue looseners worked exceptionally well. Due to the triple distillation Irish whiskey is very smooth, so one could be forgiven for drinking 'another one'. Seeing the popularity of the whiskey – it was disappearing fast as the smoothness caught most people by surprise – and happy to see a familiar drink, my mother took the bottle of 'Paddy' whiskey from her table and put it on the floor by the leg of her chair, lest it be 'accidently removed' from our table. As Christine and I went around the table chatting with guests, they all remarked how smooth Irish whiskey was and that it tasted '*incroyable*' and definitely merited '*un deuxieme verre.*' This second glass propelled the wedding into the early hours. It was gratifying to see everyone still enjoying themselves at two o'clock in the morning and not showing any signs of preparing to go home. At one stage Mam came up to me with distressing news – the bottle of whiskey by her chair leg had disappeared! She couldn't believe it. I told her with a laugh, "The Swiss don't steal; it must have been a foreigner." As the late night turned into early morning, she left with Paul and Eliane at half past five and we tried to get a few hours sleep but to no avail. The 'wedding' continued in our hotel room with Christine's cousins, Fred, and Mike and his wife until breakfast time. Everyone agreed it was 'a great night.'

We went to Ireland for our honeymoon. We stayed at home for a few days and visited family and friends. Everyone wanted to celebrate our wedding and as is tradition, a whiskey toast was offered in every house we visited. I brought Christine to Jim's house to introduce her. Jim was retired now, living in his whitewashed thatched cottage by the shore. Sitting by his fireside he could see the waves through the open door as they gently caressed the rocks just a few yards away. He worked on our farm for many years when I was young; each morning he would bring us a roll of mints before beginning his days work. We talked about the days when he brought his horse to our farm and he would let me hold the reins to guide the horse. At the time I thought this was the bee's knees as I could get the horse to move to the left or right –

like my father did years earlier with Charlie. Jim's admiration for the Boss was evident in his voice as he said: "Yer father was a great man!" We also talked about our travels and living in Bangkok or 'somewhere out foreign' as he referred to it. Any country other than the traditional Irish immigrant destinations such as England, Scotland, Australia or America was usually referred as 'somewhere out foreign'. And no rural encounter would be complete without reference to that great topic of Irish conversation – the weather, which we discussed at length. We have so many different types of rain in Ireland that we invented adjectives for them. There was 'lashin' rain', 'teemin' rain', and 'soft rain'. The common dominator was they were all wet. When I told Jim we were married he congratulated us, called his nephew over and said, "Pat, go to the field and dig 'half-a-stone' (about three kilos) of Kerr's Pinks for Brendan and his lady." Kerr's Pinks are one of the most popular potato varieties in Ireland. We left with a bag of these beautiful potatoes as his wedding gift to us. I had a tear in my eye driving away because Jim was a man of simple means and he gave us whatever he had. Planted and cared for by him, the gift of potatoes came from the heart. It was one of the most moving wedding presents we received. Christine was so touched by that gesture.

We bid farewell to my mother and drove for a few days through Connemara, Galway and into the town of Athenry. I brought Christine to see my old school, now all closed up. I went to the Principals house to say hello and he recognized me the minute he opened the door and invited us in for tea and biscuits. "You're the lad from Belmullet," he said. He was retired now and spent his time gardening and working the odd day in Galway during final exams at the brand new Regional Technical School there. We continued our journey down through the Burren in County Clare leading into Limerick city, the Dingle peninsula in County Kerry and on into County Cork. The country side was very different to that of County Mayo where I grew up. We ate in some wonderful restaurants along the way, ending our honeymoon with a great evening in a hotel in the town of Skull where a group of traditional Irish music players were performing well into the night. They were terrific. We chose this part of the country for our honeymoon because we had considered opening a restaurant in this touristic region of Ireland for the summer months and then spending the winter seasons at a ski resort in Switzerland. This was a project we had both talked about that could become a reality sometime in the future. But after a few days traveling in the southwest, we abandoned the idea when I noticed that every nice restaurant we ate in – despite the fresh, local tasty food, and excellent wines (Irish cooking had evolved tremendously since the seventies when I left Ireland) – was only partially occupied. I believed that kind of client traffic would not support a business, especially for a few short months in the summer and so we returned to Thailand.

Almost a year after our wedding my contract at the Royal Orchid was coming to an end. It was time to begin planning our move to Singapore. I had called the chef there many times: construction delays were a big problem and my contract was delayed a few times. But now he assured me I could start so I informed the management at the Royal Orchid of my departure and planned our move. We would fly to Hong Kong for a few days, fly to Europe to see my new parents-in-law, spend a few days in Ireland with my mother and then move to Singapore. Everything was lined up perfectly when I got a call from the chef in Singapore that upset all our plans. He called to ask if I could delay my start for another six months. This was a major disappointment. Now I had no work, there were two of us, and we were thousands of miles from home. How was I to know if the position would still be available in six months time? The chef insisted the position was mine if I could delay my start so I agreed, and began to think about where I could find work for six months. Asia would be difficult as many employers would not apply for a visa for such a short time. Contracts were usually two to three years duration at a minimum. I could call Klaus to see if he needed a chef and we could move to Switzerland for the winter season. All these thoughts went through our minds. In the end we decided to travel to Europe via Hong Kong as we already had the plane tickets.

In Hong Kong we stayed with the Mandarin Oriental group engineer. I had met him several times because he often ate in the grill room on visits to Bangkok. He showed us a little of the city and invited us to his private club for dinner – a prestigious club which he told us had a long waiting list for membership. Over dinner I told him of my plan to move to Singapore and how I was now six months without work. "You might just be in luck," he said. "The Mandarin Oriental Hotel in Macau is looking for a sous chef for a few months for the Chinese New Year. Why don't you call them tomorrow?" When I called, the resident manager asked me to come over for an interview.

Macau is about a one-hour journey from Hong Kong on the high speed Hydrofoil ferry.

At the concierge's desk I asked for the manager, and told them I had an appointment. The assistant concierge gestured to the elevators and led me to the executive offices. I recognized the manager straight away. He had been in the grill room at the food and beverage managers' seminar in Bangkok the year before. He did not remember me but that did not matter. Once I described my involvement in the gala dinner for the seminar and that I had worked for Mandarin Oriental Hotels for three years, he offered me the position until my contract for Singapore arrived. He agreed to let me start in two weeks and introduced me to the Executive chef Andi, a Swiss German from Basel. Andi gave me a folder of menus to study and said, "I'll see you in two weeks." I was thrilled to have found this job, to experience living in Macau and perhaps visit China and all because of a comment made during dinner at the club in Hong Kong – it was networking at its best.

We took one of the first non-stop flights from Hong Kong to London and thought the plane would never land; I had never taken such a long flight. Up until now flying between Asia and Europe involved one stop either in Dubai or New Delhi. When we arrived in London I realized it was my first time in England. As London was a common first destination for many Irish on their journey abroad, I remember thinking I must have been the only Irishman who had not been to England before travelling elsewhere.

We met my Uncle, Father Brendan O'Malley, and went to his favorite Italian restaurant in Piccadilly Circus. It was Christmas time, the streets were lit up, and shop windows were brightly decorated enticing holiday shoppers inside. As we entered the restaurant the Maître came over, immediately addressing my uncle in Italian: "Buon giorno Padre," a table for three? My uncle responded in fluent Italian confirming that we were indeed three for dinner and they talked as the Maître guided us to a table. Father Brendan was happy to speak French with us and we had one of those long Italian meals that are full of life, laughs, and recollections – and some food and wine. He told us the details of how he was nearly captured by rebels during his time with the missions in Africa. During the meal the Maitre periodically came by to see how 'Padre's' meal was progressing. "Va bene, grazie," Father Brendan would answer in Italian, then revert back to French without missing a beat. His descriptions of Africa made me realize that my stay there was a walk in the park compared to the hardships and risks he was exposed to. No wonder my grandmother asked him not to return there.

Grilled Thai Beef Salad
(Yam Nua)

TJ, the sous chef of the coffee shop in Bangkok, showed me how to make this dish. It was very popular.

Ingredients for 4 people
14 oz. (400gr.) sirloin steak tips (or tenderloin)
2 oz. (60gr.) thinly sliced shallots
Juice of 2 limes
2 cloves of freshly chopped garlic
2 teaspoons Thai red chili peppers sliced very thin diagonally
1 cucumber sliced
Two medium tomatoes sliced
10- 12 sprigs of cilantro with the stems removed
3 teaspoons Thai fish sauce (Nam Pla)
1 head of romaine or Boston lettuce (butter head lettuce)
Salt and pepper mill to taste.

Procedure
- Mix the shallots, lime juice, chili, fish sauce and a quarter of the cucumber slices in a bowl.
- Season steaks, rub with garlic and grill to medium rare.
- Slice the meat into thin strips, add to the bowl and mix thoroughly
- Add in ¾ of the cilantro.

Service
- Arrange a few leaves of lettuce on a plate. Place marinated beef in the center.
- Decorate around the edge with thin slices of tomato and cucumber. Sprinkle the remaining cilantro on top.

Tips
- Taste the spicy beef and then let the slices of cucumber and tomatoes cool the mouth before continuing.
- Some chefs prefer to sprinkle toasted sesame seeds on top for added texture.
- Instead of wine, beer tends to be a great accompaniment to this classic Thai dish.

CHAPTER ELEVEN

Peking Duck or African Chicken

I stayed one night at the Mandarin Oriental in Hong Kong on my way back from Switzerland to Macau. Christine remained in Switzerland until I got settled at work. Even though the receptionist knew I was an employee, I still received the same service as a guest. The card – in beautiful handwriting – on the bedside table, from the general manager of the Mandarin Oriental Hotel in Hong Kong read, "Mr. Cronin, welcome to the Mandarin." It was amazing to experience this historic luxury hotel from a guest's perspective. The view from my window of this world famous harbor looking across towards Kowloon was grandiose. Large ships, tiny sampans and the odd Chinese junk in full sail all vying for space in the choppy waters. Gone was the small fishing village of a hundred years ago, transformed over decades by Britain into a thriving economy. And now – after a ninety nine year lease from China – Britain would return Hong Kong Island to China in 1997, just twelve short years away. With this spectacular view still emblazoned in my mind, I left my room to visit the kitchen and meet the chef.

Even as I walked through the back service corridors, the evidence of a five star hotel was everywhere. Silver trays for service, racks of crystal glasses, polished silver wine buckets, beautiful china and tables adorned with exotic fruit baskets were ready for room service. Waiters in immaculate uniforms and chefs wearing perfectly starched hats were moving like ants in a parade of efficiency, and all because of one person – the guest. Despite language and cultural differences, employees at five star hotels around the world have the ability to make every guest feel as if they are the only one at the property – and the only one who counts.

I found the chef's office and introduced myself. Jurg, a highly talented chef, had been at the Mandarin for a few years and oversaw one of the most sought after French restaurants in Hong Kong, the Pierrot. I had heard of Jurg from many chefs in Bangkok as they praised him and the Pierrot, the height of French dining in the city offering dishes such as crayfish and fresh asparagus in filo pastry with lemon butter sauce, nettle cream soup with chicken quenelles, Ballotine of Bresse chicken with sweetbreads, truffled noodles with lobster béarnaise, and souffléed fresh fruit tartlet with raspberries and passion fruit coulis. Service was impeccable and the wine list extensive. A meal at the Pierrot was an unforgettable experience. I was able to taste some of these dishes at chef's table. Jurg had a large office with a chef's table constantly set for six people so I had dinner there as he went about his evening's work. Jurg would fly to France once or twice a year and dine in several 3 star Michelin restaurants, visit some chateaux to taste the latest vintages, then return – armed with fresh knowledge – to prepare the new menu for the Pierrot reflecting the latest trends from Europe. He gave me a great deal of advice for working in Macau with Hong Kong Chinese, Macanese, and mainland Chinese staff as the mentality of each group was very different.

The next morning I took the high speed ferry to Macau, a Portuguese colony linked to mainland China which was also set to be returned to China – in 1999. Despite colonization, Macau was decades behind Hong Kong in its development. There was no airport and very few hotels, but in contrast to Hong Kong it had a thriving casino industry and still does. The Mandarin Oriental Macau was located near the ferry terminal so when we docked, it was within walking distance. As the doorman took my luggage and ushered me through the open door, I saw an expansive hotel lobby resembling a sea of Italian marble punctuated with rugs and sitting areas decorated with spectacular flower arrangements – it was impressive. A wide red carpeted stairs led to a Chinese restaurant on the second floor where I could see a smiling hostess on the mezzanine wearing a red silk ankle-length Qipao (pronounced 'Chipao'), greeting guests for lunch. With every step, this classic split seam dress revealed discreet glimpses of her leg up to mid-thigh – an impressive fashion statement blended into her uniform which added to the elegance and mystery of the Far East. The receptionist gave me the key to a guest room with a balcony and a captivating view of the Pearl River delta flowing into the South China Sea, the gray river water creating artistic designs as it mixed with the blue ocean. This would be my accommodation for six months and I thought it to be a long way from the room in the cellar of the Schatzalp Hotel in Switzerland which I shared with Rolf for four months a few years earlier. Perhaps I had earned it?

Andi, the executive chef, was younger than me and very affable. He put me in charge of the Grillroom and I began to familiarize myself with the menu. There were a few other expatriates at the hotel: The General Manager was Swiss, the resident manager English, the sports director American, and Andi was Swiss. The Chinese New Year was approaching: the year of the Tiger. Andi explained that every year thousands of people traveled from Hong Kong to mainland China to celebrate with their families for a few days. Then they pass through Macau again on their way back home. This would be one of the busiest weeks of the year for the hotel, similar to the Macau Formula One Grand Prix week. The hotel outlets would be full all day; staff was on duty all week – there would be no day off.

Hotel operations began every morning with a meeting for all department heads. This was very useful as it helped everyone to keep in touch with events taking place throughout the hotel. The meeting took place in a board room in the business office suite. I attended on days when Andi was off. All department heads would be present and at exactly nine o'clock the General Manager – always impeccably dressed – came in through a side door directly from his office to start the meeting. He was never late. During the meeting, events of the day were discussed, VIP guests were identified, special requests were arranged and any problems were solved.

At one of these meetings the GM announced that Madonna would be staying at the hotel while shooting a film locally. Madonna requested privacy and discretion so a major part of subsequent meetings was set aside to discuss plans for her stay to ensure every department knew of her expectations and could plan accordingly. A few weeks later the singer arrived and settled into her suite. Madonna requested to use the staff entrance to avoid reporters and to use the service elevator to access her floor. These elevators were used only by employees to bring room service orders to the floors and for housekeeping to transport linen. There was a closed circuit camera in each one. The singer requested we take the camera out for privacy.

Having high profile guests in the hotel always attracted the press. There was hell to pay one morning during the operations meeting when the General Manager announced that a reporter who 'just happened' to be also a guest at the hotel snuck in to the sauna and began interviewing Madonna. Naturally the singer complained to the management. "This is unacceptable!" the General Manager bellowed at the meeting. We all got the message to step up and ensure the singer was not inconvenienced again. Later during her stay, she came to the Grillroom one evening for dinner. Once her main course was served, I went to her table to wish her 'Bon Appétit'. Madonna responded, "This is delicious!" and thanked me.

Chinese New Year celebrations are incredibly colorful and noisy. Fireworks and fire crackers are used everywhere – it is believed the noise frightens off evil spirits. I learned about the twelve year cycle and the Chinese zodiac signs named in honor of twelve animals. According to this cycle I was a horse and Christine a rat. Mr. Wong, the Chinese banquet chef, told me that in Chinese culture Christine and I would not be allowed to marry because a horse and a rat are incompatible. Marvelous, I thought. "Now you tell us, this could have serious implications on our relationship! Where were you when we needed marriage advice in Bangkok?" I remembered the pre-marriage counseling we were obliged to take in Bangkok with a Catholic priest. All he was worried about was if we would baptize our children. He never mentioned horses or rats.

I also believed the Chinese were more superstitious than the Irish. Many of their daily rituals were based on appeasing the spirits. This was evident when one day at chefs table we had a whole fish with oyster sauce and vegetables displayed on a large platter. As we sat down to eat, one of the Chinese sous chefs began to serve himself using his chopsticks, deftly removing the flesh from the back bone. Andi followed suit, and when it was my turn there was no flesh left on the top side of the fish so naturally I turned it over. Mr. Wong jumped, looking very surprised; he explained that it is a bad 'joss' – omen – to turn the fish and not good Chinese table etiquette. He told me turning the fish over is akin to the fisherman's boat being overturned the next time they go fishing. The correct way was to remove the fish bone using my chopsticks to access the delicious flesh underneath. And I thought we were bad in Ireland when it was assumed to be bad luck to walk under a ladder leaning against a wall! The Chinese took this 'joss' thing to a whole different level. It was serious stuff for them. He also taught me how to hold chopsticks so I could pick up even the most difficult pieces which was another lesson in Chinese table manners. The further away from the tip a guest can hold the chopstick the higher their station in life.

When Christine joined me at the hotel two weeks after my arrival, the General Manager – once he found out she was a teacher – asked her to teach English courses to front-of-the-house staff. So now we were both working – which was terrific – and of course, never saw each other as my work week was still between sixty to eighty hours. Christine assembled the front of the house employees, got them to commit to attending, held class every week and developed a great relationship with them. Their English began to improve as she taught hotel vocabulary they could use with guests on a regular basis. On her days off – which seldom coincided with mine – she visited the sights of Macau and Hong Kong. As a result she learned more about the region during our stay than I did

On one of our rare days off together, we decided to visit China. Other than being part of a group on a day tour, there was no way to gain access as individuals to the most populated country on earth. No visas were issued to individuals. So we joined a tour and became tourists for one day. Our tour began at The Barrier

Gate of Macao, the impressive arch that was the border post between the colony and mainland China. We lined up for immigration before a neatly dressed officer in green and red military style uniform who looked all of twenty years old. Our tour guide who introduced himself as 'Mista Chang,' translated for everyone and when our turn came to show our passports, I witnessed the round red stamp hitting the page of my Irish passport as if permanently fusing two distant cultures. The twenty year old looked me in the eye, expressionless, and handed it back. Then we stepped into the People's Republic of China – and were on our way.

We traveled by bus through the country side, rice fields on both sides of the road, oxen and people up to their knees in water – both toiling on the next rice crop. This hardship and connection to the land gave me a new found respect for rice as I remembered my childhood and the time-consuming labor of love it took for us to get our national staple – the lowly potato – to table. In both cases – whether in rural China or rural Ireland – it was backbreaking work, and a necessity for survival. We stopped for lunch and had dim sum, snake soup and fruit for dessert. There was no western cutlery – except a traditional Chinese porcelain spoon for the soup – which was not much of a problem for us thanks to Mr Wong's table etiquette lessons but it was interesting to observe how the tourists in our group went about eating. There were Europeans, Australians and Americans and all had varying degrees of difficulty with the chop sticks. Many would not eat the snake soup, some asked for 'real food,' others just ate the dim sum, disappointed there were no alternatives. Asian cuisine is not reputed for its desserts; so fruit is often the choice for this course – at least the grumpy tourists had a dessert.

Despite the complaining tourists in our group, we were experiencing an eye-opening visit to this mysterious country that I had up until now only associated with the stamp on my childhood toys, 'Made in China'. Now I had just eaten delicious snake soup that qualified for the same title. In contrast to the good food, the poverty was striking; houses were poorly maintained, residents sat outside in courtyards on rickety furniture, some were preparing food on charcoal fires and some were eating as they squatted by the fire. Holding bowls to their mouths in traditional fashion, they scooped rice and meat into their mouths with chopsticks. The Chinese are noisy eaters; they relish the taste of each mouthful, sucking in air with the food in gestures of appreciation of the taste – not unlike a wine connoisseur tasting a rich vintage.

Yet everyone smiled at us as we walked by, commenting among themselves in a language we could not understand. There were very few cars, bicycles were everywhere, either lined up on the pavements or being ridden sometimes with two or three passengers – demonstrating a balancing act par excellence. Those without bikes walked, some wore the party uniform, and some proudly sported western style clothing with various company logos. Chain smoking groups of men hunkered down playing Mahjong – a type of Chinese board game – on the pavement while chatting in Cantonese. This street scene – although it resembled a well planned set for a play on stage – was just another day in these people's lives. Our group of tourists would return to their regular lives in a few hours, but this amazing lifestyle would be enjoyed by the locals for a lifetime. It looked like we had stepped back 50 years in time. Our last stop was in Zhongshan, the birth place of Dr Sun Yat-sen – often considered one of the greatest leaders of modern China. In contrast to the surrounding houses Dr. Sun's house and courtyard looked like a palace. The entrance was guarded by a large archway with a typical Chinese green tiled roof resembling bamboo with ornaments and animals perched on the ridge tiles. Lions in sitting pose and lions in lying positions adorned the roof corners. The splendor of this Chinese architecture and the beauty of the landscaped gardens made our day trip.

As we exited China late in the afternoon, police boarded the bus at the border to check for any Chinese stowaways; using mirrors on long poles they also checked under the bus. Mista Chang bid us farewell with the following statement which has impacted me for many years. Pointing to the border gate he said, "All of you can walk through that gate without reflection; I will never be able to follow you. Please cherish your freedom to travel and remember me where ever you go." I still do! After hearing this very touching farewell, some tourists had tears in their eyes as we left the People's Republic of China and Chang, our very friendly guide, behind. One American tourist turned to her husband saying, "My gawd Jack, is there something we can do for that poor man?" Looking back at her, he shook his head.

We held many spectacular Chinese banquets at the hotel. It was impressive to see the ballroom set up for these functions, usually with round tables seating ten guests each. A lazy Susan – a revolving platter in the middle of the table – was used to pass around condiments and food platters. Food was mostly in bite size pieces so it could be transferred to guests' plates using chopsticks. Peking duck and shark fin soup were staples on larger banquets. Shark fin soup is prized for its luxury appeal, not unlike caviar in the west.

In the Chinese banquet kitchen, rows of lacquered ducks hung by the neck as the skin dried in front of large fans. This kitchen was a hub of activity; a staff of four women was seated at a table folding fresh dim sum at a speed and precision to be admired. Next to them were three choppers slicing foods on thick round wooden chopping blocks, the blur of cleavers a testament to their professionalism and dexterity. Most Chinese food is cut first then cooked to order, especially those destined for stir frying, making the wok an integral part of the cooking process. The hierarchy is different to western kitchens; the sous chef is the 'first chopper.' Then there is the dim sum chef, the fryer, the roaster and the wok chef. All cooks spoke Cantonese in very loud, almost vulgar voices. When the ingredients are all cut and portioned it just takes a few minutes to finish cooking in the searing heat of the wok. To increase this heat, air is premixed with the gas and forced through the burners by a powerful turbine – its high pitched whine a familiar noise in Chinese kitchens. This heat allows the wok master to sear the food almost instantly. In a well designed Chinese kitchen this chef barely moves from his station, everything is within reach of his ladle so he can produce dish after dish in the same wok by rinsing it out and wiping it with a bamboo brush between dishes, then returning it to the flame – the intense heat of the burner drying it out instantly.

Mr. Wong, the banquet chef, explained to me how the skin for Peking duck has to dry out so it will become crispy when cooked. To achieve this he used a piece of bamboo to blow air under the skin to separate it from the flesh. This allows the fat to melt faster and flow out during the cooking process which in turn helped the skin to become crisp. I was so impressed to see how he then carved the duck with a large Chinese cleaver using as much dexterity as any chef I had ever seen using a western knife. The meat was perfectly carved and the crispy skin placed back on top. I saw firsthand how artistic the Chinese were in the preparation of cold food platters. Often used in large banquets, the small pieces of meat and vegetable were carved and arranged on platters depicting the shape of a rooster using only a large cleaver as equipment. The rooster is believed to ward off evil spirits. It was interesting to observe how closely the Chinese intertwine their admiration and fear of spirits not only in food preparation, but in all aspects of their lives.

Much of the specialty food for the grillroom was flown in weekly from Switzerland and other countries so I was familiar with many products. Creamy Swiss yogurts, aged Gruyere cheese and large blocks of Swiss chocolate arrived every week by plane in Hong Kong as did lobsters, US Blue Point and New Zealand oysters, California asparagus and Dutch veal. We also had clear turtle soup with sherry, fresh oyster soup with saffron, and pigeon breast with endives and parsley puree on the menu.

Main courses were divided into categories such as 'specialties' and 'charcoal grilled.' The later were prepared by one of the chefs at the grill located in the center of the restaurant. The rest was prepared in the kitchen. Waiters had to be very careful in coordinating the pickup times so that steaks were ready at the grill when the specialties were ready in the kitchen as we had no intercom system. All grilled dishes were served with Béarnaise sauce and a selection of imported mustards. Some of these dishes incorporated elements of east-meets-west cooking styles such as the duck breast with sesame sauce and Chinese vegetables, but for the most part dishes were European classics with the exception of the 'African Chicken' one of Macau's most popular specialties. This grilled spicy chicken dish made with coconut, peanuts and chilies probably originated in Portugal's African colonial escapades. In any case it was very popular in Macau.

The Chinese are reputed for putting many exotic animals on the menu and even more so for eating every part as nothing is wasted. Foods considered taboo in the west are sometimes regarded a delicacy in China. Some obscure small dimly lit restaurants in the back streets of Macau and Hong Kong were no different. It was possible to walk past the animals in cages at the entrance and order from the cage. Owls, hawks, geese, bats, flying foxes, herons, cranes, and sparrows were lined up in cages all ready for the menu. The unfortunate animal was then sent to the kitchen where a butcher had it slaughtered, cleaned, and then handed it over to the cooks for preparation. A short while later the animal – now prepared with spices, vegetables, and copious amounts of monosodium glutamate – graciously appeared in person on a platter placed upon the lazy Susan for the entire table to admire.

Then Mr. Wong told me about the monkey's brain. This was a forbidden practice, but never the less available to those in the know. The monkey was strapped live to a table with a hole in the top which allowed its head to stick out a few inches above the table top. Then the top of its skull is sliced off with a swift swoosh of the cleaver, hot oil is poured in and the brain is eaten directly out of the skull using spoons while the monkey is still alive. Some Chinese believe this is an aphrodisiac. He told me he never ate monkey brain like that – it was so cruel. How could anyone eat in such a barbaric fashion? I thought if this was true, it was the height of animal cruelty.

Eventually I received my contract from Singapore. I would be the Sous chef in charge of the Chateaubriand fine dining and Grill room at the Pan Pacific Hotel. Andi and the Chinese chefs invited me out on the town for a farewell meal. Prior to this sortie I had asked Andi the proper protocol for me at such celebrations. "Given the Chinese affinity for brandy," he responded, "you should bring a bottle of brandy for each table." So I turned up at the restaurant with five bottles of Hennessey Brandy and placed one on each table. The chefs proceeded to pour for themselves during dinner after which each chef insisted to have a traditional "yum sing" – toast – with me. Unbeknownst to me, the chefs were pouring Hennessey in my glass while pouring a dark tea, which had a similar color, for them. After a few of these toasts Andi stepped in to stop the yum sing and drove me back to the hotel. Some chefs were disappointed I did not have a yum sing with them – but there was only so much Hennessy I could drink. The front of the house staff in Christine's classes took her out for dim sum but she did not have any "yum sing" to deal with. On the evening before we left, the General Manager and his wife invited both of us to his apartment for dinner. Together they cooked a wonderful meal for us.

On our way to Singapore we decided to spend a night in Hong Kong and the General Manager arranged a room for us at the Mandarin. It was a standard benefit at the time: employees could request a room, either free or at a discount, at a sister property during their travels. This depended on occupancy – guests had preference. The same handwritten note that I had received before was on my bedside table with one word added – "Welcome back to the Mandarin." This gesture made such an impression on me that I have kept that card to this day. First there was the thought behind writing the note and the carefully added word. Then there was the logistics of getting it from the GM's office to housekeeping and then to the room – the correct room. It certainly added to the five star luxury hotel setting which makes the guest feel special. We had planned to have dinner at 'la Plume' in the Regent Hotel in Kowloon. This was one of the most luxurious – and expensive – French restaurants in Hong Kong, right up there with the Pierrot. Christine's landlord in Switzerland was a personal friend of the chef, Gray Kunz, and recommended we have dinner there. We crossed the harbor to Kowloon on the legendary star ferry which afforded a spectacular view of the city skyline and the peak – the tallest section of Hong Kong Island.

As we arrived at the dining room entrance the hostess greeted us with a smile, looked at me and said, "Good evening, we have a selection of jackets for you to choose from." Jackets were required – I did not have one. Graciously she opened a concealed door in the wall paneling and in there on hangers was a selection of jackets. "Please choose one to your liking," she smiled. I took one – it felt like I was wearing someone else's jacket for the entire evening. The Maître d'hôtel escorted us to our table, possibly because I made the reservation from the Oriental in Macau, as normally that was not the Maître's job. Once seated, I discreetly gave him my card with a note for Chef Kunz and we began to study the wine list. Christine exclaimed, "Mon Dieu, they have St. Saphorin." We ordered a bottle. Just as the sommelier began to open the wine, the Maître arrived: "Stop!" He gestured discreetly to the sommelier and pointed to the wine. He turned to us and said, "The chef has ordered Champagne; he will prepare a 'menu surprise' for you and invites you to meet him in the kitchen after your meal." This was totally unexpected and an incredible surprise; we merely wanted to meet him and pass on regards from our mutual friend in Switzerland. And so the meal began: course after course arrived, superbly presented food, incredible flavors paired with the champagne and the St. Saphorin – which we decided to have anyway. It brought us back to that wonderful meal by the lake in St Saphorin years earlier. Taste memories were working overtime which made this a taste memory within a taste memory. That dinner at the Regent in Hong Kong still remains one of our most memorable meals.

Later in the evening we met Gray Kunz in his extremely well organized kitchen. He was very gracious to afford us a few minutes of his time. By now all guests were served, some were leaving, and the kitchen was being cleaned, but nevertheless he continued gesturing and commenting to the chefs as we spoke. It was amazing to see how he organized the kitchen, one which served up to 150 guests each evening – an incredible number for that level of fine dining while still maintaining quality. He mentioned that fact as we spoke. I knew from experience at the Captain Bush – which seated 100 – that this number of meals each night was a major challenge. Assuming each guest ordered at least four courses, this meant he supervised the preparation and presentation of 600 dishes each evening that had to be perfectly executed to leave the kitchen – an almost impossible feat for the level of dining offered at La Plume.

When it was time to leave, the Maître insisted he call a taxi for us and walked us to the front entrance of the hotel. He did better than a taxi – he ordered a hotel limousine to drive us back to our hotel. Arriving at the Mandarin in a Bentley from the Regent was the ultimate ending to a great evening, meeting an extremely talented chef, tasting his exquisite flavors and all this taking place in one of the most exciting and vibrant cities in the Far East. But as we entered our room, I realized I had forgotten to return the jacket!

Lobster Salad with Mango

When live lobsters arrived from France via Hong Kong and inspected for freshness, some were deemed not to last the night. We steamed them, removed the meat from the tail and claws and served them in a salad the next day. It was a light and refreshing lunch dish.

Ingredients for 6 portions:
6 cooked, shelled half lobster tails
6 cooked, shelled lobster claws
12 cherry tomatoes, halved horizontally
3 pcs. Belgian endives
6 leaves romaine lettuce, finely shredded
3 spring onions, washed and peeled
2 ripe mangos
6 tablespoons sherry vinegar
10 tablespoons extra virgin olive oil
Salt and black pepper mill to taste
Sprigs of chervil for garnish

Optional: finely cut black truffles sticks

Procedure: Salad
- Place the shredded romaine in the center of a large plate.
- Place four endive leaves around the romaine with the points facing outwards and arrange the half tomatoes in between.
- Slice the lobster tail and arrange attractively on the romaine.
- Coat the lobster with the mango sauce and decorate with spring onions and the chopped truffles. Finally add the lobster claw with the point facing upwards and add a sprig of chervil.

For the sauce
- Remove the stone and skin from the mango and cut the flesh into pieces.
- Puree in a blender and drizzle in the oil with the motor running.
- Add vinegar to taste, season with salt and pepper mill.

Tip
- Add a little sour cream or plain yoghurt to the sauce for extra creaminess.

CHAPTER TWELVE

The Chateaubriand

The lobby atrium of the Pan Pacific Hotel in Singapore was a spectacular sight. Looking up from the reception, the inner balconies on all thirty-seven floors were visible, each draped with flowers – the empty space was almost frightening. An artistic spiral of red silk suspended from the ceiling on thin steel wires reached down about twenty floors stretching to fill the enormous void. This feature combined with four glass bubble elevators gliding up the atrium wall added to this stunning appeal. It took many times of taking the elevator for me to get comfortable with my fear of heights – looking down thirty seven floors with nothing but glass between me and the void was terrifying so in the beginning I turned my back to the glass wall and looked at the doors, smiling each time to hide my fear when they opened to let guests on. As the elevators reached the lobby they descended behind a fountain creating an optical illusion of sinking.

Remy, the Executive Chef, was Swiss German, and a very dynamic chef. We had spoken many times on the phone over the past year but this was the first time we had met. Peter, the Executive Sous Chef told me, Remy was capable of working on several projects at the same time, and never sat still – always thinking of a new dish, menu concept, or a better presentation. Once open, The Pan Pacific Hotel would have ten food and beverage outlets and one hundred and fifty kitchen staff – a tremendous management task for all of us. Contrary to the Royal Orchid, the Pan Pacific promised a hard opening, which meant every outlet and every department would be operational on the first day – not an easy feat.

Due to the construction delay the hotel opening was postponed again for a few months, so Remy asked if I could work at the Movenpick restaurant downtown in the meantime. He said the hotel owners had enquired why I was already on board – with no revenue coming in they questioned the added salary expense. In order to appease the owners I agreed to help out at the Movenpick restaurant until construction advanced enough for me to begin using the grill room kitchen for recipe testing. I was not going to let a three year contract slip away because of a few months delay, and besides, my salary remained the same. I had become familiar with Movenpick restaurants in Switzerland; they operated many of the restaurant stops on Swiss highways, offering quality food at a fair price. Heinz, the Movenpick manager, was Swiss and his wife Angie was Malaysian – a terrific management couple, they were very welcoming. I felt right at home.

The Movenpick had two outlets, one on Orchard road, the other on Battery road – a short drive across the city, but a nightmare trip in traffic if the Battery road outlet ran out of a particular item during the busy lunch service. That outlet had what is called a 'satellite kitchen' – it depended on its daily supplies of raw and partially prepared foods from the main kitchen on Orchard road. Keeping the Battery road location supplied with food was a problem at that time. Its tiny kitchen provided storage space for only one day's inventory and they frequently ran out of a menu item during lunch service. So Heinz asked if I could implement a delivery system to the Battery road restaurant to prevent shortages and hopefully eliminate customer complaints.

All basic stocks, baked Quiche Loraine, salads, marinated meats and fish, ice creams, and wine and beer were delivered from the main restaurant twice daily. Despite its size, it was remarkable to see how efficient this little kitchen operation actually was. Everything had its own place. Spaces between the ranges and stainless steel tables were very tight which made for some interesting body squeezes when it got busy. Due to its location in the financial district, it filled up instantly at noon, then like a well oiled machine it ran smoothly until an item sold out and the complaints began. Many clients worked in the financial sector, timing their lunch break to end before the opening of the Stock

Exchange in New York, so service had to be fast to allow them to be back at their desks for trading.

To resolve the inventory issue, my first priority was to establish a system of checklists for the driver and set up three specific locations in the main kitchen where items could be stored for him. There was one location in the main kitchen, one in the fridge and one in the freezer. The driver checked these shelves twice daily; anything left there whether food or beverage based on the check lists went automatically to the satellite. In addition, we modified the check list for the head chef in Battery road so that every day when he closed the restaurant, he made a thorough list of every item he required for the next morning. After a week of using this system, the result was no more running out of food which practically eliminated customer complaints. It was a good start for me and helped me get the respect of the staff − a key element for supervising the multi-cultural brigade.

Any time that a chef can make work easier and faster for the kitchen brigade, they typically offer their respect in return. I put the dishwasher on extra hours and gave him the task of deep cleaning the walls, floors, and ceilings one section at a time. Then I had the kitchen painted in brighter colors and added additional lighting. In less than one week, these little improvements made me the 'chef in charge' in the brigade's eyes − without ever raising my voice − and I had not yet touched a pan or a knife. Now, with the hierarchy clearly established, we could move on to the menu. Cooking at Movenpick was like being back in Switzerland, − they even had St. Saphorin, much to Christine's delight − the familiar products were a pleasure to cook with. Swiss smoked bacon for the quiche − a best seller; wheels of raclette cheese, Swiss Gruyere, air dried beef, ham, and bacon, arrived with Swissair every week from Zurich. Even Swiss beer was imported. But the highlight of their menu − at least for me − was the amazing Movenpick ice cream. I don't know if it was the taste of alpine cow's milk or the ultra smooth texture but it tasted divine, with a silky mouth feel propelling flavor to the taste buds − my favorite was the Carmelita.

Finally, the hotel opening day was set so I moved back to the Pan Pacific and began writing menus, testing recipes, hiring staff and scheduling training seminars. This was a three month process and I was not alone. The hotel had multiple outlets – each one supervised by a sous chef: a twenty four hour coffee shop, a Polynesian restaurant, Japanese restaurant, Chinese restaurant, an Arabian restaurant, a 'Summerhouse' poolside terrace, and the Chateaubriand grill room where I would be working. There were also extensive banqueting facilities with separate kitchens, a Muslim kitchen, a cold kitchen, a butcher shop, pastry shop, and a delicatessen on the second floor overlooking the fountain by the elevators. The complete brigade would comprise of one hundred and fifty cooks spread throughout ten different kitchens on five floors.

During this pre-opening phase all sous chefs were working nine to five – a very unusual shift for a chef. After work we would talk about the day's interviews and found we had the same dilemma: everyone we interviewed was a fantastic chef – during the interview. These applicants could make a fresh César dressing, a béarnaise, a bordelaise, or a soufflé. The problem was how to know for sure. Much like in Bangkok, The Pan Pacific was one of the first five star hotels to open in Singapore in many years and staff from other hotels saw this as their opportunity to move up in their careers. We were also paying higher salaries so Executive Chefs from other five star properties did not particularly appreciate our presence as their well trained staff began to leave.

At least now these new chefs could better themselves and their families with the extra money. I remember firing one cook from the Captain Bush grill in Bangkok: I knew I was breaking his rice bowl, but he couldn't even make a béarnaise. He got past me in the interview process with his ability to look me square in the face and describe the making of a particular dish. After we opened and were able to see his inability, I gave him a week's notice and he cried at work every day for the week. Eventually with Herbert's help we transferred him to the coffee shop kitchen and he actually did quite well working with TJ. I didn't want to go through this firing process again. It was better to do the work myself than to hire under qualified cooks and have to fire them a few weeks later.

Fortunately, we found a great chef for the Chateaubriand. Mr. Soh – my second in command – helped me understand the local chefs and how best to work with them. He also knew where to find good chefs in the city. On his suggestion we implemented a system to get past the 'fantastic chefs' in the interview process and find out if they really could cook before they were hired. We asked potential chef de parties, and even the commis, to work with us on their next day off. Once they arrived in the kitchen, Mr. Soh gave them a list of duties, sauces, and the like and observed them as they planned their day. At the end of the shift, Mr. Soh and I made a decision and told the chef right away and either sent them to the personnel office to sign up, or home. This avoided having to fire any one later and the chefs who were not hired went back to their old job the next day – no harm done and I felt we had selected the best to promote this restaurant.

The kitchen hierarchy was vast and well structured. Remy had a large notice board in his office with the organizational chart of each kitchen and the names of all one hundred and fifty staff in descending order. There was a sous chef responsible for every restaurant and every kitchen in the hotel. Each of us reported to Peter, the Executive Sous Chef who then reported to Remy the Executive Chef and in turn to the director of Food and Beverage, an affable Frenchman by the name of Jean-Pierre. Then we had a series of senior cooks, then junior cooks, commis, and kitchen helpers. In addition we had a kitchen artist. He carved sculptures out of ice, butter, and Styrofoam. He had his own work room and walk-in freezer to store the ice. I often sat on the receiving dock to watch him as he transformed a simple three hundred pound ice block into an elegant swan with simple strokes of his ice chisel. These sculptures would be flood light in a prominent position on food buffets adding to the elegance of the decor.

Housee was Mauritian and sous chef in charge of the 'Tiki', the Polynesian restaurant on the first floor. He was a great chef, brought the island flavors to life and was always ready with a smile or a joke. I loved his French Creole accent – we spoke mainly French together. His wife and son remained at home in Mauritius and he supported them from Singapore, a familiar immigrant tradition for me. Hassan was Moroccan and the sous chef in charge of the Casablanca, an Arabian nightclub and lounge serving an array of Middle Eastern fare. He was a little more serious by nature, had just finished a contract in Saudi Arabia, and was reveling in the freedom Singapore offered. Fritz our butcher was German and came from Canada for this position. He was very quiet but made some of the best sausages and charcuterie I had ever tasted. He had his own kitchen resembling a small sausage factory and worked with two cooks usually from six in the morning to four in the afternoon. Josef, from Switzerland, was the baker and pastry chef; he was very tall, quite shy, had a bushy beard and always spoke with a smile. He also had an incredible facility resembling a Swiss bake shop with the equipment, ovens, and staff necessary to provide all the breads, pastries, breakfast Danish, ice creams, chocolate confections, and desserts for all outlets at the 800 room hotel, in addition to all the banquets.

Then there were the local sous chefs for the coffee shop, the cold kitchen, the banquet kitchen and the Muslim kitchen. The latter provided all food for Muslim dishes for the banquet kitchen and some Muslim dishes on the coffee shop menu. The sous chef for Hei Tien Lo, the Chinese restaurant – which had a commanding view of three countries, (Indonesia, Malaysia and Singapore) from the thirty-seventh floor – was from Hong Kong. Akio came from Tokyo and was the sous chef for the Japanese restaurant. This beautifully decorated space on the third floor was set amid its own outdoor Japanese garden, complete with a well stocked fish pond and wooden bridges. It was touted at the time as the largest Japanese garden in a hotel outside of Japan. Inside the restaurant were various Tatami rooms, a Sushi counter, Tempura counters and a Teppan-yaki counter. Lastly, there was me in the Chateaubriand grillroom – from Ireland.

During the three month hiring process, discussions about staff interviews were frequent among sous chefs. Given the diverse cultural backgrounds of all of us, it was a wonder we were able to employ anyone at all. Once we began to cook however, there was progress. Remy selected an unused store room on the second floor and had it turned into the chef's dining room, installing a large table surrounded with 15 chairs. As we prepared dishes and began looking at possible food presentation layouts for all outlets, this room became the tasting room, a kind of central command room for all sous chefs. One day we ate Japanese, the next day Chinese, then Polynesian, followed by Moroccan, Singaporean, Malay, and French until we had the menus in every outlet complete. It took weeks of testing. Later when the hotel opened we kept that room for our regular chefs table and made a roster for our meals. Every day all sous chefs, together with Remy and Peter, ate lunch and dinner together. We had foods from the different outlets in our own dining room – meals were always a surprise, and I rarely knew in advance what food we would eat for any particular meal. All I knew was that it would be of 5 star quality or it would not make it past the door.

As in Bangkok, Christine and I were given a suite in the hotel. This one overlooked Marina Bay. Long hours were the norm so I seldom had time to admire the view. Most of the expats lived on property as it was cheaper for the hotel to provide rooms for us rather than rent apartments. This meant we were also available whenever the situation required our presence in the kitchen. Expatriate contracts at the time typically included accommodation and food, and depending on seniority, a flight home every one or two years. General Managers would have a car and driver provided and some may have schooling costs paid for if they had children. My contract included a tax free salary, health insurance, and two flights home during the three years. In return I spent eighty to ninety hours a week ensuring the restaurant worked – whatever that took. And it was great fun.

The Chateaubriand restaurant was named after the steak of the same name – a dish created for Count Francois René Chateaubriand in the 18th century. This French Count – a writer and statesman – had a great appetite and always ordered a larger steak than his fellow diners, approximately sixteen ounces. So his chef created 'Le Chateaubriand' which is typically a double fillet steak cut from the head of the fillet, grilled and usually served for two on today's menus. Because of its expensive nature it is presented on a silver platter surrounded by turned buttered vegetables, some form of potato, Béarnaise sauce or perhaps a bordelaise sauce. Carved at the table with elegant movements of the knife by the Maître gave this dish the standing it commanded on the menu.

The restaurant had an open kitchen, which was a new feature for me. Separating the kitchen from the restaurant was a beautiful copper lined bar over which a row of suspended infrared polished copper heating lamps kept food warm for pick up. Behind this bar were table top counters with built in fridges and a water bath for holding some hot foods. On the back kitchen wall were the stoves which meant chefs had their backs to the guests as they cooked. Only the grill chef faced the guests. The open kitchen was dominated by the charcoal fired grill, beautifully designed; the grill bars precisely angled to create perfect markings on steaks and fish. It quickly became an attraction for guests.

This exposure of kitchen staff to the guest meant everyone – including myself – had to be trained differently as our movements and actions were constantly observed. It was as if we were on stage. Things such as gestures, food hygiene, noise levels, uniform cleanliness, personal hygiene, daily shaving, wearing a hat and the likes became paramount. We had a back kitchen that was not visible to the guest which provided a space to prepare seafood platters, shuck oysters, cook mussels and conduct general preparation for the menu – and it allowed us to get off the stage. In the beginning, every time I walked through that door to the open kitchen I became conscious of our customers' gaze until it eventually became second nature. However, during a busy service there was tendency to forget this and noise levels increased. Then the Maître would come to the counter and say "Brendan! The brigade is too loud," and we would tone it down.

The main attractions on the starters menu were French oysters, fresh seafood platters, Abalone soup, fresh crab bisque, and a spicy crabmeat crêpe in a money purse fold – and of course, caviar, a majestic beginning to any meal. Main courses included a large selection of US and New Zealand charcoal grilled steaks, a Chateaubriand, Kobe beef, New Zealand lamb, king prawns, lobster, and a local fish called Silver Pomfret. In addition, we had two specialties from the grill: the Chateaubriand Sword and the Mermaids Brochette. One was a selection of meats served on a sword, the other a variety of fish and seafood also on a sword. Both these items were served in a spectacular fashion. The waiter would pick up the flaming swords from the grill chef behind the copper bar and walk in a stately fashion to the guests table followed by the commis carrying a starch, vegetables, and a selection of sauces. With a few deft movements – using all of his table side skills – the waiter elegantly removed the meat or fish from the sword, arranged it on a plate with its garnishes all while having a discreet conversation with the guests. Every time we served these swords, other guests' eyes would follow the flame, imagining the flavor – they could see the taste. It was food entertainment and my first exposure to providing another dimension that would please our guests that went well beyond the preparation of excellent food.

By now I was moving away from using flour to thicken sauces and soups and turning more to corn and potato starches, and rice flour. Sauces thickened this way are much lighter than using wheat flour or a roux – butter mixed with flour – and leave practically no flour after taste. I also began thickening the crab bisque with slices of toast bread pan-fried in clarified butter. To make the bisque, I would begin by sautéing a mirepoix in butter with crab shells with the gills removed – the gills give the base a bitter taste. Then flambé with brandy, add some tomato paste, sauté that to add more flavor, then lastly add a light fish stock. When it had simmered enough to extract the crab flavor I would pass it through a very fine strainer and set it back on the heat. Now was the time to add the toast and once it softened I blended the lot, seasoned it, and added a little cream. The result was a light creamy rich-textured bisque using very little cream. The final touch was the pinch of cayenne, not spicy – just highly seasoned. It was such a simple recipe that anyone could make it at home.

It took a while to get the crab crêpe just right for the starter. If the crêpe – a thin French pancake – was too thin it would break during the folding and filling process and could not be served. On the other hand, if it was too thick it became chewy. We needed a crêpe that would hold together the spicy crabmeat that we could tie with a chive or a strip of blanched leek, and not break or split open until the guest cut into it. They had to look like real money purses – what some people referred to as a 'beggars purse', a money pouch closed by means of a draw string – from the time they were prepared, to withstanding being transferred to a baking tray, heated, transferred again to the plate and garnished with sauce. During recipe testing, the first crêpes fell apart when removed from the oven. This could mean disaster during a busy service. As we experimented with the crêpe's thickness we discovered that by making the center of the crêpe slightly thicker than the edges it would strengthen the bottom and hold in the crab meat better.

With a little practice, the vegetable chef became very good at making crêpes like this; they later became very popular among our starters. Presentation was also a challenge. Our first attempt was to pour a mirror of crayfish sauce – similar in flavor and color to the crab bisque, but thicker and made with crayfish – on the plate, decorate it with a swirl of thick liquid cream and set two hot 'crab purses' in the center of the sauce. It looked nice until the waiter picked it up and the law of nature kicked in. Because the crab purse was not touching the plate and resting only on the sauce, it moved with the waiter's motion and by the time it got to the guest it looked as appetizing as a dog's dinner – unacceptable. Food had to look the same from the time it left the kitchen until it was placed in front of the guest. We solved that problem by putting the purses on the plate first and adding the sauce afterwards. Now the waiter could have run in circles if he wanted to and the purses wouldn't move.

It was this kind of detail that took time. Every recipe was tested and retested. During the pre-opening phase the management came to taste every day during lunch. We scheduled sessions on fish tasting, beef tasting, oyster tastings, and seafood platter presentation sessions until it was agreed we had the right combination of portion size, flavor combination, and acceptable presentations styles for all dishes on the menu. It was exhausting work trying to please everyone and we still had not served a single customer. Such ground work was necessary as we were the first restaurant of this kind to open in the city in five years. We would be scrutinized by our competition and the press. Better to do this now than have the customers tell us later – or worse, have a negative review in the press by a pen-happy food critic. The Chateaubriand would be crucified before we even got out the starting gate.

Caviar – the delicate roe of the sturgeon, a common food at its source in the Caspian Sea and Iran, but elevated to almost cult status once exported – was presented in spectacular fashion befitting its eminence. The kitchen artist prepared a miniature hollowed-out ice sculpture of a fish which was placed on a starched napkin folded in the classical 'artichoke' style and then laid on a silver platter. Inside the ice we placed two small batteries connected to a flashlight bulb, illuminating the sculpture – and bringing it to life. The classic blue tin of 'Malossol' (lightly salted) Beluga Russian Caviar was placed on the top, nestled in some crushed ice – with the lid removed but also placed on the ice for authenticity – and served with its classical garnish of finely chopped, cooked egg yolks and whites and lemon wedges. In addition, we served Melba toast, Russian blinis – a buckwheat pancake – and some *crème fraîche*. As it was brought to the table, other guests gazed inquisitively at the ice sculpture which by now radiated crystals of light in the dimly lit dining room. Guests helped themselves to the caviar directly from the tin using mother-of-pearl spoons, their non-metallic nature leaving the taste and texture of the caviar unaltered. Caviar – served with champagne – was the ultimate precursor to a sumptuous meal experience, and we had many.

Because the hotel was planning a hard opening and every outlet was training and doing menu testing, we invited secretaries and directors in small numbers every day for lunch to give us feedback well before the official opening day. We were actually going through the motions of a soft opening for all outlets but with employees as guests. We even had real guests staying on the lower floors so the reception and housekeeping could work out any kinks in the check-in and check-out system and test the communication between the departments.

The seafood platter was predicted to be a very popular starter. The platter would rest on a raised circular metal frame placed in the center of the table. We first placed a layer of ice on the platter and added a little fresh seaweed for decoration. On this we placed freshly cooked halved lobster tails still in the shell, cooked, cracked lobster claws, crab claws, jumbo prawns, French 'Belon' and 'Fines de Claires' oysters on the half shell, as well as cooked mussels in the shell and decorated it with steamed periwinkles and lemon stars. It looked spectacular and as Jean-Pierre predicted, it became a best seller once we opened. We served a selection of sauces and vinaigrettes to accompany the various shell fish. One was a simple French vinaigrette made with red wine vinegar, chopped shallots and crushed black pepper. Then there was a garlic mayonnaise, a chili mayonnaise and a European cocktail sauce. These platters were so simple to make, but when they arrived at the table it was magical to see the guest's expression – their eyes lighting up – anticipating the flavor, and the comments – ooh and aah!

The Shiitake mushroom consommé baked with a puff pastry crust was a little more complex to make and also took us a few tries to get it right. We made a traditional beef consommé like I learned in Switzerland and now using the Shiitake stems for additional flavor. I then sliced the Shitake caps, sautéed them in very little butter and filled oven-proof bowls with the strained consommé. Once the mixture was completely cold, we cut rounds of thinly rolled puff pastry – which Josef made in his pastry shop – and sealed each bowl using egg wash to bind the pastry to the porcelain. Decoration was simple, a few leafs made with pastry, or sometimes just a design using the prongs of a dinner fork. When we tested the baking process, many pastry covers shrunk and fell into the soup rendering them un-servable. After many baking trials we found that when the pastry was very cold it baked properly every time so we knew then that the soup had to go directly from the fridge to the hot oven. When a soup order came in we placed the bowl in the oven for 15 minutes and when it came out, its shiny dome looked like a Christmas present waiting to be unwrapped – which the waiter did at the table, to the guests' delight. I often observed – from the kitchen – the expression of joy on guests' faces as the waiter cut away half of the pastry, releasing the delicate Shiitake aroma – these were food memories in the making – and I was a food memory creator. The guests' expressions and gestures made the long hours and the recipe testing all worthwhile. Making people happy is what chefs do! Anything less and it is not worth getting out of bed in the morning.

Not every recipe turned out perfect even when we were open. Many customers complained that the consommé was salty. This was the same consommé I had made in Switzerland, Bangkok and Macau. After speaking with many guests we determined they did not like the highly seasoned consommé so I had to scale back on the salt and then everyone was happy. It was a good learning experience for me on how various cultures have different relationships with seasoning – particularly salt.

The Maître was French – very French. A tall thin man with a shortage of hair, he had a commanding demeanor as he walked through the restaurant. His moustache looked like handlebars on a bicycle, and he was in the habit of twisting them up with his thumb and forefinger whenever we talked. Despite being very strong minded – which resulted in us arguing a lot because of his inflexibility – he was an excellent Maître. He was in charge of the wine cellar and made it his mission to implement the open bottle system which was to be a feature on our wine list. He would suggest a particular wine at the table and then invite guests to the cellar to sample. This cellar was located in the center of the

Chateaubriand separated from the restaurant by a smoked glass wall. The Maître would open any bottle of the guest's choosing so they could taste it in the cellar prior to ordering. If they did not like that particular wine, he would open another, let them decide, and if it was to their liking, walk them back to their table, the bottle balanced neatly between his right palm and forearm – label facing upwards. This was a new concept for Singapore and we believed it would make the Chateaubriand stand out.

He repeated this scenario constantly throughout the evening; guests loved the individual attention and the ability to taste the wine before actually ordering it. Wines opened that the guest did not like were sold immediately by the glass to other guests. Waiters would 'up-sell' this as a special feature, offering an expensive French wine by the glass – a very affordable way to taste French wines normally offered only by the bottle and sometimes financially out of reach for many customers. It was a great way to promote wine sales and demanded a strong personality which is why this Maître was such a success.

The most expensive item on the menu in the Chateaubriand was Kobe beef, imported directly from Japan every week. Akio used most of it in the Japanese restaurant, but I sold a few portions every day. Because of its expense –we charged per gram – steaks were individually cut and weighed at the table so guests knew of the cost before they placed an order. We had an entire sirloin always ready on a carving board in the fridge. When a guest requested Kobe, the carving board was placed on a trolley with a large kitchen knife and a weighing scale and wheeled to the table. The Maître moved the knife along the meat to whatever thickness the guest requested and before cutting the steak informed them of the approximate price. If they agreed he cut the steak, weighed it, gave them the exact price and brought the steak to the kitchen with its cooking designation, rare or medium. An order of 'well done' for such a delicacy would be a sacrilege – although we had a few. A two hundred and fifty gram steak – about nine ounces – cost ninety Singaporean dollars at the time, approximately four times more expensive than a US steak of the same size. It became very important to have it grilled correctly as the expense of grilling a replacement greatly affected our food cost – not to mention the unsatisfied guest having to return the steak. I constantly worked with the grill chef so we got the timing right. After grilling, each steak was moved to a warm section of the grill for a few minutes 'to rest' and brushed lightly with a strong demi glace which gave a wonderful sheen and added even more powerful flavor. This allowed the meat juices to redistribute in the steak which made the difference between a good steak and a great steak. I would prefer to have the guest wait a few minutes longer while the steak finished cooking rather than have a Kobe steak sitting under the heat lamp waiting for pick up. It was all in the timing.

Since the kitchen was visible to the guests I began to recognize many regulars. Some came in for lunch, some only for dinner. Mr. Chan, a Chinese businessman with an affinity for French oysters and Kobe beef, ate frequently at the Chateaubriand. The first few times he came in I would nod to him to acknowledge his presence or give a slight bow of the head from behind the copper bar. On later visits as we all got to know him better, I began to approach his table to welcome him and perhaps explain about a special. When he came in with other business people I always made a point of going to the table to personally welcome him and his guests and to let him know that a fresh shipment of Belon Oysters – his favorites – had just arrived. If I did not see him coming in one of the waiters would be sure remind me. "Chef, Mista Chan is here la." And I would visit his table. There is an unspoken language that takes place in restaurants when the chef comes to the table with a brief greeting or a special comment for a guest. Sometimes, the less said the better. It's all in the gesture. Mr Chan knew what thoughts this gesture instilled in his guests' minds – admiration and respect for him ensued. Other guests wondered why the chef only went to that table and not to theirs – that particular person must be a special guest, or a VIP? We made sure Mr Chan was always happy. Eight portions of Belons on the half shell and 8 Kobe steaks with two bottles of Chateau Mouton Rothschild left no room for error.

Every evening our resident musicians, a Hungarian trio, played in the restaurant. One played the cello, one the accordion, and the third played the violin. They were amazing musicians, strolling among the tables stopping at each one to serenade guests, paying attention to avoid businessmen in deep discussion. The trio was always trying to get tips from guests – which the Maître forbade. The Hungarian violinist would often put a ten dollar note in the strings of his violin and lean in towards the guest while playing so the money was waving right in front of their nose. Then the Maître would discreetly call him over and remove the money. A short time later the money was back again. They played the *Schwarzer Ziguener* – The Dark Gypsy – for me and believed it was their best melody for guests celebrating a special occasion. They knew it was my favorite.

Often during a busy service they would walk by the copper pickup counter and the accordionist would whisper to me in his thick Hungarian accent, "Chef Bredan, ve are going to play ze *Schwarzer Ziguener* for table six." I would respond "Ok la," and Mr. Soh would smile at my imitation of the local grammar. As the violinist played, the accordionist began to sing in a low baritone, *"Du Schwarzer Ziguener, komm spiel mir was vor. Denn ich will vergessen heut', was ich verlor."* There was a tremendous welcoming and relaxing atmosphere in the restaurant as the waiters carried flaming swords, the Maître walked guests from the wine cellar with a wine bottle on his arm, flames shot high above the copper bar from the charcoal grill, waiters discreetly served food, and all of it with the crooning of the *Schwarzer Ziguener* in the background. The restaurant resembled an edible theatre. Guests loved it. We repeated this scenario every evening like a well rehearsed play – which in many ways it was.

Shortly after the hotel opened, work life took on a sense of regularity. All outlets were open and hotel occupancy began to increase. We were competing with the new opening of the Westin Stamford Hotel located just a few hundred yards away with rooms available at exactly the same price, seventy nine Singaporean dollars per night. The Pan Pacific Hotel was part of a city within a city and linked to the adjacent shopping complex in Marina Square, which was being promoted as the largest shopping complex in South East Asia at the time. Two other hotels completed the commercial development: The Mandarin Oriental Singapore and the Marina Mandarin Hotel.

We were fortunate to get a favorable review in the Singapore *Tatler Magazine*, in which the entire hotel was featured. The main picture was of the lobby looking skywards, a spectacular sight. There was also a picture of the Chateaubriand and its wine cellar, a caption noting that the open bottle concept was new to Singapore. Around the same time Singapore's Best Restaurants guide gave us a glowing review. They used symbols to highlight quality in four areas. Four symbols was the highest rating for each category. They used symbols of chef's hats for the food, dollar signs for price, wine bottles for the wine list, and bow ties for service. We were awarded four symbols in each category – one of the few restaurants in the guide to get all four. I was very happy with this review. It was days like that which made all the hard work and long hours worthwhile. The review mentioned some of the dishes and described the shiitake mushroom soup with puff pastry in great detail. The Kobe beef was mentioned, even describing how each animal is massaged with beer daily to achieve the marbling for which Kobe beef is famous. The Chateaubriand steak was also mentioned, describing how it was served for two people and the poached lobster tail with mango and the passion fruit soufflé were also described. After the review was published these dishes became even more popular.

To promote the hotel, we had a large marketing department. It was my first experience in this domain and I quickly realized that it is an art form. The hotel was independently responsible for marketing itself worldwide. There was a marketing manager responsible for the Middle East, another one for Europe and yet others for Oceania and the USA.

They all reported to the marketing director, an affable Australian called Mark. He would entertain guests in the Chateaubriand and as he walked past the copper grill on his way to his table, he would wave and say: "G'day Brendan." Once his table was served I usually passed by to say hello to his guest who was always a VIP linked in some way to increasing business at the hotel. I once asked him, "Mark, how do you manage to fit all this work in one day, you seem to be always in the hotel with some guest or other?" He responded, "I come to the office at three o'clock in the morning and achieve more before nine o'clock than I could on most days because there are no interruptions." Then he would have breakfast with his family and begin his regular day's work. Thanks to his excellent marketing strategies, the hotel prospered. One of the marketing directors, Cynthia, was English; she was responsible for promoting the hotel in the Middle East, spoke fluent Arabic and was an avid gourmet. She was also very concerned about her appearance, her skin, and her hair, to the point she would ask me for foods she believed would enhance her beauty. "Brendan" she would say, "I want to eat mushrooms today. They contain zinc which is good for my hair." Then I would prepare a mushroom toast for her and she would tell everyone later how the mushrooms were responsible for her beautiful hair and that she ate them at the Chateaubriand.

The Chateaubriand closed on Sunday so that became my day off and was a reason to leave the hotel for the day. There was an outdoor hawker's area at Newton Circle that did a fair job of providing food and dining late into the night, and we often ate there. It was a collection of food stands with vendors preparing very tasty meals with little effort and few utensils. Fish head curry made from red snapper and Bak kut teh were popular dishes; the later was a tasty Chinese soup made with pork ribs, herbs and spices such as star anise, cinnamon, cloves and garlic, usually served with noodles and a light soy sauce. Many hotel chefs congregated there in the evenings. It was not the most dynamic night spot in South East Asia but it filled a void. The night life in Singapore at the time did not come close to that of Bangkok or even Macau or Hong Kong for that matter so many evenings after work, Christine and I went to visit other hotels which like the Pan Pacific, were also cities within a city – just smaller cities. They often had foreign bands rotating every few months. The lobby bar in the Hyatt Hotel was a welcoming place for a few quiet drinks, which was what I appreciated on my evening off – to get a break from the fast pace of the restaurant. At one point they had a wonderful Filipino band that played my favorites from Harry Belafonte. "This is my island in the sun…" and "Daylight come and I wanna go home."

On our way home we usually stopped in the Casablanca night club in the Pan Pacific for a few drinks and listened to our hotel's resident band, the Tigers. This was a six man Syrian band that played excellent music. Johnny the band leader sang in English, French and Arabic. Every time we entered the Casablanca they would sing in French for Christine, "Cheri je t'aime, Cheri je t'adore, Como la salsa de pomodoro." They were one of the best bands in Syria and highly sought after in other Asian countries at the time. Many Middle Eastern guests came to the Casablanca just because of their music and Hassan's great Moroccan food. Osama was the lead singer and did not play any instruments. He told me how important it was for him to sing as much as possible in Arabic so he could preserve his voice and pronunciation. If he sang too much in English, Middle Eastern guests would complain he was losing his great voice. I understood this as I knew that traditional Irish singers faced the same dilemma when they sang mostly in English – they would lose the proper Irish pronunciation which is so important when singing – or speaking in Irish.

The following month as we were celebrating Christine's birthday at the Casablanca, a belly dancer performed and Osama was singing beautifully in Arabic when the strangest thing happened. The Saudi Arabian ambassador was at a table two alcoves from us. The club was full; no one was dancing except the belly dancer. All of a sudden the ambassador got up and walked onto the dance floor and right up to the dancer. He began throwing handfuls of money at her, one handful after the other as he reached into his pockets for more, jumping and clapping his hands at the same time. He then retreated to his seat. The money was lying all over the dance floor: at the girl's feet, on the drums, in the strings of the guitar, and on the stage but the music never stopped and neither did the dancer. I had never seen such an exhibition of Middle Eastern generosity before.

So when I met Johnny the next day, I asked him about the money and he finally explained. He said, "Brendan, it was the Ambassador's way of expressing his appreciation for the dancer and the great music; it is quite a common gesture in Middle Eastern countries." He went on to say it also meant the band could not take a break or even touch the money until the Ambassador left for fear of insulting him. Johnny said, "I had to remind the band to keep playing. We kept looking at the money lying all over the stage, but to stop playing would be an insult, and to pick up the money while the Ambassador was present would be an even greater insult." So they played nonstop until the ambassador left about half an hour later.

Hainanese Chicken Rice

The following dish was very popular in the "Five Domes" twenty four hour coffee shop. It is delicious and very easy to prepare.

Ingredients for 6 servings

1 oz. (30gr.) garlic chopped
¼ cup (1/2 dl.) soy sauce
3 oz. (90gr.) cucumbers sliced
1 oz. (30gr.) chicken fat
2 oz. (60gr.) onions sliced
3 ½ cups (7.5 dl.) chicken stock
Salt and white pepper powder
4 lbs. (1.8kg.) whole baby chicken
3 1/2oz. (115gr.) pickled sliced ginger

¼ cup (1/2 dl.) sesame oil
1/2 oz. (15gr.) salt
1 oz. (30gr.) chives chopped
2 oz. (60gr.) fresh chilies
1 lb. (454gr.) Thai rice

Preparation

- Season chicken inside and out with salt, ginger and half of the garlic.
- Bring water to boil in a stock pot and place chicken inside. Poach for 45-50 minutes (simmering, just below boiling point).
- Remove from stock and baste with a little of the sesame oil seasoned with salt and pepper.
- Cut chicken into pieces, remove bones and arrange in a serving dish.
- Garnish with sliced cucumbers and decorate with fresh chilies and chopped chives.

For the Rice

- Heat chicken fat and sesame oil in a sauce pan.
- Add the remaining chopped garlic and onions.
- Fry until golden brown.
- Add rice and fry for one minute.
- Add chicken stock, season with salt and pepper to taste.
- Cover and simmer for 15-20 minutes until tender.

Assembly

- Serve the chicken with the rice pilaf, soy, and Asian chili sauce separately.

CHAPTER THIRTEEN

Charlie

As I entered our hotel suite one night after the restaurant closed, I saw the book on the coffee table and knew. Christine came in from another room, put her arms around me and said: "Guess what good news I have?" I looked at the book, then looked at her and thought: there must be room for one more in this marriage. Then she told me she was pregnant. This was unbelievably good news for both of us. Although it was not exactly unexpected news, it was extremely joyous never the less, and we were ecstatic. Soon there would be a young Cronin running around. The birth of a child would change our lives. As we wanted to wait for the birth to find out if it was a girl or boy, we nicknamed it 'Charlie' in the interim. The baby names book created interesting discussions between us. What name to choose, Irish or Swiss?

I suggested if it's a boy we could call it Connor. Christine said if we live in a French speaking country later, that name will be shortened to Con – meaning stupid in French. Needless to say Connor got nixed. Another one was Siobhán. Christine once again came to the rescue saying the French pronunciation was similar to *cheval* which means horse in French – not a flattering name in any case, except for the horse. And so began the long process of name choosing and as time went by we shortened the list. Christine's doctor reserved the hospital bed months in advance of the birth; this was due to Singapore being a popular destination for mothers from surrounding countries to give birth. Singapore had some of the most modern hospitals in South East Asia at the time. The doctor told us an interesting story about an upcoming date, one which many Chinese parents would love to have their child born on – the eighth of August nineteen eighty eight. The date included four eights ensuring great life – and much luck to babies born on that auspicious day. The words luck and eight have similar pronunciation in Chinese, making number eight a very lucky number for them – Charlie would be born long before then, however.

By now Mr. Soh was capable of running the kitchen and could be left in charge for a few days on his own. It was around this time that Remy asked me to go to our sister property, the Pan Pacific Hotel in Kuala Lumpur, to assist with a ten day Irish food promotion. I took the short flight to KL – as it is often referred to in Asia – and began preparing the menu with Wolfgang, the executive chef. I admired Wolfgang instantly as a very competent and likable chef; he had good knowledge of classical Irish cuisine and had many of the recipes already in place. I brought my mother's Irish Soda bread recipe and we put it on the menu. Irish stew was a hit as the Malays love lamb. Boiled bacon and cabbage was a different story due to religious restrictions. Wolfgang had an innovative presentation for Irish stew. He wrapped the boiled vegetables in a cooked cabbage leaf and presented them like a small parcel on top of the lamb stew, sprinkling the lot with chopped parsley. The dark green color contrast of the parsley was beautiful. I was impressed that he knew so much about Irish cooking – which was not exactly world renowned.

On opening night I was introduced to the Malaysian Minster for Tourism, local business owners, and interviewed by the press as the "Irish Master Chef" flown in from Singapore. There was no point trying to tell them that I was not a Master Chef – I would have liked to become one, but as of yet, I was not. My interviews with the Malaysian press was the first time I learned that not everything said in an interview with the press is printed correctly. The promotion ran for two weeks with a full house each night. It was a tremendous success, I believe in part due to Malaysia's British past; many of the foods we offered had similarities, particularly desserts.

The day before my departure for Singapore, Wolfgang invited me out for drink. We chatted on various food and travel topics, but at one point he changed the conversation and said: "Brendan, I am leaving Malaysia and moving to Australia. I will be the Executive Chef on the opening team of the next Pan Pacific Hotel on the gold coast in Eastern Australia. Would you be interested in the Executive Sous Chef position?" I was surprised at this offer: I had only worked with him for two weeks, but during that time we got along very well. I also wondered if he had told Remy he would be offering me this position. I replied: "Wolfgang, that is a tremendous offer, thank you for considering me. At the moment we are expecting our first child and I am only half way into my three year contract in Singapore. Can you give me some time to think about this?" We agreed to keep in touch. I thought to live and work in Australia would be a great experience – it was relatively close to Singapore so moving there would be easy.

The morning after I returned to Singapore, Peter was having coffee on his own at our chefs breakfast table in a corner of the coffee shop. He asked me how the promotion went and we chatted for a while. Then he said: "Brendan, I will be leaving in a few weeks. I am moving to another property. I am letting all the sous chefs know one by one." This was another surprise but not unusual, given the international circuit in which chefs revolve. He was the person who brought me from Bangkok to Singapore; we had worked very well together to open the hotel. He was an excellent chef, highly organized, and produced great flavors. I would be sorry to see him leave.

The next day Remy asked to see me in his office. This was not an unusual request as we did this many times to discuss menu items, food presentation and the likes while the other sous chefs and Jess – the secretary – came in and out as the door was always open. This time was different, however, as there was just the two of us – and he closed the door. Remy always addressed me in the formal regardless whether we spoke French, German or English. This conversation was in German. "Herr Cronin," he began, "as you know Peter is leaving and we need an Executive Sous Chef. I have been watching your work over the last eighteen months and I believe you are ready to take on that position. If you agree, I will recommend you for the job to the Food and Beverage Director. What do you think?" I was surprised and very grateful for his positive comments on my work and responded: "Thank you for the offer, I am happy to accept it." We shook hands, and I went back to the Chateaubriand to prepare for the dinner service. What I didn't expect was that this promotion would be in addition to my current work schedule. I would remain on as sous chef of the Chateaubriand while simultaneously taking on the Executive Sous Chef position and the responsibility of all outlet kitchens – and one hundred and fifty staff – ensuring their smooth operation, while reporting directly to Remy. It was a lot of added responsibility, but I suppose I couldn't look a gift horse in the mouth – and I got a raise.

This promotion changed my work day dramatically. I explained to Mr. Soh that he would have to take on more responsibility, which was not a bad thing for him; he was ready for a more senior role. He had proven himself as a dedicated chef since the opening. I would be leaving the hotel one day and he would be ready to take over. This was actually a stipulation by the Singaporean government in my contract. During my time at the hotel, I was to train a local chef to a level that would allow him to take over my position after my three year contract was over.

So I moved into the chef's office with Remy and Jess the secretary, and took over Peter's desk. This position involved more paperwork than I was currently used to. Jess was a fantastic organizer and kept us all on track. She helped me tremendously with my transition to the number two spot in the kitchen. A petite girl, she would walk through the busy, noisy kitchens handing out Banquet Event Order sheets to department chefs, getting time sheets signed, and sending staff schedules over to payroll. She would chat in English and Chinese with the local sous chefs, dodging in between trolleys of food, large butter and ice sculptures never once getting upset.

My new daily schedule began in the coffee shop at nine o'clock where I would check that breakfast was running smoothly. This was a twenty four hour outlet and provided breakfast for all hotel guests including room service so it was not uncommon to serve one thousand breakfasts before ten o'clock. If there were no issues there I headed to the office and my first job was to read the night auditor's report which included revenue generated from each outlet and banquets. I was particularly interested to see if the revenue from large functions held the previous day was credited the same day as the function. That was crucial because the food cost was charged each day and if the revenue did not offset it, our general daily food cost would rise dramatically. This figure would be in a report to the General Manager which he read by mid-morning. I had to have any errors identified and relayed to Remy first thing every morning so that if the GM called him about the food cost, he was prepared to answer.

After an hour in the office, I left on my rounds of the outlets and banquet kitchen to meet with each sous chef and talk about their day, any special menus, reservation numbers, VIP's and any private parties. So vast was the hotel that this task took me about two hours. Meeting the other sous chefs and having a chance to chat with them was the best time of my day in this new role. They did not need me for any cooking advice; they were all very professional in their own right. My new role was more of an organizer and ensuring food orders, staff scheduling, and over all food costs were in line. Sometimes the Chinese sous chef would order a large shipment of expensive shark fin on the last day of the month. Essentially we would incur the cost in the last few days of the month but only get the revenue to offset it in the beginning of the following month, which greatly affected the month end food cost. In these instances it was better to order in the new month. To help eliminate this problem I asked the purchasing manager to call me if a large order of expensive food items was placed near the end of the month. Then I would go to the sous chef in question and see if we could reduce the amount to help keep the food cost in line or have it delivered on the first of the following month.

Most of my work day was spent in this fashion, helping the other sous chefs and ensuring their outlets were running smoothly. My day usually ended around eleven o'clock at night when the night shift for the coffee shop arrived. Once they arrived at work I knew the coffee shop could run smoothly through the night, room service orders would be filled and one thousand breakfasts would be ready by six in the morning and hopefully I would get a quiet night's rest without any phone calls.

My new role was not always easy. Prior to this I was just one of the sous chefs but now I was their supervisor of sorts. It was a balancing act. Fortunately for me the hotel provided training for recently promoted mid-level managers; it was invaluable in helping me make the transition while remaining on good terms with all kitchen staff. Despite the training, there were times when discussions with Remy got heated. We would meet in his office and ask Jess to go to the staff canteen for a coffee break. When she closed the door we lowered the blinds on the windows looking into the various kitchens and argued our points of view. It was a good way of clearing the air, and no one ever saw us, no one lost face, and when we finished we both went about our duties and Jess came back from her coffee break and opened the blinds – she knew why they were closed. We made a point not to let disagreements linger – spit it out and get over it! Tomorrow was another day. Remy was fantastic at that, and I learned so many managerial traits from him.

As Executive Sous Chef, I also met many of the vendors. Singapore had strict policies governing the relationship between vendors and purchasing managers – to the point that contracts with major suppliers were only valid for thirty days. After that time vendors had to bid on contracts again. It kept everyone on their toes. It was a constant task to know which vendor was supplying a particular product in any given month. One vendor in particular was extremely helpful. He was an American named Bob. He owned his own company in Singapore which imported American foods – some of which we had on the menu, notably US beef, conch and abalone from the Caribbean. He would come to Remy's office in August to get our order for American turkeys for our Christmas menus. It would take that long to have them ordered and shipped by container to the Far East. It usually took us a few days to compile the order.

Our first task was to write the Christmas menus then calculate how many turkeys would be sold in each outlet and check with the banquet sales office to see how many holiday parties and banquets were reserved. Then we could give Bob the final count and place the order. It was around this time that our weekly supply of Dutch veal and Swiss dairy products from Europe were refused entry to the country and were returned by the Singaporean customs. There had been a nuclear explosion at a power plant in Chernobyl in Russia and the radiation fallout fell over Europe. The Singaporean customs determined the food unsafe due to the levels of radiation and had it sent back to Europe – apparently it was ok for Europeans to eat. Our suppliers then began importing from New Zealand, South Korea and more from the US.

Bob invited Christine and me to his apartment for dinner to meet his wife, Joan, an avid tennis player, who was also pregnant with their first child. We soon became good friends and helped each other with lots of solid advice on doctors, nursery furniture, and the likes as both couples were navigating new waters by having a child in a foreign country so any information we could share was beneficial to both. We have remained good friends to this day.

Now that I was visiting each hotel outlet on a daily basis, I observed in-depth how the sous chefs ran their outlets compared to how I was running the Chateaubriand, and I began to see how we could help each other during busy periods. It was common for one outlet to be very busy while another was quite slow so we began to cross-train staff to help in situations like this. We cross trained between the Polynesian kitchen and the coffee shop and between the Chinese kitchen, the Japanese kitchen and the Chateaubriand. As staff exchanged roles the system began to pay off. It allowed each sous chef to have back up staff trained for their menus during busy periods. As this cross training was taking place I spent some time in the Japanese kitchen. The discipline was admirable. To see these chefs in action with a simple kitchen knife was humbling. And I thought I could use a knife correctly?

Akio frequently prepared eel for robatayaki – a form of Japanese grilling. Eels were delivered live and stored in a fish tank. Preparing a slippery live eel is very difficult but Akio made it seem so easy. He kept the eels in a bucket of ice water on the table which slowed their metabolism so they wiggled less. Using a chopping block with a small hole at one end, he removed one eel at a time from the ice water, placed its head over the hole and drove a large nail through its head pinning it to the board and killing it instantly. Now that one end of the eel was tethered, with lighting speed he inserted his knife under the eel's chin with his right hand while holding the body in his curled left hand. With the thumb of his left hand on the back of the razor sharp knife he guided the knife down the length of the eel's belly slicing it open and removing its insides all in one swift movement. The entire episode took less than 15 seconds and gave a new meaning to the term 'fresh fish.' He cut off the head, rinsed the flesh and cut the eel in four inch lengths, then slid them on skewers. Then he reached for the next eel. Marinated with soy sauce, this eel would be on the menu as eel robatayaki that same evening. While he was making these skilled preparations, Akio never stopped explaining to me how the Kobe beef was produced.

By now Charlie's birth was approaching fast. Christine was getting impatient as the tropical heat and humidity did not make it easy on her. Never the less she walked everywhere, keeping active despite the heat. She joked when we had dinner together because her belly stuck out so much that she could place her plate on it without it falling. On our second Christmas day in Singapore she joined all the hotel expats who were not involved in food production for lunch at Raffles Hotel. So while this group was enjoying Singapore slings at the long bar and a traditional Christmas lunch at Raffles Hotel, I was a few hundred yards away with a full restaurant keeping guests happy. We were never together on holidays and special events. This was not a new phenomenon – work took precedence and now with added responsibilities, my work week was even longer. The following menu was served that Christmas at the Chateaubriand. We also had a Christmas turkey lunch for any guest who requested it.

Sliced poached lobster tail on crisp greens with mango and pickled tamarind topped with walnut champagne vinaigrette

Pheasant consommé with lentils

Atlantic salmon steak in a light fennel cream

Blackcurrant sherbet

Poached beef tenderloin with
apple horseradish cream

Clove soufflé

Blue Mountain coffee
Or
Earl Grey tea
Les griottes

To prepare the turkey I removed the legs and deboned them –
leaving the breast on the bone. I then made a meat stuffing, adding
raisins marinated in brandy and glazed chestnuts. I stuffed the legs
with this, rolled them and tied them with butcher's string. On
Christmas day I roasted the legs. In a separate oven I roasted the
breast; when it was almost cooked I removed the flesh from the
bone and kept it warm in a shallow tray with a little demi glace to
prevent it from drying out. Now the turkey was completely boneless
which allowed me to get more portions per pound than if I roasted
it the traditional way and the flesh did not dry out – a major
challenge for most restaurants. Dry turkey was not worth sitting
down at the table for.

Christmas was a special time at the hotel which was highly
decorated for the festive season. A tall pine tree was flown in from
Canada for the lobby. The Executive housekeeper and engineering
staff decorated it with lights and ornaments. Christmas songs
played throughout the hotel – the sounds floating up the atrium.
Josef made a large gingerbread house which was placed by the
fountain in the lobby, and his Dresden Stolen – a typical Christmas

fruit bread originating from the town of Dresden, in Germany – was widely available. Each outlet entrance was decorated with smaller Christmas trees and they also had Christmas carols playing. Christmas foods were on every menu; I added roast turkey to the Chateaubriand menu with my mother's bread sauce. Listening to Bing Crosby singing 'White Christmas' despite the thirty degree Celsius heat outside was a stark contrast from my winter season in Switzerland which were dominated by freezing temperatures and snow.

Charlie was born a few days after Christmas at Gleneagles Hospital. It was a girl and we named her Shannon. We were both overjoyed. She was home a few days later in time for the New Year celebrations. As we were leaving the hospital room Christine reached to pick up Shannon, but the nurse touched her arm and said, "Both of you can go to the front entrance and I will bring the baby to you." I asked: "Why can we not carry the baby ourselves, we have waited a long time for this moment?" Apparently it was hospital policy not to allow new parents to take their baby from the nursery for fear of mixing up babies. After hearing this, I asked her, "Have you looked at this baby recently? Can you imagine an Asian mother bringing home a blonde blue-eyed Caucasian baby? There would be some serious explaining to do in that house." The nurse just smiled at me. We followed her advice and walked to the front entrance. I kept thinking how could anyone get their baby mixed up with ours? The infants all had Asian features except for one. All of the Asian babies neatly lined up in little cots, with a much bigger cot to hold a much bigger baby at the end. It was clear to me who each belonged to. But I did not mention this and did not make a scene so we waited patiently for Shannon at the entrance. The last step before check out was a signature by me onto an official government document stating that Shannon would not claim Singaporean citizenship later in life. Apparently this was a standard procedure for all foreigners born on the Island of Singapore – then after signing, we could leave with our precious family addition.

Since my promotion to Executive Sous Chef I had become the go-to person for all one hundred and fifty staff in the kitchen, and anyone else who needed help with something or other involving food – including guests. The phone rang in our suite at three o'clock one morning. I picked up quickly before it woke the baby. It was the reception desk. "Good morning Mr. Cronin, we are sorry to wake you up. There is a VIP guest checking out in four hours and he requested six deluxe in-flight meals for his private jet at Changi Airport. Can you arrange that?" Could I prepare something? Of course I could. What else was I to say? Tell him to call room service? 'No' was not an option in a five star luxury hotel. There were no nine to five rules here, just get the job done and keep the guest happy – whatever it takes. So I responded: "I'll be right down." The receptionist gave me the list of foods the guest requested. After reading it, I realized that at least I had not been called out of bed to make ham and cheese sandwiches – they wanted the works. Lobster, caviar, foie gras, prawns, smoked duck, wines, Perrier water, homemade chocolate pralines you name it, and they wanted it now. After running around to all of the hotel outlets during the middle of the night collecting the most expensive foods from each menu I finished the list by seven o' clock and had everything packed, ready for pick up and charged to the master bill. The pilot and a stewardess came to pick up the food and signed for it, not even looking at the price. Then I had time for a coffee with Christine and Shannon before starting my regular day.

I was fortunate to be able to visit many hotel departments on my daily rounds. A visit to the reception generally began by walking directly across the expansive marbled lobby floor, greeting guests as they passed by. Management asked all expatriate chefs to be visible in the outlets and hotel in general – they felt from a marketing standpoint, it was important for guests to meet and interact with European chefs. This was a big contrast to my time at the Hotel Elite in Switzerland where I was told to stay out of sight for exactly the same reason – because I was a foreigner.

At the reception I would inquire on the status of the presidential suite occupants; perhaps they may make a dinner reservation for the Chateaubriand? On to the business office to check on an invoice, the loading dock to verify a food shipment, the stewarding department to inspect the new chafing dishes, and the banquet kitchen artist to check the ice carving for a VIP function that evening. Then the laundry room to pick up a freshly starched hat, and a chat with Lan, the laundry manager, to show him a picture of one of his starched hats as it appeared in The Straits Times – the Singapore daily newspaper– on my head. His reaction was precious; he smiled saying "Thank you la" because he too, although indirectly, contributed to guest's satisfaction – a difficult situation for him as he only got third party compliments.

It's the staff that makes a great hotel great – not the guest; the guest comes in because of what a great staff does.

When the presidential suite was occupied, it was important that everyone knew the guest's name and treated them as a VIP. Every outlet hostess knew the guest's name in case they called to make a reservation. The hotel operator knew, the concierge knew, and the outlet managers knew that when guests left the suite to move around the hotel – either to the bar, the pool, or to an outlet – it was all hands on deck for the staff to ensure satisfaction. The guest's favorite flowers were noted in the guest history file, as well as favorite drinks, most ordered food items, favorite color, and so on. It was all part of trying to exceed their expectation.

At one point we had a sheik staying in the presidential suite for a few weeks and as usual the entire staff was made aware of his presence. He ordered all his meals through room service, had a fully stocked bar installed, and was generally undemanding – the type of guest hotels love. He paid his bill every week and invited senior management for cocktails at his suite once every ten days as a gesture of genuine Middle Eastern hospitality.

One morning at four o'clock there was a call to room service from his suite with an order for Mechoui – a whole roast lamb – and of course room service called me. When a guest in the presidential suite orders anything out of the ordinary, the answer is always yes. Then we figure out how to do it. I called Hassan. "Hassan," I shouted on the phone, "the sheik is hungry, he wants a Mechoui." Hassan could not believe it. "Brendan," he said, "it takes four hours to cook and I don't have a whole lamb in the house!" I replied, "We'll have to go to the market to get a whole lamb. I will meet you at the reception in ten minutes with money and a driver." I sent Hassan off in the hotel limousine to the market to get a lamb and went to the kitchen to heat up the oven, make coffee and wait for him to return. With a pending room service order from such an important guest, I could not possibly return to bed.

The coffee shop kitchen was busy preparing for breakfast while also serving regular room service food orders, and they had no room to roast a lamb. I decided to heat up an oven in the main kitchen instead. The adjacent bakery, which also worked through the night, was in full swing as the bakers prepared Danish and breakfast breads. I had croissants and coffee ready when Hassan returned. "I bought three lambs. The sheik will order another Mechoui, I can assure you," he said, laying the lambs on the stainless steel table. Hassan began to wipe the lamb inside and out with vinegar to clean the meat of any bacteria, a procedure quite common in countries where meat is bought in open markets. He marinated the lamb with cumin, garlic, lemon, coriander, butter, and made incisions in the thick parts such as the leg and put it in the oven to roast. He told me traditionally the lamb would be roasted over an open fire or in a Mechoui pit or oven in the ground.

Then we sat down and had coffee and the croissants while the lamb cooked, he told me about life and work in Saudi Arabia – and he described the public executions. He explained how the people gathered round the square after morning prayers to witness the spectacle. The victim was brought out, blindfolded and put kneeling facing Mecca. The executioner would remove any hair from the back of the victims neck, then step back and using both hands and all his strength, and with one swift swoosh of the Scimitar sword, sever the victim's head while leaving an inch or so of flesh so the head did not fall on the ground – apparently a faux pas in the executioner's profession according to Hassan. As Hassan described this he stood up, raising both hands over his head and lowering them in a swoosh mimicking the swing of the Scimitar.

He went on to explain how the body was removed, the market stands were put back and everything returned to normal – everyone got the message. It was a very detailed description and one that put the hair standing on the back of my neck, which gave me goose bumps – now I was even afraid to shave. It was an amazing experience: there I was at five o'clock in the morning in the large banquet kitchen, an Irish chef sitting on an empty milk crate having coffee and croissants with this fantastic Moroccan chef, listening to a cold-hearted description of a public beheading in Saudi Arabia. All while we were cooking Mechoui for a sheik in the presidential suite. However, it was just another day at work in the belly of a five star hotel.

Hours after the sheik's call, room service delivered the Mechoui to his suite, which Hassan had presented on a large silver platter. He prepared a light couscous with peas and cumin, Harrisa (a spicy North African sauce), and some yoghurt-based dipping sauces to go with the lamb. Watching Hassan carefully arrange the Mechoui was evidence of his caring attitude. It was as if he was sending this food to the guest with love and hope that they would enjoy it. The next evening as we sat around the chefs table for dinner, Hassan described how the sheik asked to meet him and invited him to the presidential suite that morning. Hassan told us in detail: "I was nervous taking the guest elevator, as I did not know if a complaint or a compliment was in the offing. I entered the presidential suite and an aide ushered me to the main room where the sheik was sitting on a couch. He complimented me on the Mechoui saying it was the best he had ever eaten and gestured to me to sit down. I thanked him. "Would you like a drink?" he asked. "No thank you," I replied. But the sheik insisted and asked the aide to pour a whiskey. I refused again, citing my religion, while glancing at the fully stocked bar. Then the Sheik asked me, "How much do they pay you here? I will pay you more if you come and cook for me. You are wasting your time and talent here." I was unsure how to answer for fear of insulting a hotel guest, and politely refused his offer, thanked him and I returned to the kitchen.

It was a great story coming from Hassan who described the sheik as this majestic figure, his black goatee contrasting with the flowing white robes, his aides waiting on him, and how Hassan thought he could have easily become one of them – travelling around the world cooking Mechoui.

Andi, the Executive Chef from the Mandarin Oriental in Macau, was visiting Singapore and came to see me at the Pan Pacific. He had left Macau, and was now in Switzerland teaching cooking in a Hotel Management School. It was great to see him again. We had worked very well together for six months in Macau. I found him to be extremely well organized and well respected by the Macanese and upper management. After our initial greetings, he asked me: "Brendan, how long more will you remain in Singapore?" "I have just one more year left on my contract, why do you ask?" I responded. What he said next took me completely by surprise. "There will be a teaching position open in a few months in a school in Switzerland and I think you should consider it." When it rains it pours in the Cronin household – I had received one offer from Wolfgang for Australia and now another offer in Switzerland. I was blessed to have such opportunities in my work and to have met so many chefs who believed in me and my cooking abilities. As I sat there with Andi, I thought about the possibility of living in Australia – it would be an adventure of a life time, just a short flight from Singapore. It would be a step towards opening my own hotel as Executive Chef and developing my career with the company, maybe traveling to more locations in the South Seas and opening new properties.

I heard stories of chefs who became opening specialists. Remy was one of them. They assembled an opening team, developed restaurant concepts, wrote menus, trained local chefs and took care of the thousands of details it takes to get a new hotel opened; they would run it for two years, and then move on to the next opening with another crew. Was this the life that is in store for me? Or was teaching in my future? I was not sure. It was a very difficult decision to make. The teaching avenue had many advantages. As a professional chef, I was always at work when the baby was awake. The long hours did not matter much when it was just Christine and me. I worked hard and then we went out on the town and partied hard. Now with Shannon on board, I recognized that this changed things, and I began to realize that I did not see both of my girls as much as I would like. On the other hand I loved my work, the excitement of the hotels, meeting the guests, working with the staff, and experiencing the adrenaline rush of service. But I was still working eighty hour weeks and not getting any younger. The prospect of having weekends and holidays off was very appealing.

But then the doubt crept in – I was not sure I could cook well enough to teach it. And I would be leaving the luxury hotel circuit in South East Asia where I had begun to build a network of chefs. I knew I could make a good bisque with my eyes closed, but to teach someone to do it was another matter altogether, especially if they were not professionals. I mentioned this fact to Andi and his response made me think more seriously about his offer. "Brendan," he replied, "what have you been doing since you left Switzerland seven years ago? You have been teaching kitchen staff in different countries how to work together, cook, season and present food the way you want it. Now all you have to do is the same thing using classroom guidelines." I hadn't thought about it like that, but I realized he was right. I told him I would think about it and we agreed to stay in touch.

Christine and I talked every day about these two offers and what they entailed for our future. We weighed the possibilities of each one from my professional career standpoint and from her working ability standpoint. We loved living in Asia and had traveled a fair amount. We wanted to continue that lifestyle. My exposure to the many different foods enriched my knowledge of flavors and food combinations – if we moved to Australia that would continue. If we moved to Switzerland it would most likely stop. On the other hand I had not had a Christmas day off in almost 20 years; the same went for New Year's Eve and many other major holidays. I was spending less time with my family than what I would have liked. So after all these discussions we finally came to an agreement – I wrote to Andi to tell him I was interested to begin learning about teaching.

After a few months, the time came for us to leave Singapore. Ironically Remy was also leaving around the same time, moving on to open another property. The kitchen staff organized a barbeque at a park off the East Coast Parkway overlooking the bay. There, with the warm tropical evening sea breeze fanning the charcoal flames we laughed, joked, and cheered. They gave me gifts and letters of thanks. Some were crying and so was I at times. Many friendships were built during my stay. Remy gave a little speech and thanked me for all my hard work. We took pictures together and we said our goodbyes. We had spent three years in this beautiful city island nation. Three unforgettable years, during which I met wonderful people, great chefs, eaten incredible foods, received great restaurant reviews for the Chateaubriand, and made many friends for life. We arrived as two and were leaving as three. For both Christine and me, Singapore would continue to have a special place in our hearts – it would always be Shannon's birthplace.

Raspberry Butter Sauce
(Beurre Blanc Aux Framboises)

This was a very popular sauce – offered as a side – at the Chateaubriand. It is easy to prepare and can be served with pan-fried or grilled chicken, fish, scallops, prawns (shrimp) or grilled or broiled lobster. It is also ideal with roast vegetables. Guests loved the sharp taste and creamy mouth feel this sauce added to the meal. Make it at the last minute as it is tricky to keep warm.

Ingredients for 5-6 portions:
¼ cup (60ml.) raspberry vinegar
¼ cup (60ml.) dry white wine
¼ cup (60ml.) pureed raspberries
1 oz. (30gr.) finely chopped shallots
4½ oz. (130gr.) cold unsalted butter (garlic clove-sized cubes)
Salt and black pepper mill to taste

Procedure:
- Using a heavy bottomed stainless steel saucepan reduce the vinegar, wine, and shallots on low heat to 1/3 of the original volume.
- Add the pureed raspberries and remove the pan from the heat.
- Whisk in the butter cubes one at a time – ensuring the first one is almost melted before adding the next.
- If necessary return the pan briefly to low heat to keep the mixture warm enough to melt the cubes – but do not let it boil.
- If desired, strain out the shallots – personally I leave them in for extra flavor.
- Season to taste with salt and black pepper mill.

Tips
- Keep warm until required.
- The consistency should be creamy.
- If it looks like melted butter it has been heated too much.

CHAPTER FOURTEEN

Back in the Classroom

After seven years working in wonderful hotels in Africa and South East Asia, I was back in Switzerland – still cooking, but from a very different perspective. My career was entering a new era. Gone was the excitement, fast pace, and unpredictability of the large hotels, now replaced with the routine and precision of a Swiss Hotel Management School. Nevertheless, I quickly realized that my travels, hotel experience, and languages had prepared me very well for this opportunity. It would be easier to learn the principles of teaching than to accumulate hospitality industry experience to use in teaching. Literally overnight, my hotel experience – something I had taken for granted up to now– became a valued skill. My understanding of how hotels operated, the guests' expectations, and the staff's trials and tribulations all became a library from which I created anecdotes to illustrate particular points during class.

But bringing examples of my previous work to the classroom was a major challenge for me. Working in hotel kitchens was always an endurance test: the rough language expressed in loud voices coupled with hand and facial gestures required no translation; this was no place for softies, timelines were set and met at all costs because the guest was king. But the school was different: the students – the next generation of hotel leaders – were here to learn management principles. They were the 'new guest.' I would have to change and adapt to get the message across.

We were living in the small village of Bluche in the Swiss Alps and home to 'Les Roches' – one of the more renowned Hotel Management Schools in the world. Bluche – located next to the world famous ski resort of Crans Montana – holds the Guinness Book of Records title for being the smallest village in the world with the most nationalities – an accolade attributed due to the large resident student population spanning over sixty countries. The transition to small town life from the bustling city of Singapore was a difficult transition for both of us. Christine and I no longer took taxis everywhere as in the cities. There were no major shopping complexes or large cinemas, no major hotels to go to and sit in the lobby sipping Singapore slings while listening to Filipinos playing Harry Belafonte. It was very different – but it was so enjoyable.

Being both from rural backgrounds we embraced the outdoors, skiing, and hiking. Our life style changed and we became interested in different things such as picnics by the river, biking, and long walks in the alpine forests. I was off every weekend and we began to explore other towns and historical sites in the valley. The additional regular time off had been the single most important factor that affected my transition from industry to academia because it affected my family. I now had time to spend with them. I went from working an eighty hour week to a fifty hour week while continuing to do what I loved. The school was a ten minute walk from our apartment – I didn't even have to drive.

We had been in Switzerland for about a month when I began to notice Christine was not settling in as quickly as she did every other time we moved. I assumed it was just a matter of her needing more time to readapt so I was very surprised when one evening during dinner she said: "I think we should return to the Far East. I am not happy here." I nearly choked on my food – this was unexpected. We had made the decision together to leave Singapore and return to her country, and she should have felt at home by now – after all, I was still the foreigner. To start questioning our decision now, after the move, was disturbing to say the least. I was working all day at the school and putting in extra hours on weekends to learn the necessary material to prepare myself for taking over a class of my own and had not paid much attention to how she was adjusting – until now. Christine had not yet met many people in the village to interact with.

She was experiencing severe reverse culture shock to her own country and believed returning to Asia would alleviate it. After living for so many years in South East Asia, Christine did not recognize her country anymore and could not see herself settling back into the highly structured Swiss lifestyle. She felt the people were very distant – the warmth of the Asians was missing. I had to agree. After Singapore and previously, Macau and Bangkok, a city of 11 million people, living in a village with a population of 500 required a major cultural adjustment. It was true that compared to the warmth of the Asians, the Swiss were a little cold and we both knew it would take some time for us to readjust. But she insisted and asked me to call Wolfgang in KL and see if the Australian position was still available – maybe we could move to Australia? I asked her to be patient at least for one semester and if that did not work out we would consider returning to the tropics.

Andi – the person who brought me to Bluche – began to guide me in learning the techniques of teaching cooking to non-professionals. There were five chefs and three pastry chefs each teaching different courses. We had many similarities: many of them had traveled to different countries during their careers, working with large hotel companies. Some, like me, were also farmer's sons and had completed a similar circuit, Africa, the Middle East and Asia – and some wore moustaches! The majority was Swiss, some were Swiss Master Chefs and some were studying for the Master Chef exam.

Les Roches had burned to the ground three years previously and the owners rebuilt it in a spectacular fashion on the edge of an alpine plateau one thousand two hundred meters above sea level. They had the latest equipment installed with modern classroom design, functional reception areas, and a lobby coffee bar, a sun drenched south facing terrace with a breathtaking alpine view, landscaped gardens and a swimming pool. Every kitchen had copious amounts of windows providing spectacular views of the surrounding Alps and the town of Sierre visible in the distance as it spread out on the valley floor hundreds of meters below – a tremendous change from the many windowless kitchens of my professional career. Sierre boasted over two hundred days of sunshine per year.

The school was spotless, and the kitchens even more so. Temples of stainless steel, white tiled walls from floor to ceiling, red tiled floors, and filled with the most modern equipment, made them the ultimate working paradise for any chef. Every conceivable piece of equipment was available to demonstrate cooking techniques to students. Tilting frying pans, tilting stockpots, induction stoves, vacuum packing machines, steam injection ovens, pressure steamers, and a computer were just some of the equipment I had to get used to while preparing food with students.

On the first day of my teaching career, I was assisting Rudi, a highly dynamic chef who had worked for major hotel companies in Africa, the Middle East, and in the Philippines and had been teaching for a few years at Les Roches. The practical class schedule began at seven in the morning in the production kitchen, the largest kitchen in the school. Students had already eaten breakfast at six thirty. During roll call – to put the students at ease – Rudi spoke a few words of Swahili to the East Africans in the class, gave a greeting in Arabic to the Middle Eastern students and then finished with some Tagalog for the Filipinos. They would respond in kind, sometimes giggling among themselves – looking strangely mal adroit in their chef's uniforms.

The class objective for the day: cook and serve a two course lunch for five hundred 'guests', who happened to be their fellow students. The third course – dessert – would be prepared by a pastry teacher with another class in a different section of the kitchen in addition to baking fresh bread and dinner rolls. There were twenty five students in the class originating from twenty two countries on five continents – sixty five nationalities were represented in the entire school. It was imperative they got along together. Ingredients were arranged on large trays and students were assigned in groups based on menu components. One group prepared the starch, another prepared the vegetables, still another made the soup, and yet another group prepared the main course. In addition we selected two students to prepare vegetarian dishes.

After the initial briefing, the groups assembled at their pre-assigned stations throughout the kitchen. Rudi and I rotated between them to ensure the food was prepared according to the recipe. The simpler the recipes were written, the easier it was for students to prepare it, and the more time it gave the instructor to move between groups ensuring a positive outcome. These students were not professionals and had no intention of becoming professional chefs, but rather hotel managers. They could not be left on their own for any length of time for fear of an accident or ruining the food, or in some cases, getting up to some devilment. I chatted with students as they chopped vegetables, trying to hold back my frustration at seeing the vegetables cut unevenly, or the inappropriate way the knife was held, or when food fell on the floor due to their inattention. I was surprised to see so many Asian students in class and I talked often with them about their customs, foods and my travels to their home countries. Their eyes would light up when I mentioned I had lived or traveled in their homeland and knew a little about their culture. During these exchanges, their longing for home and family often emerged as a tremor in their voices. I had to remember they were in unfamiliar surroundings and very far from home – I had been in that situation most of my professional life so a little empathy went a long way. If Christine experienced culture shock moving to Bluche, I could not imagine what it was like for them.

It was during these classes I realized the difference in teaching non-professionals compared to the professional chefs I had worked with. Up until now in my career, I would ask a chef to prepare such and such a dish with the expectation that they had the skill, understood the terminology, and also knew the cooking steps to complete it correctly. I never taught anyone how to use a knife before. That was an accepted basic requirement for any position in the kitchen – except perhaps an apprentice on their first day. Now I had to teach students how to hold and use a knife, which was often bigger than any knife they had ever seen. Chopping a vegetable – or any other food – without looking at it is a skill practiced by most chefs. The coordination of both hands – the first knuckle of the middle finger of the left hand guiding the blade of the knife along the food – is so ingrained in professional chefs that it becomes second nature with time, and not even considered a skill. So it surprised me when students would ask how I could look at them, ask and answer questions, all without looking at the food I was chopping. It was a difficult question to answer, and I realized that I did not know! I never thought about it. It was like asking someone, "How do you breathe?" I had always done it like that. But such an answer was not good enough in the classroom – it did not serve the student. There was no learning in such answers.

Despite all my experience, I now had to learn the simple steps of how to teach chopping a vegetable to non-professionals, so they could use the knife like professional chefs. It sounded like a joke but made me realize that it's one thing to perform a task, it's another matter entirely to describe or demonstrate it to another person or audience with such detail that they also can do it – with precision. Once I mastered the sequence of simple-to-follow steps, it was easy to teach it and then have the satisfaction of watching students prepare five hundred portions of almost perfectly chopped vegetables without any bits of finger mixed in. It was my first time differentiating between knowing a subject and being able to teach it with a positive outcome. The key to a successful outcome – in the case of chopping vegetables – was to let the body of the knife blade touch against the first knuckle of the middle finger with the tip of that finger curled inwards towards the palm – away from the edge of the blade – while keeping the other fingers behind the middle finger. Using the first knuckle as a guide, the tip of the middle finger was always half an inch away from the cutting edge of the blade, which if practiced correctly, makes it impossible to cut one's finger.

The class was programmed to the minute. It was like a theater, every performance a mirror of the previous one. In essence it was very similar to the Chateaubriand. I began to use the same approach with the students as I did with the chefs in the restaurant by bringing in a little humor. I was determined that in my class students would not experience the fear I did as a boy in the National School. I believed that if an upbeat atmosphere worked for chefs in a professional kitchen then it would also work for students in the classroom and create a more conducive learning environment.

Rudi led the students by designating task after task and when they were finished, they were given another task – there was no down time. If there was, it would be a time students began thinking – and acting – stupidly. After all we were in a professional kitchen, and they could not always notice the dangers invisible to non-professionals: sharp knives, scalding water, hot oil and slippery wet floors – horse play was unacceptable.

The first day's lunch menu included a fresh vegetable soup with a 'Paysanne' – cut carrots, leeks, celeriac, turnips, cabbage, potatoes, onions and a little smoked bacon. Paysanne translates from French as: "the farmer's wife". She certainly knew how to make a good soup! The main course was a pan-fried pork steak with mustard butter, buttered 'Macedoine' of vegetables and 'Parmentier' potatoes. Macedoine is a quarter inch cube cut, usually reserved for vegetables and Parmentier is slightly larger but is a term only used for potatoes. Needless to say this menu involved a lot of chopping and was purposely designed to have students learn basic knife skills in the first week of class. For students on the sauce section it was a daunting task for their first day in the kitchen. They had to pan fry five hundred pork steaks and have them all the same flavor, color, degree of cooking and lined up on large gastronorm pans – food pans.

Demonstrating pan frying was a little easier. But first students had to add flavor with a good seasoning mix. I showed them how to first place a layer of seasoning on the tray by sprinkling the seasoning by hand from about a foot above the tray so the seasoning mix resembled falling snow – providing an even coat. They laid the steaks side-by-side on this seasoning and then seasoned the topside. The next layer of steaks went on top of those, season again, and so on. They had to have the same amount of steaks in each row, in each layer, and on each tray, so counting them later was fast and accurate. I used the labor cost analogy to demonstrate the amount of time wasted counting five hundred steaks four times. Count them once and be accurate.

Now it was time to pan fry. The steaks were laid in lines of 20 in a large tilting frying pan. Students got a little stressed when there were four lines of 20 in the pan: managing 80 steaks at one time became a big challenge as they all had to have the same color and degree of cooking. They had to be turned over to brown the other side. This took time, so students had to be fast and we pressed them to work even faster lest some steaks became too brown. During this process of pan frying, students would always ask me, "How can I tell if the steak is cooked?"

To demonstrate this I would show them how to press their right index finger into the fleshy muscle which attaches the thumb to the left hand, near the heel of the palm. Once they had identified that feeling or resistance, I told them that this is the same feeling as touching raw meat – which is what the thumb essentially is – and to now touch the raw pork for comparison. Then they made the connection. Now we went to the next step. I asked them to put the tips of their thumb and index finger of the left hand together and then touch the same spot again and note the more firm resistance. This resembles the resistance of a rare steak. Continuing with the tips of the middle finger and thumb – the resistance is even firmer corresponding to a medium steak. The remaining fingers represent medium well and well done. Students could not believe they had learned such a simple solution to an age old question.

The class had their thirty minute lunch break at eleven o'clock and ate in a section of the dining room. Precise timing – a Swiss phenomenon – was also a hallmark of the school so when the dining room doors opened for lunch it was exactly twelve noon on the large clock in the lobby. The doors closed at five minutes past twelve so if a student was late and they went without food, it usually only happened to them once. It happened to a few students in the first week of every semester – many cultures have different ideas as to the length of a minute.

Shortly after twelve noon food orders came in to the kitchen. Soup was served and then the student appointed expeditor called out to various class mates for protein, starch and vegetables which they presented on silver platters and placed under the lamp. Expediting food for five hundred people was a challenging task for a non-professional because they were right in the middle of the action. For this reason we appointed a different student every day to expose them to a little challenge. Having to shout out orders to their fellow classmates brought students out of their comfort zone and instilled self confidence − a quality I observed was lacking in many of the younger generation as I developed my academic career. The students, upon hearing the expeditor's orders, responded with a loud − yes, you guessed it − OUI CHEF! This actually made me laugh as I reminisced.

If the expeditor didn't shout loud enough, they wouldn't be heard over the noise of the kitchen which resulted in the order not being prepared and led to a delayed service. Since we had only one hour to serve a 3 course meal to 500 'guests', time was crucial. If I organized the class correctly, during service I could simply stand to one side and watch the action − twenty five students from different countries, cultures and creeds working in unison with food. It was very satisfying. If I got it wrong − which I did many times in the beginning − I would run like a blue-arsed fly from one station to another urging the students on so we could make our deadline, trying not to shout or show concern in my voice. In the dining room a similar class was serving the student body as they sat around tables of eight. These 'waiters' were under the same stress and time constraints. When lunch was over the morning class cleaned the tables, equipment, switched off all appliances, swept floors, and gathered around the kitchen table for a debriefing at a quarter to two.

At this time, the kitchen looked as clean as it did at seven o'clock that morning except that now the afternoon sun shone through the windows, glinting off the stainless steel tables casting strange light shapes on the ceiling, and giving the kitchen an even cleaner effect. Rudi evaluated the morning class, gave comments, constructive criticism, asked questions and finally gave out homework for the next day. Class ended at two o'clock and would be back for a repeat performance tomorrow morning at seven on a different menu and so on until Friday rolled around. As the students were leaving the kitchen, I could overhear comments about how tired they were. I suppose a seven hour shift on your feet with one thirty minute break was a big challenge for them and it was only two in the afternoon – half of the 'normal' day I was used to.

The smaller a la carte kitchen was more intense – also offering two classes per day. One class with twelve students cooked a three course prix fixe lunch with each student cooking for a table of four. This class also began at seven in the morning and finished at two in the afternoon. In the evening a separate class of twelve students cooked a complete a la carte menu taught by yet another teacher. This was a dinner menu where each student cooked alone at a self sufficient station, with their own food, equipment, and gas range. I rotated between the kitchens for my first semester, working with each teacher to learn how they organized the teaching process to ensure students learned and the food was good. My objective was to gain enough proficiency to take over the class as soon as possible. Work flow and timing were crucial to ensure every meal was ready exactly on time; a miscalculation in the kitchen by the teacher could mean the entire school would not have a quality meal. There was no fall back. Students were learning – they would not see the mistakes – which meant that if I did not see the problem before it occurred, no one else would. This was very different to my work in Singapore where I was surrounded by professional chefs looking out for every detail.

As I was learning these lessons – some of which was new information for me including the theory of cooking, food science, and nutrition – Andi, who had just finished his Master Chef's exam, said to me: "Brendan, what you are learning now is similar to the course material taught for the Masters. You should think about studying for the exam." The other chefs agreed with him and told me how much passing the exam helped them with their teaching. The Swiss title of 'Chef de Cuisine Diplomé' is a protected title awarded through a federal program offered in Professional Development Schools in Switzerland. No chef can use this title – which translates in English to Master Chef, the highest culinary title for any chef – without passing an intensive series of examinations. This is a two week grueling challenge with a very high failure rate, offered only in French, German or Italian. Only a handful of native English speaking chefs had ever passed it and to the instructor's knowledge no Irish chef had ever passed the exam. What great encouragement this was for me. Still, despite my hesitancy, I felt this was an opportune time for me to take this exam and fulfill my long-time dream of becoming a Master Chef – like Herman from the Hotel Elite. I had so much admiration for him at that time many years ago and it inspired me to become a Master Chef like him – but I never pursued it; instead, I traveled. So now, back in a learning and teaching environment, I began to imagine that finally the revered title of Swiss Master Chef might just be within my reach. What I had dreamed of all these years might now come true.

Many of the kitchen teachers had passed the exam and encouraged me to begin studying. But doubting my ability was a major factor for me. I thought the exam was easier for them because they were Swiss, spoke the language fluently, and had all completed an apprenticeship to begin their careers which was much more complex than the training I completed in Athenry many years ago. Much of the material in the Master Chefs exam was based on the foundational learning of the Swiss three year chef's apprenticeship which all Swiss chefs must complete. I began to doubt my ability to pass the exam for many reasons. I was a foreigner, Irish, non-deserving, I had not done a Swiss style apprenticeship, and all the examiners were Swiss...and the self-created list went on – then there was the slight problem of language.

After many weeks of self-doubting and finding excuses justifying why I would fail, the team of Master Chefs at the school won the argument and I began the one-year course which would lead to the series of practical, oral and written exams. Classes were held in the town of Basel every Wednesday – an eight hour round trip by car from Bluche. I would leave the house at four in the morning and drive to Basel to be in time for classes at eight. We studied many subjects during the day, had a one hour lunch break, then more classes until five in the afternoon when I drove back home arriving at nine in the evening. I kept that schedule every Wednesday for one year, hail, rain or snow, and I never missed a class. The team of Master Chefs I worked with at Les Roches went above and beyond to cover my practical classes on those Wednesdays.

My Master classes in Basel were in German. I requested to take the exam in English but as that was not a Swiss national language I had to choose from German, French, or Italian – all Swiss National languages. However, upon my request, the examiners' commission agreed to let me take the oral sections in German and the written sections in French. It was the best I could hope for. My written French was fair but I knew Christine could help me improve it. My spoken Swiss German was almost fluent at the time – to the point that many people I spoke with believed I was Swiss German. I could also read the language but as I never took any German courses, I never learned to write it properly – a regret I have to this day.

Despite the very heavy schedule and the stress of learning in a second language, there were lighter moments in my Master classes, many at my expense, as I tried to understand the subject matter in German, switch it into English in my mind to ensure accuracy, and then regurgitate the answer back in German – not always accurately. Once during nutrition class the teacher was explaining the various digestive organs and their roles. He had a plastic dummy on the table from which each of us in turn had to remove and identify specific organs and describe their function in the digestive process. It became a class joke with me in this subject because I always got confused between the German words Organismus and Orgasmus. Needless to say I got it wrong while identifying the organs in front of the teacher and everyone in class

– even the girls – laughed, and of course the teacher was in stitches. Standing there at the top of the classroom looking at everyone laughing at my grammar, I had no choice but to laugh also. It became the class joke during breaks when the rest of the class would ask me whether I had seen an Organismus or an Orgasmus. I got used to it. I had to.

I had been studying with another chef from Germany who also taught at the school. His name was Franz – ironically he also joined the school from Singapore. I met him many times there and did not know he was coming to Bluche until I saw him on my first day at the school. We drove together every Wednesday to class and studied every Saturday at the school and he was extremely helpful with my German translations. There were chefs from many sectors of the industry in our Masters class. Chefs from corporate food companies, state education, university hospitals, and convalescent homes; each of us considered the Master's exam a qualification that would promote our careers. As we approached the finals, there was talk of the actual exam and of course the horror stories of chefs who failed it. For those who had friends who completed the exam there were stories of the letter arriving in the post notifying them of their success or failure. Even down to the details of how the first sentence was structured: "We are happy to inform you"…. was enough – no need to read further. On the contrary, it could also read: "We regret to inform you…." As the exam date approached such conversations of joy or disappointment punctuated our coffee breaks as we imagined reading our exam results and reactions to both scenarios.

After one year of intensive theoretical and practical studies I felt I was finally ready to take the exam. I had studied the subjects intensively, and did practical work every weekend at the school making classical desserts, pates, terrines and mousses. I spent many Saturdays working with our fish and poultry supplier to learn and identify various breeds and types of fish and game birds. I attended separate cold kitchen and pastry courses in Lausanne and Berne and wrote many letters in French for my correspondence subject. Christine spent hours teaching me French grammar and punctuation – which compared to English punctuation, was more like Algebra mixed with geometry: every letter had a different decoration on top. So in the end, I was ready to get it over with. These studies had dominated my life and the family's life for one solid year. Weekends with my family were sacrificed; evenings after class were dedicated to studying and practicing my French correspondence. Literally every free moment was devoted to some aspect of learning – the high failure rate always on my mind. I wanted to get back to some sense of normality and perhaps do something other than studying on the weekends.

The week of the exam arrived. I stayed at the Professional Development School in Weggis in central Switzerland for the duration of the written and oral exams. I shared a room with Franz and we made a pact. We would not discuss the content of exams when we regrouped between sessions. Both of us agreed it would distract us from the next session – especially the accounting where there was only one correct answer. My first oral exam was equipment identification. I entered the room and the examiner walked with me to several tables laden with all kinds of kitchen equipment, knives, and utensils, and asked me to identify each one in German and explain its usage. Thanks to my training at the school and working with students for the past year, there was no utensil on the table that I did not know its name and usage. Many of these items were not always used in regular kitchens; some were text book examples so we had them at the school for demonstration purposes. As we exited, the examiner shook my hand, thanked me in very formal Swiss fashion, wished me well for the next exam, and advised that it would be to my advantage to tell the other examiners to speak in High German as he felt I did not understand him very well. There are many dialects within the Swiss German language; I did not speak all of them but I understood his point. Nevertheless I decided to stick with Swiss German. High German was not a favorite language for Swiss Germans...I needed all the help I could get here. No need to get these examiners on my back because of a dialect. The next oral exam was nutrition, and then there was law, legislation and government, and lastly, cooking techniques and food product identification. The following two days involved written exams on subject such as: menu writing, menu translation from French to German and vice versa, the complexities of managing apprentices, the laws, academic components, and overall structure of the three year Swiss chef's apprenticeship. Then there were exams on the principles of teaching apprentices, proper lesson plans, an exam on menu composition in German and French, and finally an exam on the history of cooking. After these exams Franz and I returned home for a short break before beginning the practical exam the following week.

The practical was a complex two day series of exams. One exam involved the preparation of a four course meal for six people and a master's dish. The next – cold kitchen – involved producing a series of pâtés, terrines and mousses and presenting them on aspic coated platters. The last exam was pastry, my weakest area. For each exam I was assigned an apprentice. I would be judged on how I incorporated him into my planning and how much I could teach him while still completing my exam on time. If I was filleting fish, examiners would expect to see me demonstrating to him the correct filleting process, and perhaps let him fillet one or two fish, which I did, while hoping he got it right, for the final product was my responsibility. Not his. There was an expectation that Master Chefs would have some teaching role in their careers, hence the apprentice.

The morning of the exam, we were assigned our dishes and together with the apprentice I began planning the menu and allocating tasks between us. We had one hour for this section which involved calculating ingredient amounts, delegating tasks to the apprentice, and constantly following up with him. We had to create a time line which guaranteed the menu would be ready within the allotted exam time and then it was off to the kitchen to begin cooking.

For my masters dish I was given nine hundred grams of monk fish, twelve large prawns and six shelled scallops with roe. I was to add a starch and two vegetables of my choice, together with sauce and garnish, and the cost could not exceed three francs per person. We had to create a dish by incorporating as many cooking methods as possible while demonstrating the techniques to the apprentice and letting him do some of the work. I had to prepare a platter for four judges to be served in the restaurant and two individual plates for the examiners to taste in the kitchen. I decided to give this menu an Asian flavor:

Pan fried monkfish with grilled jumbo prawns and steamed scallops

Chinese broccoli with toasted sesame seeds

Oriental vegetables sautéed with
Chinese five spices

Steamed Thai rice with roast pumpkin seeds

I began by marinating the monkfish with soy sauce, the prawns with garlic, and the scallops with ginger. As I began to prepare a Thai red curry sauce with coconut milk I noticed there was none on my ingredient tray despite it being on my ingredients order so I called the examiner over and told him. "Wait one moment," he responded, and left the kitchen in the direction of the store room. Coconut milk is usually found canned in the west so I was a little surprised when he returned with a whole coconut and said, "Can you do anything with this?" As he handed me the brown hairy hard shelled nut I realized this was a test: whole coconuts were unusual in Switzerland. All I could do was to thank him.

Now it was his turn to be surprised as I called the apprentice over and did a one minute explanation about the coconut, making sure that it was an educational moment for the apprentice. I even told him the story of when I was in Africa on the beach with Christine, and how the African children – for a few cents – would offer to climb the coconut tree to get a fresh coconut for us. To see those children climbing up to thirty feet bare foot on the slim but rough tree trunk was spectacular, even as it swayed back and forth with the ocean breeze – they never fell. Back on terra firma with the coconut, a few swift movements of a machete – which appeared out of nowhere – revealed the cool coconut water that was so tasty on that hot tropical beach as the smiling children said "Merci Yovo" when I paid them.

Then I took out my largest chopping knife and while holding the hairy coconut in my left hand over a stainless steel bowl, hit the nut very hard three times in quick succession with the back of the knife near the handle while under my breath muttering "Open Sesame" in English, with a few Irish expletives added in for good measure – thinking this better work or I am in trouble. The nut split, the coconut water flowed into the bowl and I was able to show the apprentice the white coconut flesh and how to extract it. As he began this task, I started on my Thai curry sauce. The examiner came over to me and referring to the coconut asked, "Where did you learn how to do that?" "In Bangkok," I replied. He raised his eyebrows. It turned out he also worked in Bangkok at a different time period to me and now was Executive Chef at the Badrutt's Palace Hotel in St. Moritz. Good, I thought. He may look more favorably at my work! However this process with the coconut delayed me, because the liquid that I collected was coconut water – much thinner than the coconut milk my recipe required. Now I had to make coconut milk. To do this I got the apprentice to grate the flesh very finely then he blended it with a little warm water to form a thick liquid. We strained it through muslin cloth to get the milk and saved the pulp to give back to the examiner which could be dried to make desiccated coconut flakes. This was to demonstrate efficient use of leftovers – now I could get back to my dish.

During all this time I tried to ignore the examiners for if I saw them writing on their clipboard I automatically assumed it was negative. Andi had advised me not to look at them during the entire exam. So I continued with my dish and tried to keep my eyes on the food and the large clock on the kitchen wall. I steamed the Thai rice with lemon grass and using the coconut milk finished the curry sauce ensuring it was very mild to suit European taste buds. In the end I had to thicken it because the milk I made was not as thick as the canned version – I used a little potato starch diluted in cold water and stirred it into the hot sauce, and was relieved when it worked perfectly.

The examiner signaled that my time window for presenting was approaching. I began to plate the food. The apprentice – who was very involved in helping me – was doing his best to work in tandem. We presented the dish garnished with pumpkin seeds, sesame seeds, and spring onion stems cut into decorative flowers. The vegetables were a colorful mix of Chinese and Shiitake mushrooms – on which I had carved a decoration into the caps – together with soy sprouts, snow peas, and carved carrots Thai style all tossed in a little sesame oil and flavored with five spices. I watched the examiners at the end of the kitchen taste the food, talk among themselves and make notes. It was over, and I knew that what was done was done. I turned to the apprentice, thanked him, and began to clean up so we could get out of the kitchen.

The next two days were similar in style: performing under great stress to produce food in classical fashion while constantly teaching the apprentice, keeping the workstation clean, separating trimmings into reusable or not and always watching the clock. Finally the last exam was over. It was such a relief to have them all completed. After one year of constant focus on the Masters, so many details always in my head, worrying if I had forgotten a particular technique or calculation – and now the emptiness, it was a welcome relief. I was drained of energy and mental stimulation.

It was a relief to finally be home and know that I felt I had done my best. I would have to wait a few weeks for the results. Christine checked with the post man everyday to see if my 'special letter' had arrived. She said that if the letter arrived in the morning post she would bring it to me at the school during the break and we would open it together. And so one day two weeks later she turned up at the school during the main morning class break with the letter and as I held it in my hand thoughts of the discussions with fellow classmates about reactions to the news came back to me. I opened it, read the first line, and handed it back to Christine. We hugged. I did not know what to think, whether to laugh or cry. It was incredible news to receive after all the work I had put in over the last year. The letter read: "We regret to inform you….."

I had to get back to class; twenty five students were waiting for me and five hundred more salivating in classrooms, imagining the tastes, aromas and satisfaction of eating lunch. My failure of the Master's exam was not something they worried about – and why should they? I continued with the class and during our lunch break, broke the news to the team…there was silence at the table. Needless to say I was very disappointed and thought that at least I gave it my best shot. Andi broke the silence saying, "You will pass it next time." I was not sure I wanted to try it again and he replied, "The failure rate is very high…you are not the only one who failed, you will sign up for the next exam offered in a few month's time and pass it second time round." It sounded like an order, but then everyone on the team had an interest in my success; each one of these chefs played a major role in covering my classes while I was at school every Wednesday. I owed it to them to try again. I would think about it, but for now I needed a time away from studying.

It was around this time that I met Serge. He owned a carpenter shop, and I often watched him from the classroom window as he prepared large wooden beams in his shop adjacent to the school. A cheery man with a weather beaten face, he constructed many chalets in the region – a true craftsman. He also sang in the choir, which is how I met him – at one of the choir's public performances. Like many people in the valley, Serge made his own wine. I became every interested in this process and offered to help him with the heavy duty work involved in wine making. He had the perfect wine cellar tucked away beneath his carpenter's shop where he taught me how to crush the grapes, ferment the juice and then wait for the second fermentation, filtering, and waiting – the most difficult of all tasks. I went once a week after class to his cellar to taste the wine as it passed through the various stages of maturity. We would taste the new wine from the barrel and compare it to previous years' wines. Serge's taste memories were so strong that most times he did not need to taste previous vintages to compare, but did so anyway for my benefit.

I began to appreciate wine more and changed my drink preference from whiskey and beer to wine, and as we were living in an incredible wine region, began to collect some vintages. On weekends I washed the wine bottles for Serge and arranged his cellar as thanks for the knowledge he passed on to me. We had many great discussions in his cellar just a few meters from the classroom but many worlds apart in a sense. He told me how he built up his business beginning as a carpenter's helper to the present day as a chalet builder with two employees in his shop. We discussed the types of wood he used and the modern kiln wood drying techniques and how they affected his choice of building materials. We also talked about my travels, the foods I cooked, the people I met and how I ended up teaching at Les Roches. I realized most of the students, from other countries and cultures would never get to know the people that lived in the village in any other capacity than to say "Bonjour." They mingled among themselves forming lifelong friendships; for the most part the cultural divide between them and the people of the village was too wide to bridge. They would not experience this side of Switzerland like we did – just by living in the same village.

In August, Serge told me: "We must prepare to bottle the wine. We need to empty the barrels in preparation for the next harvest." A Saturday was chosen and Paul, my father-in-law, came to help. We set up an assembly line in the cellar to deal with the volume. Serge filled the bottles from a filtering machine which was connected to the barrel by an electric pump and passed them to Paul who corked them. Christine put the labels on and I sealed the sleeves and stacked the bottles in crates on the floor. Wine – unlike spirits – ages in the bottle and in time we would use this vintage as a benchmark comparison. We finished bottling the Pinot noir, Riesling and Fendant by lunch time.

Serge's wife was a very pleasant woman whom I always addressed in the formal. I spoke in the informal with Serge but she – being older – never initiated the informal with me. She prepared lunch with platters of air dried beef, local raclette cheese, cured air-dried bacon and a special air-dried ham from the Valais together with dark rye bread – another local specialty. We sat around a table outside the cellar door in bright sunshine eating and admiring our work – droplets of nature sealed in bottles for future generations. Serge opened some of his Fendant and Pinot noir from years past, poured for everyone, and raised his glass saying "Merci a tous" for the help. During the meal he offered to help me make my own wine for the following year. I thought this was a tremendous opportunity – too good to pass up and so I agreed. He said, "We will begin in the spring by pruning the vines so you can learn the entire process."

By now we were well settled in to village life. It was such a pleasant experience walking through the village on my way to work, chatting with people, greeting students, and breathing in clean mountain air. On one particular day I took a short cut through a small wooded area practically in the middle of the village where I came across an abandoned chalet situated on a level clearing facing south towards the Italian Alps. I thought this would be the perfect house to rent – we were living in an apartment on the third floor of a six apartment building without any elevator. Neighbors told me the chalet was a holiday home and only used once a year. I eventually contacted the owner who lived in Chamonix. We drove into France and up to a beautiful Alpine resort to meet him. It turned out he built the chalet as a holiday home but rarely used it. We rented the chalet with a one year lease and bought it at the end of the lease. Although it was very small, it had three bedrooms, an uninterrupted view of the southern Alps, was only a few minutes' walk to the school, and it had a perfect cellar for my wine.

To add to the surprise of finding this wonderful house in which to create a home, Christine had even better news: she was pregnant. We were so pleased at this wonderful news, and again, we decided to wait for the birth to find out if it would be a girl or a boy. And the baby name book was back on the coffee table.

During our years together Christine had become an accomplished cook, to the point that she could cook dishes at home much better than I. She learned so much during our travels, particularly from Jabeen – Freddy's wife – in Bangkok. They often cooked together in her apartment at the hotel while I was at work. Christine collected many recipes during that time. Jabeen was Fijian and brought island flavors to her cooking. For Christine's thirtieth birthday we invited a few friends and Christine cooked a spectacular meal for all of us. She was already using Freddy Girardet's recipe book *'The cuisine of Fredy Girardet'* to create dishes for us at home. Fredy Girardet was arguably one of the best Swiss chefs at the time – his book stated: "He was the greatest chef in Europe" and renowned for his restaurant in Crissier, for which he was constantly rated by Gault Millau with nineteen and a half points out of twenty – an incredible feat. While I was in Singapore, Remy tried to get Girardet to come to the Pan Pacific for a two week promotion. He wrote back declining our request saying that if guests waited three months for a table at his restaurant in Crissier, he felt he should be there to greet them and not be off in some foreign country. It was a fair argument.

Using his recipes, Christine prepared a cream of tomato soup with basil. It was like drinking velvet, smooth and tangy to the taste buds. Then she served 'en papillote' of salmon with shallots, white wine, lime, and ginger. This is a dish cooked in the oven in a parchment paper pouch called a 'papillote' which seals in the flavor. The salmon cooks in the steam created by the wine as it evaporates inside the papillote. When it is opened at the table the steam releases the aroma to the guest's delight, setting the stage for an exceptional meal and driving the taste buds into a frenzy of anticipation. She served it with a quinoa pilaf – an ancient grain, common to the Incas which has a nutty flavor and unlike rice, a slightly crunchier but tender bite. For dessert she made a Raisinée tart. This tart – typical of the canton of Vaud – is made with Raisiné mixed with eggs and cream and baked in a pie crust – similar to a fruit tart. The Raisiné is made from pear juice reduced to thick syrup – not unlike the process for making maple syrup, but much thicker. The taste was delicious and the guests were surprised as they expected I would be the one cooking. I just poured the wine! This continues to be a common occurrence in our house when we entertain.

It was around this time the first Gulf War began. We had Iraqis and Kuwaitis in class together as well as students from many other Middle Eastern countries. We set up a television in the lobby for them to follow the news and tuned it in to a new American news channel recently available in the valley named CNN which provided twenty four hour coverage – a new feature for Switzerland. It was painful to see the students so devastated, trying to comfort each other, not knowing if their families were safe as they watched the bombings on the television. Phones rang constantly as families tried to get in touch with them. Teachers met to discuss class protocol on how we would deal with war discussions in class particularly in a highly multicultural school. We still had material to cover and despite the war, we all agreed to keep discussions and questions on that topic for break time, particularly given the amount of nationalities involved. It would lead to a never ending class discussion which could easily become heated.

By now the time was approaching for me to take the Masters exam a second time. Andi told me candidates were only allowed to take the exam three times – I hoped it would not come to that. The results from the last exam, despite that I failed it, were encouraging. I had passed all the written exams with the exception of menu calculation. I also passed all the oral exams, and the pastry exam. I had to repeat the hot kitchen and cold kitchen exams as well as menu calculations and a Master's dish.

On the day of the exam I was back at the Professional Development School in the same kitchen, which gave me a sense of familiarity. For my dish this time I was given sturgeon. This fish is famous for producing caviar, but it is also a delicious fish in its own right. As it is a fatty fish I decided to hot smoke it and serve it with a horseradish *beurre blanc* – French white wine butter sauce with horseradish – together with a raw beetroot salad, herbed vegetables and a potato spinach roll. It was not a difficult dish to prepare. The objective of the exam was the see how chefs could perform under stress, be organized, teach the apprentice, practice proper food, kitchen and personal hygiene, and cook good food on time.

I smoked the fish with oak chips on low heat. Hot smoking cooks the fish during the smoking process – which is much shorter than cold smoking, typically reserved for salmon. Smoked trout is usually hot smoked which is why it falls apart and cannot be carved like smoked salmon. For the potatoes, I puréed them, added egg yolk and seasoning then spread the mixture out in a one inch thick layer on a sheet of plastic wrap. I sautéed the spinach in butter, seasoned it with nutmeg, salt and pepper, and spread that evenly over the potatoes. Then I rolled it up like a Swiss roll and let it cool in the fridge. To make the *beurre blanc* I reduced white wine with a little vinegar and chopped shallots to fifty percent of the original volume. Then I whisked in chilled butter cubes waiting for each one to melt before add another while all the time carefully balancing the temperature and finally adding grated horseradish. If the sauce became too hot, the butter would completely melt and resemble just melted butter with shallots – not exactly appetizing. When the sauce was ready I began with the potatoes by removing the plastic wrap, cutting the roll into one inch slices, coating them in breadcrumbs and pan frying until golden brown.

The second time around I did not pay any attention to the examiner. It was as if the apprentice and I were the only two in the entire kitchen. This mind set helped me to remain calm and focused. The sturgeon was smoking in the small smoking oven I had brought with me from the school. I added rosemary and juniper berries to the oak chips for flavor. The secret was to have smoke with some heat but no flame as that makes the fish bitter. Essentially the oak chips should just smolder. I had selected two vegetables, salsify and zucchini to serve with the sturgeon. I blanched the former and added it to the zucchini and tossed them in butter with chopped chervil. Now I was ready to present. I felt good about my effort. We cleaned the kitchen and left. Tomorrow was a big day. I had my last test – the cold kitchen.

For this exam I was given a whole pike to present as a classical cold platter dish. I decided to stuff the fish and serve it in classical fashion – sliced and glazed with aspic – on an aspic lined platter with a selection of garnishes. I began by scaling the fish then deboning it through the belly leaving the back intact. It was important not to pierce the skin on the back as I wanted that part of the fish to be prominent in the presentation. I made a light stuffing with some of the flesh, egg white and cream to which I added truffle bits, red capsicum dice and pistachio halves for flavor and color. Then I laid the fish in a mould skin side down, layered it with blanched spinach leaves, piped in the mousse and folded the fish to close the mould. I wrapped the lot in plastic wrap and steamed it.

While it cooled I prepared the platter with aspic. I set the platter on a level shelf in the walk in and poured on the liquid aspic jelly a quarter inch deep. I had flavored it with Chardonnay. It was imperative during this process not to stir the aspic as it would incorporate air and form bubbles which would be impossible to remove when cold. One tiny bubble on the platter would not escape the examiner's attention. Now that the platter was prepared I removed the fish from the steamer and let it cool. Then I began to make the garnishes: stuffed half quail eggs with truffle dust, mini Zucchini cups with poached shrimp and palm heart logs filled with three colored capsicum dice. I also prepared a light tarragon mousseline sauce.

It was time now to slice the cold stuffed fish. If I had stuffed it correctly each slice would have an outside layer of flesh, a thin ribbon of spinach next to that, then the white mousse speckled with black truffle, green pistachio and red capsicum. I had blanched the capsicums before adding them to the mousse so they would not bleed red and also not produce steam during the cooking process which would create air pockets throughout the mouse – a definite faux pas. As I began slicing, the examiner watched carefully – each slice had to be identical in thickness and be laid out for glazing in the same order as it was sliced. This would ensure I put it on the platter in the opposite order so it resembled the whole fish from head to tail when served. The apprentice glazed each slice three times being careful to avoid any minute bubbles. Now I was ready to assemble and present. It was important to have a symmetrical presentation for the fish as well as the three garnishes so I made a diagram on parchment paper to guide me. Once I let the slice of fish touch the aspic on the platter, I could not move it again because it would leave an imprint which would 'smudge' the final dish. I laid out each fish slice on the aspic coated platter so that the presentation flowed from head to tail and each slice looked the same despite slight differences in the speckling of the truffles.

I finished the platter and presented it to the examiner on time. He made only one comment – which nearly devastated me. "I have never seen a square fish." I had used a square mould to shape the fish during poaching. There were other moulds available which I did not see, some were round. Well now it was finished and his comment put doubt in my mind as to whether my effort was enough to pass the exam.

Having returned home I was once again waiting for the letter with my results. The examiner's comment constantly stuck in my mind creating doubt with every thought. Christine and I set up the same system to bring the letter to school once the postman delivered it. Two weeks later it arrived. Christine brought it to me, we both looked at each other and I opened it. I looked at it in disbelief, it read: "We are happy to inform you…"

I could not believe it! I had actually passed the exam. I was so happy I went in to tell the entire class. There were great cheers, and students came over to shake hands with me. All the teachers came over during the break; everyone was overjoyed for me. Finally I was the proud owner of the title: Eidg. Dipl. Küchenchef –Swiss Master Chef – one of a handful of native English speaking chefs to ever pass the exam, and so far as anyone on the examiners commission could tell me, the only Irish chef to do so. My dream had come true. After all those years of thinking I might one day become a Master Chef, my thoughts turned to Herman who had inspired me to pursue this dream many years ago. Unfortunately I had lost contact with him. I would have loved to call him and let him know the "Irish Boy" was now a Master Chef – just to hear what he would say.

Raclette

Raclette is one of the most popular dishes in the 'Valais'.

Ingredients for 4 people
1½ lbs. (700 gr.)   Swiss raclette cheese
6 oz. (180gr.) gherkins   6 oz. (180gr.) pickled pearl onions
Pepper mill to taste
1 lb. (454gr.) small potatoes boiled in the skin

Procedure
- This dish, which is typical of Switzerland and even more so in the 'Valais' where we lived, requires a special type of overhead grill to melt the cheese in thin layers.
- The melted layer is then scraped off directly on to the guest's plate.
- Seasoned with pepper mill, raclette is eaten with small boiled potatoes served in the skin, gherkins, and pickled pearl onions.
- Guests have multiple portions so the meal goes on for ever.
- If you do not have this type of grill, use the following procedure.
- Cut the boiled potatoes into ¼ inch slices and lay them on a baking sheet (with or without skin).
- Cover with ¼ inch slices of cheese – cut to the same size as the potato slice.
- Bake in a hot oven until the cheese melts. (Approximately 5-6 minutes)
- Be careful not to over bake which lets the cheese separate so that the fat runs out.
- Serve immediately.
- Make several small batches as the meal progresses.

Tips
- Due to its rather heavy nature, Raclette is typically served during the colder months.
- Other than white wine, avoid drinking ice cold beverages with this dish.
- It will lead to an upset stomach as the cold beverage impedes digestion.
- A fruit brandy – schnapps – is a great digestive with Raclette.
- Also avoid very cold or frozen desserts afterwards.

CHAPTER FIFTEEN

So You're a Chef, Huh?

By now Christine was getting tired of carrying the next generation around and we were impatient to meet this addition to our family. Even Shannon was wildly excited to meet 'bebé'. We compiled a list of names but for some reason seemed to have mostly girl's names. It was only on the way to the hospital that we selected a boy's name from our list. Before Christine went into the delivery room the doctor, a thin man with a pencil moustache, approached me: "Monsieur, would you like to cut the umbilical cord when the time is right?" Hesitantly, I said: "Yes, yes, of course." After a short labor period the baby was born, the cord was clamped and the doctor gave me a very sharp sleek stainless steel scissors – which I instinctively thought would be a perfect implement for trimming fish, despite the fact that he had other uses for it. I nervously held the scissors in my right hand, wondering if Christine or the baby would feel anything. I had enough experience with cuts to know how painful flesh wounds could be. As if reading my mind the doctor said: "Do not worry Monsieur, Madame and the bebé will not feel anything." So I went ahead. The crunching sensation and noise felt like I was cutting through the outer part of a chicken wing – slight resistance but cutting never the less. It was a strange feeling to be severing this most intimate liaison between mother and child but also a tremendous privilege for me to be part of this birth and to be the one releasing our child from its maternal biological support – leaving it free to thrive on its own. Then the doctor lifted the baby into Christine's waiting arms and she said, "Bonjour Ryan." It was a momentous occasion. The two of us gently hugged him.

Back in the hospital room, there was a lady in the next bed to Christine who had also just given birth; her husband came in every evening and brought her a flask which she drank from throughout the day. Christine was curious and enquired what was in it. The lady described the mixture of white wine, simmered with honey, cinnamon and sugar – an age old family recipe used to build up the body and reduce bleeding – hence the cinnamon. This story reminded me of how my father bought six bottles of Guinness for my mother when she came home from the hospital after the birth of my younger brothers. Every culture had its own household remedies for ailments and rejuvenation. Ryan's birth also created great excitement for the grand parents. Paul in his haste to drive up the valley to see his only grandson got a speeding ticket and Eliane, while minding Shannon in Les Diablerets ,burned the rösti potato cake – a definite faux pas in her culinary repertoire. They both fondly remind me of these facts to this day.

We brought Ryan home and put him in a cot in his own room. Every morning as we went to bring him downstairs, the view from his window was captivating and spectacular. The panorama of the Alps etched out against the blue sky always stopped me in my tracks. Such a pristine view of nature merited a moment of silence and appreciation. All three bedrooms had the same uninterrupted Alpine view. A soothing visual alarm clock with the background sounds of birds singing. It was almost tempting to wake up early so we could wait for it, ready to listen with admiration – afraid of missing nature's powerful start to the new day.

Now that I didn't have to study on weekends, I had a lot of time on my hands and so began distilling fruit brandy. This was highly illegal in Switzerland much like Poitín in Ireland but I knew some people nearby who distilled their own brandy and they could advise me – and would keep it a secret. It wasn't as risky as working illegally so I felt the reward was worth the risk. I thought my heritage had prepared me well for this adventure so I bought a barrel to store the 'wash' and decided my first flavor would be apricot. Apricotine was my favorite fruit brandy, made from the abundant fruit crop in the valley. I spent many evenings sitting in our very dry cellar stoning the fruit, letting it ferment and then distilling. To make the still I rigged up our one gallon stainless steel pressure cooker to a length of copper tubing and ran that through a barrel of cold water, exiting it at the bottom. It took two hours for the pressure cooker to boil off a gallon of wash, condense it in the copper tube, and collect it in a glass bottle. While I waited I graded student's papers. Jean-Claude, one of our neighbors, often came to help and offer advice. Even though he had a hoarse voice from years of smoking, he still sang in the choir. He also distilled his own brandy which we always referred to as '*La soupe*' when anyone was present. We discussed many topics on those long evenings as we sat in the cellar waiting for the still to complete its function. One evening, he told me about his very bad stomach ulcers. After multiple visits to the doctor he decided that there was no cure and gave up hope of finding any relief from the pain. It was then he met a village elder who recommended he eat '*le limace vivant*' – live slugs. So bad was the pain that he eventually decided to try the remedy. It involved putting the slug on his tongue and allowing it to crawl down his throat – apparently the saliva alleviated the pain before the slug got killed by the stomach acids. "Brendan," he said, as he stuck out his tongue, making retching noises, "the first few times I tried it I threw up because the feeling of the slug in my throat was more than I could handle. *Mais, j'ai persisté!*" he exclaimed, "I eventually mastered the discomforting feeling and let the live slug slide down my throat every morning and to this day I have never had an ulcer." I had never heard of this remedy but he told the story with such enthusiasm – punctuated with gestures and twisted facial expressions – that it had to be true. As we talked, I filled up the pressure cooker every two hours.

Distilling the entire barrel of wash was a process that took several days. Now I had a few gallons of brandy at about thirty percent alcohol by volume, which tasted like apricot flavored sugar syrup – undrinkable. It was time to prepare the second distillation, and I ran this mix through the still again which increased the alcohol to seventy percent – lethal stuff! The final step was to dilute it with distilled water down to forty two percent alcohol by volume. Brandy with content higher than forty two percent alcohol masked the fine fruit flavor. Then I bottled the lot and stored it for the winter months. Distilled water was easily available at the chemists but purchasing a large amount caused suspicion so I distilled my own. Many villagers knew who distilled illegally in the region, so it would be easy for them to inform the police. I did not want the local paper headline to read, "Hotel Management teacher fined for distilling illegally." It was possible to distil legally in Switzerland, but for that I would have to buy a few cows. Farmers are allowed a few liters of home distilled brandy per head of cattle as medicinal remedy for sick animals. The following year I made plum, pear, and marc brandy. I gave most of it away as Christmas presents.

At the time it was uncommon to find a native English speaking chef in hotel schools in the country. Nevertheless we sometimes received requests for English speaking chefs to present at one venue or another. Most times we declined such requests due to the intense nature of our class schedules. The DuPont de Nemours Company was holding an international conference in the Alpine resort of Zermatt and contacted us to enquire if we had an English speaking chef who could prepare and present a cooking demonstration. No one on the kitchen team was interested so I volunteered. I would be presenting a paper on classical chefs for the ladies' program in conjunction with a tasting demonstration.

I traveled to Zermatt and was met at the train station by the driver from the Hotel Zermatterhof with an open sleigh drawn by two beautiful horses decked with jingle bells. It was an amazing experience for me to be in an open sleigh in the middle of winter gliding down the Banhofstrasse in Zermatt, jingle bells ringing and all the while sipping *Glühwein* – which the driver discreetly kept in a flask by his feet. People were looking at the sleigh gliding by and then at me, looks of wonder on their faces, as if to ask – who is that person in the sleigh on his own? I felt like an important person.

I was invited to the cocktail reception and dinner that evening and introduced to the guests as their chef for tomorrow's program. There were people attending from all around the world, some speaking French, Italian, and Spanish, but most spoke English. I sat with some researchers from America and we discussed Teflon® – a famous non-stick product invented by this company. I told them how helpful it was for today' chefs – making rösti for example – and I thanked them for inventing it. I talked about how difficult it was to make rösti – and even omelettes – before the advent of Teflon® pans and described how I learned the hard way in Adelboden when the grated potatoes would fall on the floor or stick to the pan. The following day, after my program concluded, the ladies presented me with a beautiful casserole lined with the famous non-stick material. I still have it in our kitchen to this day.

Later that year in October, the grapes were ready to harvest to begin making my own wine – a Pinot noir. Serge helped, and we crushed his grapes at the same time – I would have my own barrel of Pinot noir in his cellar. Like last year, I came often to taste the fermenting wine – mostly after class when he would be closing down his shop for the day. He taught me how to identify the changing tastes in the wine and showed me how he got the oak tannin in the wine – he had just begun to use stainless steel tanks instead of the traditional oak barrels, so he simply took a piece of oak from his carpenter's stock, cut one foot lengths on the circular saw, rinsed off the sawdust, and put them in the wine. Every two weeks we tasted – this time for the amount of oak – and when it had the correct depth we removed the piece of wood. If it required more oak 'depth', Serge removed the wood, ran it on the plane to expose fresh edges and then put it back in the wine. I purchased the bottles and designed a label in preparation for the first vintage of the Cronin winery.

In the meantime, teaching had changed my life. I could now spend my holidays and weekends with the family. My mother came over to Switzerland a few times to see us. She loved to sit on the sunny side of the house and admire the view of the Alps. There was a field next to our small chalet. In the summer, cows – their bells ringing – would lean in over the fence to lick her hand. Then she would kick foot ball with the children, read stories to them and helped with cooking and household work, as was her nature – never a woman to sit still! We drove up the narrow mountain roads and along cliff edges which made her nervous due to the vertical drop. She ate at the student run restaurant with Christine while I was teaching, and enjoyed the food. She told me how the students were nervous when they found out who she was – always thinking they would be judged differently. She would be sad leaving as I drove her to the airport. As we said our goodbyes, to cheer her up, I repeated her own words: "Sure you have to leave to come back."

We went often to Les Diablerets on the weekends and stayed with Christine's parents Paul and Eliane, They loved minding the children which allowed us to ski, and go out in the evenings when the children were asleep. Sometimes they came to stay with us and although the chalet was small they had a great time playing with the grandchildren – Paul doting over his only grandson. At this point we had been in the Alps for seven years – it seemed my life was a journey of seven year segments. We had a house with a stunning view of the southern Alps – which like the ocean view, changed constantly as weather patterns moved up the valley. I had my Swiss Master Chef's diploma, and we had two children – whom my mother referred to as 'a gentleman's family', a girl and a boy. We considered our traveling days over, at least until the children grew up, so it was very unusual upon returning from an evening out with Christine's choir to hear about the 'telephone call'. Elaine had been babysitting and answered the phone; the caller spoke in English so she understood very little. All Elaine could tell us was: "There was a phone call from America, they would call again tomorrow." I did not know anyone in America accept my Uncle, Tex O'Malley, who lived in Queens in New York and he did not have our number and even if he did had no reason to call us unexpectedly. The 'Girls in America' were retired and living back in County Mayo in Ireland, so who could this caller be? I would have to wait for the next day to find out.

Over the past year the school decided that to better compete in the international market, it should have American accreditation to bolster its marketing image around the world. American visitors and accrediting teams came to the school several times during that year. I met many of them as they wanted to meet with each teacher to discuss courses and the like. One man in particular stood out. He was a tall broad shouldered amiable man with a ready smile who talked enthusiastically with everyone he met, including me. He had also worked in Africa, developing educational programs and we spoke about the differences in culture there and the important role education plays in reducing poverty. Now he was visiting the school as a member of the accrediting team that would determine if we qualified for American accreditation.

Our curriculum underwent many fundamental changes. Course titles were modified – cooking was now called 'Culinary Arts.' Reactions at the school were mixed. "What's wrong with the name 'cooking'?" "Why must it now be called Culinary Arts?" And so on went teachers' comments. "Why are Americans telling us what we should be doing?" "They don't understand. All they know about food is hamburgers and French fries," – a common belief outside the United States. But if we were to be granted American accreditation – and this was the school's objective – we would have to change not only the course names, but syllabi content and exam formats as well as many operational systems school wide.

The next evening, as arranged, the phone rang. It was Anna calling from America. Anna had been a management stagiaire – trainee – in the school's a la carte kitchen with me the previous semester. She worked with me for the entire semester and we got on very well. She assisted the Maître – the service instructor – as we served forty eight students from our a la carte menu. She was extremely organized, always on time, empathized with students and simply got the job done. Now she had graduated and was working in a Hospitality Management School at a college near Boston. The reason for her call was just about the last thing I expected. After pleasantries about the weather, my family, and the school, she asked me: "Mr. Cronin, would you consider coming to America to teach?" I was speechless. It was impossible. How could I leave a house, my wife, two children and go to America? She explained they were looking for a Swiss Master Chef to teach in their Hospitality Management School. She went on to explain that

Daniel, also a Les Roches graduate, was already working at this school with her. I couldn't believe this. We were not planning to move again. Without ever really discussing it, Christine and I both thought our move from Singapore was our last – at least until the children grew up. The start date Anna mentioned was in a few months which meant I could not do it in any case because of the semester schedule. So I declined.

At work, I kept this phone conversation to myself. Sometimes things have a way of sorting themselves out. Discussions began to emerge during the kitchen teachers' coffee breaks about the owner's concern of the number of Swiss Master Chefs on the payroll. We had one of the largest concentrations of Master Chefs for any one employer in Switzerland at the time and definitely for any hotel school. It would be a pity if one of us had to leave because of labor cost. Most of the other chefs were like me: bought a house, had children in school and had settled down. The only down side – unlike a city with multiple hotels to choose from – was that here there was only one hotel school. So as these discussions became more frequent, I began to think that maybe we should move before being asked to. Christine agreed. I called Anna and told her I was still interested. Christine and I would fly over to the US for a weekend to see the school.

We arrived in Boston two days after the Oklahoma City bombing. Flags were at half mast, and the country was in disbelief that such an atrocity could happen on U.S. soil. There were dozens of people killed in the attack. Televisions in the airport were streaming gruesome images, with reporters giving running commentaries.

We were given a room on campus and were told we would meet the president of the college the next day to discuss the details of a contract. The campus was next to the ocean, a sprawling area surrounding two central lakes with large geese, some swimming, and some grazing on the surrounding lawns. Tree covered pathways led between buildings and across a foot bridge spanning one of the lakes. Anna, Daniel and the hospitality dean brought us to a local restaurant. It was our first meal in an American restaurant and very different to anything we had experienced previously. The waitress introduced herself by name which was unusual as in Switzerland that was not the norm. She greeted us with the classical American greeting "Hi, my name is 'Buttercup' and I will be your server this evening." I was not sure if Buttercup was a real name, despite that it was written on her name badge. In a Swiss restaurant even if a guest was a regular they would most likely not know the waitress's name, and even if they did, the interaction would be much more formal – her first name would be replaced with a polite "Mademoiselle." I ordered a US beef fillet which was listed on the menu in American culinary terminology as 'tenderloin.' It was very inexpensive compared to US beef in Switzerland. It was also very tender. Christine ordered a lobster.

The next day we were shown to a large stone building on campus with the lettering 'College Hall' over the doorway. As we walked Anna, Daniel and the dean talked about the president and how involved he was in the operation of the school while each one wondered at the outcome of the meeting. We climbed two flights of stairs, entered the president's office, and Anna said: "I would like to introduce the president of Endicott College, Dr. Richard E. Wylie." It was a major surprise. This was the same man I met in Bluche one year previously when he was a member of the accreditation team. He never mentioned then that he was a college president and I neglected to write down his name. He came around from behind his desk extending a firm handshake, welcomed me and we spoke again about Africa and the time he spent working with Haile Selassie building educational programs in Ethiopia, and my time in Togo. Then he went into detail explaining his vision for hospitality education and his ambition of integrating a European style student-run restaurant in the School of Hospitality Management on the campus. This restaurant – unlike the one in Les Roches – would be open to the public allowing students to learn the intricacies of Food and Beverage and the details necessary for the operation of a fine dining restaurant while providing a foundation for their hospitality education. He had observed this learning model at Les Roches and was impressed by its practicality.

The question now was: were we willing to move to America and accept this new challenge in education.

I liked the school, the area, and the challenge. It was like opening a new restaurant all over again. To help get a sense of the local scene, Christine spent some time being driven around trying to estimate the cost of living. She went to a supermarket to calculate the cost of a week's shopping for four people, and called a real estate company to determine rental and house prices. We met for lunch; she had a rough idea of the cost of living and I had the proposed salary. We agreed it would work and at the end of the day I signed a contract. To celebrate our decision, we were invited by the dean, Anna and Daniel to dinner in Boston at Durgin Park restaurant. I had to order the US prime rib I had heard so much about. Christine had lobster again. The plate of beef I received could easily have fed a family for a week and the rib bone would have kept a dog alive for just as long. It was my first introduction to American sized portions which at first I thought were obscene because most people do not need so much food at one meal. Nevertheless the taste was unbelievable.

The next morning before leaving for the airport, we walked on Mingo beach – one of three beaches on campus. It was very warm compared to Switzerland which was still snow covered at that time despite being late spring. It was on that beach we asked ourselves what would happen if the children did not agree to the move – we had not told them we were going to America for the weekend. By now they had made friends in the village and at school. If they were not on board it would make the move much more difficult. After much discussion, we devised a plan.

When we returned to Bluche we sat them around the kitchen table and told them we were all going on the most exciting journey ever. Could they guess where that might be? After the usual answers like visiting the grandparents, going to Ireland, and the circus, we told them we were going to visit Mickey Mouse in America. Their response was priceless. They asked in unison: "When are we leaving?" It was a done deal! Having them on board made everything else about our move so much easier – and every day they asked: "When we are leaving?"

After we returned to the valley everything moved very fast. We sold the house and had a farewell party for friends and family. As we were packing our house, I had several cases of our 1994 Pinot noir which had not been labeled. I stayed up all night ensuring I placed labels and sleeves on each bottle so we could bring some to America. Everyone in the small village could not believe we were leaving the valley – and the country. "Are you sure you're making the right decision?" many neighbors and friends asked with genuine concern in their voices. Immigration is not a Swiss phenomenon, not at least to the extent the Irish have perfected it. In addition, the Swiss distrust of anything foreign surfaced constantly –"America is so far away." Nevertheless for us it was a major move especially with two young children who spoke very little English at the time. Paul and Eliane were very sad seeing us leave. They promised to visit us. Paul took many years to get over the fact we were no longer an hour away by car.

Once everything was packed we traveled to Belmullet to visit my mother on our way to the U.S. There we had what is often referred to as an 'American wake,' where neighbors and friends came to bid us farewell. This was a tradition that began in the early nineteenth century, during the Irish Famine, because of the long journey to America and the probability that the emigrants would never return, so they were given a big send off. The 'Girls from America' – now retired in Ireland – were there. Both were employees of the Waldorf Astoria in New York City for many years and were so happy to see me 'finally' getting to America. Auntie Grace told me some of her work stories, which surprised me because she never mentioned them in all the years we talked about hotels.

Both she and Auntie Kathleen were room service order takers for the 'Towers' – which catered mostly to VIP's and celebrity guests. They always worked side by side on the same shift. One day the phone rang from a guest room in the towers: it was Bob Hope placing an order with room service. Unknowingly,

Auntie Grace answered the phone: "Room service, this is Grace, how can I help you?" "I'm Hope," the guest said. Without hesitation, she answered back: "And we're Faith and Charity!" Normally a room service order taker could be fired for being so open with a guest, but not my Auntie Grace. Because of her way with words and her strong Irish accent – the guests loved chatting with her. Bob Hope responded: "By God that was the quickest one-liner I've ever heard. I'm going to hang up and come right down to where ever you are in the building to meet you!" And so he came down to the reception and asked to be brought to see "The Irish girl, Grace O' Malley." He gave her a signed copy of his picture and then chatted for several minutes and placed his room service order directly with her. Each time he returned to the hotel he would ask for her by name when placing his room service order.

My Auntie Grace was a true hospitality professional. She would take the room service orders from the guest when they called down, put it through to the kitchen and then call the guest back to chat, mostly about Ireland – a definite faux pas in any hotel. No employee places an unsolicited call to a guest's room. Yet the guests wanted to chat with her. Gregory Peck, Floyd Patterson, Henry Kissinger, Bob Cummings, Elizabeth Taylor, she called them all back to "have the chat," as she said. She told me that they were the nicest people. They just wanted to be treated like anyone else and they respected her for how she accomplished that without any fuss.

Years later, during their retirement, Gregory Peck was visiting Ireland and wanted to connect up with his "Irish girls". Not having their address or telephone number, he did what any normal person would do. He put a request on the front page of the Irish Independent – the national Irish newspaper – asking them by name to call him at the Shelburne hotel in Dublin. They saw the ad and called him. He invited them to stay at the Shelburne; they had a tremendous time as his guests as he was finally able to return their Irish hospitality. Listening to my aunt tell this story was so entertaining. I learned more that evening about her work at the Waldorf than in all our previous encounters.

We celebrated our departure in McDonnell's pub in Belmullet's late into the night. As happens often when the Irish get together for a celebration, we sang many songs, and Mam was no exception. An excellent singer, she sang one of her favorites: 'The Red River Valley' as an ode to our journey.

From this valley they say you are leaving.
I will miss your bright eyes and sweet smile.
For they say you are taking the sunshine.
That has brightened our pathway awhile.

Come and sit by my side if you love me,
Do not hasten to bid me adieu
But remember the Red River Valley
And the girl that has loved you so true.

At one point, Mam leaned over to me and said, "I always knew you'd end up in America! I hope you'll be happy there." The next day we flew to the States – twenty three years after I had first left home.

We arrived in Boston's Logan Airport and joined the queue for customs and immigration. I was nervous about this part of our journey and worried constantly that our paperwork and visas would not be in order. We had heard so much about this process over the years, from Irish friends and family who would wait for months to get a working visa to enter the country and have a shot at a better future, only to be refused at the border due to lack of a particular paper or other and have to fly back to Ireland. If our visa was not in order we could be sent back to Ireland on the next plane. The American Embassy in Dublin – where we obtained our visa – was an unfriendly place despite its efficiency. If it was any indication of how immigration officials treated travelers to America, then I was expecting more of the same as I approached the officer with our passports.

He was a well built man wearing a blue short-sleeved uniform shirt with shoulder lapels, his hair slightly graying at the temples and a tanned face which told of the outdoors. I put our passports on his desk. "Is this your first visit to America with your family?" he asked, glancing through my passport. "Yes sir, it is" I replied. He continued thumbing through my passport noting all the stamps from other countries I had visited. "You travel a lot!" he said. I nodded. "What is the nature of your visit?" "I will be teaching in a college north of Boston," I replied. By now I was conscious of the long line of passengers behind me, waiting to pass through customs and hoped this officer would not find fault with our paperwork and delay everyone. Two Jumbo jets had landed simultaneously, one from Ireland and one from New Delhi, and passengers were anxious to pass through immigration, meet their families or continue their journey.

"What do you teach?' he asked. "I am a chef and teach Culinary Arts." "So you're a chef, huh? Ever cook deer?" "Yes," I replied, "many times. I love deer meat." "How do you cook it?" "Well...first I marinate it, then...." he held up his hand. "Marinate? What do you marinate it with?" "I use red wine, juniper berries, vegetables, bay leaf ...." He held up his hand again. "Wait a minute; I need to write this down." He pushed the passports aside, took a plain sheet of paper and began to write. "What was that again? Berries?" "Yes... juniper berries, red wine, bay leaf, onion, and celeriac." "What's that?" he asked, as he continued to write. "It's like a yellow turnip but white, it has a great aromatic flavor," I explained. Now the line behind me was even longer, and people were looking at the young family who obviously had some serious problems with their paperwork because the immigration officer was writing so many notes.

He was a very friendly immigration officer – which changed our impressions from the American immigration staff in Dublin – although he did not seem to care about the long line behind us. As he wrote, he told me how he loved hunting deer in the state of Maine but could never get it to taste good. Now he was happy he had a recipe from an Irish chef that he would try during the upcoming game season. He finished writing the recipe, then reached for the large stainless steel stamp and hit the open page of each passport in rapid succession. Although for me it all happened in slow motion, I watched as the dull sound of the stamp hitting each page made me breathe a silent sigh of relief. This was the vision which millions of people around the world dream and fantasize about – coming to the U.S. We were in!

He handed me the passports, looked me directly in the eye and with a smile said: "Thanks for the recipe, welcome to America!"

Pan-Fried Venison Loin With A Redcurrant Demi Glace

This is the recipe I gave the immigration officer:

Four servings:

2 tablespoons olive oil
2 oz. (60gr.) finely chopped shallots
2 oz. (60gr.) redcurrant jelly
4 fresh rosemary sprigs
2 cups (4.7dl.) demi glace – brown stock
1 bay leaf and 5 crushed black peppercorns
8 escallops of venison loin (4 oz. each, fat, and sinew removed)

3 cups (7dl.) red wine
Salt and pepper
¼ cup (0.5dl.) heavy cream

Procedure

- Combine 2 ½ cups of the wine with chopped shallots, bay leaf and the crushed peppercorns in a small saucepan and reduce over low heat until a quarter of the liquid remains.
- This reduction concentrates the wine flavor.
- Add demi glace and continue to reduce until liquid begins to thicken.
- If necessary, thicken some more using a little corn starch diluted with red wine.
- Set the sauce aside.
- Season, and panfry the meat in a very hot skillet with olive oil.
- Brown on both sides, reduce the heat and cook until medium.
- Remove the meat from the skillet and keep warm, drain off any excess oil and pour in the remaining wine to deglaze the pan – reduce by half.
- Now add in the demi glace, redcurrant jelly, and cream.
- Bring to a boil, strain and adjust seasoning if necessary.

Assembly

- Serve the venison hot and coat with the sauce, garnish with sprigs of fresh rosemary.

Tips

- Poached apples or pears, sautéed cherries and grapes are excellent accompaniments for venison.
- Autumn vegetables such as: celeriac, braised red cabbage or Brussels sprouts are a good choice, potatoes in any shape or form are nice as well as Spätzli or buttered fettuccini.
- Last but by no means least, roasted or glazed chestnuts give this dish a special touch.

Epilogue

That encounter with the nice immigration officer took place almost 17 years ago. With hindsight – looking back over the years – I realize I have lived a great life. I met amazing people along the way, some believed in me – others not, but that's all right. Not all the guests I cooked for liked my food either, but I am grateful to the tens of thousands of people I cooked for around the world and the compliments you bestowed on me. The satisfaction I received from making you happy at the table – even if only for brief moments – continues to be my driving force. It's what chefs do.

I have been blessed to have met Christine during a great time in my life, and together being able to travel and create a loving family who continue to impress me on a daily basis. During the years I spent teaching in the U.S. I met some wonderful people, got to know great students, and saw our children grow in to accomplished adults. Arriving in America has been one of the defining moments of my life. I have traveled to many states and have come to the realization that the United States is really a world recipe, a combination of events and people who together have built a country that is the envy of millions – but not always understood by the world. It is a recipe attributed to millions of people – immigrants like me from around the globe who were given a chance to make a difference. I have learned a great deal about people, tolerance, ignorance of the world, and compassion: that it is hard to believe such an amazing country with so much world influence could be founded on such simple principles as freedom and equality.

Over the past years in the U.S., I have witnessed the emergence of great chefs, terrific restaurants, fantastic food, cooking principles, and the acceptance of quality wine, coffee, pastries and breads. It is bewildering why such fundamentals were not discovered and appreciated earlier. There are now many great schools in which chefs can learn the fundamentals of cooking and progress to become master chefs in their own right, open restaurants, and fulfill their dreams whether that involves traveling, teaching, or just simply hanging a shingle over the door with their name – a tremendous accomplishment in itself, one that I did not aspire to.

I still remain in contact with some of the people who helped me along the way. Herbert lives in Manilla and runs a great deli. Peter – from the Royal Orchid in Bangkok – is the General Manager of a fantastic property in East Africa. Jurg – from the Mandarin Hong Kong – owns a restaurant in Hawaii. Andi from Les Roches, teaches in Zurich. Jabeen and Freddy live in Sydney. My mentor and inspiration to become a Swiss Master Chef, Herman from the Hotel Elite, died many years ago. Other directors of my past years of employment live in Hong Kong and work for prominent hotel corporations, and some are retired in France. Bob and Joan live in Napa Valley in California. Remy owns a restaurant in New Zealand. Serge still makes his own wine and we chat on the phone every year on his birthday. Many others are retired and I respect their privacy. Paul and Elaine have an active retirement, hiking and skiing at three thousand meters and visiting us when they can. Klaus and Anne are retired; their son now manages the Eurotel. Monsieur Urvieder died a few years ago – I still walk by his farm where I bought the calf, with fond memories on my visits to Les Diablerets. Werner is well and lives in Gstaad, I visit him on trips to Switzerland. Daniel is the General Manager of a luxury hotel in Newport, Rohde Island. Anna and her husband are at the newly opened Raffles Hotel in the Seychelles.

My mother is in good health and still lives in our family home with my brother, his wife, and their children. She still uses the turf fired range, makes her own brown bread every week (in the same gas cooker), makes black pudding, plum pudding and her special Christmas cakes every year. She has visited us in the U.S. many times. She was my inspiration for writing this book. During one of her visits to America I gave her some short stories to read that I had written for a school project. After reading them, she said:

"Brendan, you should think about writing a book." After all, she was the one who got me Cheffin' in the first place.

As for me, I continue teaching 'Culinary Arts' together with a variety of Hospitality Management courses – and traveling when I can. But as we say in Irish: '*Sin scéal eile*' – that's another story.

The End

Cheffin' by Brendan Cronin

About the Author

Brendan Cronin – the only Irish chef to attain the prestigious Swiss culinary title of 'Chef de Cuisine Diplomé', Swiss Master Chef – currently teaches Hospitality Management classes at Endicott College. He lives on the North Shore of Boston, USA with his wife, Christine.

Cheffin' by Brendan Cronin

Made in the USA
Charleston, SC
12 February 2013